Irony
IN THE AGE OF
EMPIRE

Irony

IN THE AGE OF

EMPIRE

COMIC PERSPECTIVES
ON DEMOCRACY
AND FREEDOM

Cynthia Willett

Indiana University Press

BLOOMINGTON AND INDIANAPOLIS

This book is a publication of

Indiana University Press
601 North Morton Street
Bloomington, IN 47404-3797 USA

http://iupress.indiana.edu

Telephone orders   800-842-6796
Fax orders   812-855-7931
Orders by e-mail   iuporder@indiana.edu

*The paper used in this publication meets the minimum
requirements of American National Standard for Information
Sciences—Permanence of Paper for Printed Library Materials,
ANSI Z39.48-1984.*

MANUFACTURED IN THE UNITED STATES OF AMERICA

Library of Congress Cataloging-in-Publication Data

Willett, Cynthia, date
Irony in the age of empire : comic perspectives on
democracy and freedom / Cynthia Willett.
p.   cm. — (American philosophy)
Includes bibliographical references and index.
ISBN 978-0-253-35166-1 (cloth : alk. paper) —
ISBN 978-0-253-21994-7 (pbk. : alk. paper)
1. Comedy—Political aspects—United States.
2. Comedy—Social aspects—United States.   I. Title.
PN1929.P65W55   2008
809'.917—dc22
2007048894

1 2 3 4 5   13 12 11 10 09 08

For Stefan, Liza, Joe, Lori, Leslie, Carlos,
Gabrielle, Julie, Randy, Dylan, Chloe,
and my parents, Ellen and Joe

CONTENTS

ACKNOWLEDGMENTS

I wrote this book over the years when my children's tastes in comedy were changing from Rugrats to *The Colbert Report* and Hollywood romantic comedies. Much of the research for the book owes to Liza and Joe's collaboration as well as their endless stream of jokes. Meanwhile, Stefan Boettcher counts as my chief collaborator on several fronts at once.

Some of the richest occasions for thinking about the ideas that went into the book were spent in delightful evenings with Pam Hall, Lynne Huffer, and Elizabeth Bounds. Their good-humored support and lively conversation kept me laughing even through the more serious parts of the work.

Chad Kautzer offered strikingly good ideas for revising several of the chapters. Yoko Arisaka, Beth Butterfield, Dan Conway, Amy Coplan, Duane Davis, Tom Flynn, Kathryn Gines, Gertrude Gonzalez de Allen, Lewis Gordon, Patricia Huntington, Lawrence Jackson, Martin Japtok, Claire Katz, Donna Marcano, Rudi Makkreel, Bill Martin, Martin Matuštík, Noelle McAfee, Eduardo Mendieta, Darrell Moore, Kelly Oliver, Lou Outlaw, Jeffrey Paris, Michael Sullivan, Shannon Sullivan, Ron Sundstrom, Jim Winchester, and Shannon Winnubst, among so many friends and colleagues, offered valuable insights at various stages of the project. My exceptionally talented editors, John Stuhr and Dee Mortensen, together with two anonymous readers, enabled me to bring this work to a conclusion. Peter Milne and Alessandra Stridella served as excellent research assistants. Audiences at Stony Brook, University of San Francisco, Penn State, DePaul, Southwestern University, Trinity College, University of Georgia, North Texas, Vanderbilt, Spelman, and elsewhere encouraged me to clarify my thoughts and inspired me with new ones. And finally, I owe much thanks to many awesome students over the past several years, including my doctoral students Lina Buffington, Denise James, Sara Puotinen, Yael Sherman, and Ericka Tucker, and the fantastic participants in my seminars in new critical theory in the spring of 2007 and on comedy and tragedy in the spring of 2006.

PROLOGUE

ON TRUTHINESS

On September 11, 2001, the radical Islamist group Al Qaeda largely succeeded in carrying out a plot to destroy the U.S. World Trade Center towers and embarrass a mighty power. The United States responded with two invasions. The retaliatory invasion of Afghanistan arguably made sense given that the country served as the main headquarters for Al Qaeda. However, the invasion of Iraq, even as it was staged as a war for freedom, struck most of the world as a case of imperial arrogance, and a risky one at that. The American government's charges that Iraq was harboring terrorist organizations, including members of Al Qaeda, and was concealing weapons of mass destruction not only lacked sufficient evidence but turned out to be little more than lies. Meanwhile, the invasion went awry, unraveling not just all semblance of order in Iraq but the international credibility of the United States as well. It appears that the rash decision of the ill-fated Bush regime has, sadly and with no small degree of irony, furthered key aims of the terrorist agenda. It has helped foster the appearance that the U.S. superpower is the bully its critics claim it to be, and thus damaged its international reputation and prestige.

How could this American fiasco have happened? Two factors were decisive. First, a lackluster mainstream news media failed to do its job, that is, subject the administration's foreign policy objectives to serious public scrutiny and critical analysis, or give any serious coverage to oppositional voices. At the time these voices were flippantly discounted as fringe or, worse yet, unpatriotic, and yet many of their predictions have unfortunately come true. This failure of the media rendered many Americans blind to the likely significance of the Iraq invasion and, ironically, undermined the liberal imperialists' claim to bring basic rights, free speech first among them, to the Middle East. For how could we claim to bring free speech to the Middle East when there was a lack of meaningful political speech or debate at home? Second, the moral rhetoric of neoconservativism captured the national imagination and defined the terms of the debate. This moral rhetoric configured the world into a melodrama of good versus evil and targeted Iraq as a nodal point of an Axis of Evil. Such cartoon morality blocked any respect for the subtleties of international politics and set the United States up for "blowback" from its heavy-handed use of power.

The mainstream news media, caught in a blinding force of moral pieties, thus shored up the radical foreign policy goals of the neoconservatives. At the time one had to wonder, where might one find an effective counterforce to the inflated moral rhetoric of such self-deceived deceivers? Enter the late-night satirists, featuring most prominently Comedy Central's dynamic duo, Jon Stewart of *The Daily Show* and Stephen Colbert of *The Colbert Report*. For what else to do when the mainstream media serves as a conduit for bombastic posturing but to laugh? And what more appropriate force for deflating rhetoric and exposing self-deception than irony? So when comedian Stephen Colbert was invited to celebrate an elite cadre of journalists at the White House Correspondents' Dinner, his satirizing pose as a right-wing stooge of the president hit right on target. Ridiculing both the president and the self-important reporters who have for the most part served only to insulate him from public debate, Colbert quipped: "Now, I know there are some polls out there saying this man has a 32% approval rating. But guys like us, we don't pay attention to the polls. We know that polls are just a collection of statistics that reflect what people are thinking in 'reality'. And reality has a well-known liberal bias" (April 29, 2006). In response to the spectacle of a visibly uncomfortable president, there were those who said that the satirist had crossed a line. There were others who thought he was doing what the press had failed to do, speak truth to power.

The truth-telling of the satirist is not the same as that of the public moralist or political debater. In certain circumstances, it can be more effective. Consider Colbert's notorious riff on the "truthiness" of the Bush administration—the administration's tendency to speak not the truth but something closer to what philosopher Harry Frankfurt glosses as "bullshit."[1] The riff has been repeated on a string of episodes of *The Colbert Report* since it began airing in the fall of 2005. Colbert poses as a blustering though sincere pro-Bush news pundit in order to challenge the conservative bias in the mainstream news media and to expose the media as an uncritical vehicle of the administration's untruths. The satire does not counter moral claim with moral claim or political argument with political argument, and for good reason. Direct challenges to the radical agenda of the neoconservatives have not been effective because the debate has already been framed by their rhetoric.[2] The genius of a satirist like Colbert is that he avoids straightforward attacks (counterposing argument with argument) and takes aim at the target's posturing (the underlying hubris) instead—this is not unlike the tactic used by Charlie Chaplin in *The Great Dictator* (1940), Roberto Benigni in *La Vita E Bella* (*Life Is Beautiful*), and Dave Chappelle with his character Clayton Bigsby, a blind white supremacist who doesn't know that he is black. Indeed, where the source of the concern is not only with the moral claim per se, but with the bad-faith arrogance that underlies the claim, what better weapon than the humor of the ironist? Much pleasure comes in exposing to laughter the bullshit of the high and mighty. Satire certainly packs a punch that straight moral discourse and argument lack. The satirist draws upon this potent force when speaking "truthiness" to power.

No doubt, ridicule cannot take the place of either moral discourse or argument in public debate. It cannot capture the moral pathos of war or the horror of suffering. Nor can it substitute for an extensive analysis of a political position. But ridicule has advantages that serious speech lacks for a democratic political ethics. It can offer a democratic equalizing of the discursive terrain when the Habermasean unforced force of the better argument has the rhetorical deck stacked against it. And, of course, laughter is contagious, and sometimes disarmingly so. We find ourselves laughing when we really do not want to be. Laughter can capture us from outside and reveal aspects of ourselves even against our own will. And, strangely, this experience can be emancipatory.

But, of course, none of the genres of comedy is guaranteed to be a force for the good against the powers that be. In fact, there is nothing inherently moral about comedy at all. It is not even certain to counter the arrogance of power. On the contrary, laughter can just as easily disenfranchise the weak and prop up their tormentors as knock them down. Consider the prevalence of racially encoded jokes about welfare moms and their crack babies in the 1980s and '90s, and the dismantling of the welfare state that followed. As the right-wing talk shows of the period illustrate, ridicule can just as easily augment arrogance as expose it, enabling those with power to eliminate liberties for others. But comedy can also liberate us from oppressive social forces as well as our own lack of authenticity or bad faith. Think of the edgy race humor of stand-up comedians such as Richard Pryor and Dave Chappelle, the subversive laughter of queer camp, or even, as we shall see, the happy endings of romantic Hollywood film comedy. Comedy can open dimensions of freedom that are absent from the narrow discourse that frames our standard moral and political debates. This book is about locating through various genres of comedy that larger social vision of freedom.

Given that this country was founded on an ethics of freedom, one would think that the concept would be richly developed in major philosophical works.[3] After all, the rhetoric of freedom frames our key political documents and serves as the source of our normative discourse as well as of our hypocrisies. It has defined the goal of the civil rights movement as well as the war against terror. Even if the notion readily serves as a mask for predatory domestic and foreign policies, any civic definition of U.S. citizenship (as opposed to an ethnic, racial, or nationalistic one) surely lies in some egalitarian concept of freedom. Moreover, freedom not only lends its name to our political ambitions, it also speaks to our most intimate personal aspirations. Our spirituals and folk songs, expressionist art and Hollywood films, appeal to the value of freedom, and so do commercials.[4] Yet while freedom names our most sublime personal and political goals, there is no American statement of freedom that matches the Oxford eloquence of Isaiah Berlin's "Two Concepts of Liberty" or the intellectual tour de force of Jean-Paul Sartre's *Being and Nothingness*.[5] How could this be?

A scholar of American humor has said that in the United States, freedom is less a principle or a law than a speech and a gesture.[6] Communities of inclusion and exclusion, judgments of character that place the burden of proof on some and not on others, and patterns of ridicule sustain a groundwork of feeling for a free life. If this groundwork for a free life has not been well served by abstract intellectual prose, perhaps it is because it does not easily lend itself to such an analysis. Yet the social dynamic of communities, the virtues and vices of character, and political arrogance and moral blindness are all central topics of U.S. comedy. There in comedy our much-needed discourse on freedom might find fertile ground.

Comedy is especially relevant now as a progressive political force.

Since the 1980s, the language of freedom in the United States has been laden with a radically conservative political agenda and a strident moral tone. Concentrated wealth and restricted ownership of the media have threatened the means of free speech by narrowing considerably the range of views that are heard in the public realm. Given the pervasiveness of the conservative agenda, some of the most searing and effective critiques of American hypocrisy (e.g., of its imperial wars of liberation) have been found not in an often self-righteous moral discourse but in the leveling spirit of ordinary satire.

One might even argue that in the United States today no discourse expresses the stakes of freedom better than comedy. Martha Nussbaum contrasts the tragic sense of inevitability that one finds in high European art with a comic mindset that prevails in American culture.[7] Some would vehemently disagree with such a grand claim. Cornel West for one points out that the optimism of American life readily slides into an arrogant triumphalism when it does not attend to suffering (see chapter 2). And yet West's own tragicomic refashioning of an optimistic American pragmatism rekindles a spirit of resilience from the bleakest chapters of U.S. history, and this insurgent comic spirit provides one of the most important sources for a philosophical discussion of freedom.

Just as there are many modes and genres of the comic, so too there are many dimensions of freedom. The comic can appear as a lawless element for subverting staid conventions or serve as a leveling force against hierarchical societies. It can alter a perspective and shift the balance of power. The comic can destroy traditional social bonds, but it can also generate new ones.

Once we turn to the comic for a glimpse into freedom, we see that conventional liberal theory gives an account that is incomplete and even off-center for what we value most. The standard liberal view is that freedom signifies an individual entitlement to make decisions over one's own life and thus that any person who is rationally coherent exhibits what it means to be free. Simply put, freedom is rational autonomy. In theory, this view may sound good enough, but in practice rational autonomy is not always the key ingredient for a free life. Consider Kwame Anthony Appiah's example of the butler in Kazuo Ishiguro's comedy of manners, *The Remains of the Day* (chapter 5), which he uses in his defense of this understanding of liberalism.[8] Appiah argues that while few of the novel's readers would aspire to a life of servitude, here portrayed in the butler's sadly ridiculous character, the butler chooses his service to a master, and this fact alone essentially makes him not servile but free. If a character reflects on his life and makes a choice, then that element of considered choice renders his life free, and this is true regardless of what others might think, or what servitude might follow.

Still it would hardly strike any ordinary reader of the Ishiguro comedy of manners to describe the butler as living a life that is free, and this difference of perspective is significant. The novel presents us with a man who is, as even Appiah observes, not only "mildly ridiculous" but also "self-deceived," indeed who is ridiculous precisely because he is self-deceived. We can agree with Appiah that the question of the character's freedom should not revolve around his career choice to be a butler rather than procure some apparently more dignified position. The life of a butler may appear to be servile, but if it is indeed a free choice, who are we to say that it is wrong? Indeed, a so-called lowly class position as a servant may accompany a more fulfilled life. Compare the staid butler of the Ishiguro novel and, say, the irreverent valet in the 1981 film comedy *Arthur* (dir. Steve Gordon). But if one may enjoy a relatively free life as a servant, as perhaps *Arthur*'s valet does, Ishiguro's butler does not. The difference between the two characters is signaled by the fact that while the butler is the target of our ridicule, the valet is not; on the contrary, the valet is the agent of it. This is because the valet is sufficiently self-aware of his own needs and those of others in a way that neither the valet's master (the spoiled millionaire played by Dudley Moore) nor Ishiguro's starchy butler is. This lack of awareness on the part of the butler manifests itself in the decision to remain in service to a master who barely knows him rather than marry the woman who is his only true friend. Tragically, the love from this one true friend is precisely what awakes in the butler some vague sense of his deeper needs, which he then leaves unfulfilled. Thus the butler's life plan may be "rationally coherent" and "freely chosen" from a liberal perspective, as Appiah claims, but it hardly amounts to what a satirist would typically portray as a free life. As in this example, an external, satiric perspective on a character can trump a self-reflective, rational one.

Thus a comic perspective (whether from a comedy of manners, a romantic comedy, or satire) can bring into sharp focus what liberalism is never more than dimly aware of: that much of the groundwork for our experience of freedom lies in deeply felt and poorly understood desires, including those that bind us to friends, antagonists, and burdened communities. Our participation in a libidinal sphere as this sphere is teased out in comedy sheds light on crucial and neglected aspects of who we are and what it means to be free. And if meanings of a free life can be discerned through the medium of comedy, we should not be surprised if a comic perspective could overturn views of freedom typically proposed in liberal theory. The rational autonomous agent favored by philosophical liberalism (and its rational-choice sibling, *homo economicus,* so favored in the social sciences) does not reflect the ways in which ordinary persons, like literary characters, orient much of their lives through the claims and challenges of others. Comic portrayals of our multidimensional social lives supplement and may even exceed liberalism's polar logic of autonomy and dependence. In comedy the unfree character is not the one who refuses to give her life a coherent rational plan, and thereby succumbs to the point of view of others. The unfree character is the one who suffers from social vices such as vanity, arrogance, or self-deception—vices that require for their correction the ironic perspective of others.

Indeed, what the philosopher praises as the rational man may come across in comedy as the straight man, if not the blind fool, while the Hollywood screwball may turn out to bear much of the comic insight. Think of the contrast between the boorish scientist played by Cary Grant and the madcap heiress played by Katharine Hepburn in Howard Hawks's 1938 film *Bringing Up Baby* (see chapters 4 and 5). Hepburn's zany antics make no sense whatsoever to the overly rational Cary Grant and perhaps not even to herself. Grant's first encounter with Hepburn is on a golf course, where his serious, all-work-and-no-play demeanor is disrupted by her playing his golf ball and then insisting that it is hers. She proceeds to bang up his car, which she also insists is hers. Eventually, she involves Grant in a crazy search for a leopard that she claims is a missing pet named Baby. Grant may not understand what all he is getting into with Hepburn, yet he is drawn to this zany character against his own will. In the end his commitment to her is experienced as emancipation.

The freedom that we encounter in comedy often lends itself best to paradoxical statement. This is because while the characters may go to ridiculous lengths to free themselves from oppressive norms or relationships, comedies typically end happily only when these same characters find themselves enmeshed in obligations and social bonds not fully (or at least not fully consciously) chosen. In *Bringing Up Baby,* Grant tries his best to escape the predatory Hepburn (not to mention her leopard) and resume his life as a scientist. But by the end of the film, and against all reason, it seems he wants to be "taken captive" by her. Abstract discussions of liberal freedom focus too narrowly on the reflective, self-contained individual rather than the attunement of the libidinal individual to himself and to those who matter to him. Paradoxical though it may be, freedom often finds its happy ending in a welcomed sense of bondage (chapter 5).

Our turn toward the comic as a locus of freedom should be viewed as a part of the history of the evolving meanings of freedom in U.S. culture over the past few centuries. This history appears, broadly speaking, in three stages.

In the early days of the American republic, freedom was located in the head of a productive household. The ownership of productive property (slaves included) was thought to cultivate the republican virtues of citizenship. The (male) citizen established through his effective management of property that he could master his own desires as well as control his less than fully rational dependents for the sake of the common good. That there were slave children who often enough looked a lot like their master didn't seem to count against him.

The democratization of freedom in the 1800s shifted the meaning of freedom and the basis of citizenship from ownership of property and republican virtue to self-ownership and personal freedom. As productivity moved out of the household and into wage labor, freedom was redefined as the capacity to plan and control one's own life. This view of freedom culminated in the right to a private space symbolized in the nineteenth- and twentieth-century imagination with having a home (or for women, even just a room) of one's own. The home relieved of its productive functions (the ones that were rewarded with money) became a place to pursue leisure-time activities and affectionate relationships of choice.

More recently, as global capital uproots workers from communities, families, and countries of origin, a third locus of freedom is emerging. For a highly mobile and displaced people (we might think of our nannies, if not ourselves), the absence of freedom may be felt as the loss of various forms of social and political citizenship, including effective participation in communities, family life, and unions of all kinds.[9] As a writer for the dispossessed, Toni Morrison speaks of freedom as a place one can call "home," but she does not mean by home either a productive household or even just a bounded realm of privacy.[10] Her novels testify to the yearning for a larger sense of connection with communities, histories, and redemptive futures (see chapter 1). Even in a novel as bleak as *Beloved*, the slave, Sixo, while being burned alive by his captors, breaks out into laughter as he calls out, "Seven-0! Seven-0!"[11] This laughter is not sheer madness, although it is on the verge. Sixo has just come to realize that his pregnant "Thirty-Mile Woman got away with his blossoming seed" (see chapter 5).

We are not the self-contained, choice-driven creatures of standard conventional liberalism, but the relational creatures who cultivate our identity from our obligations and connections with others. Against the rational, self-engaged life with all its proclivities to disconnect from historical memory and participation in social and political life, comedy sets the stage for freedom as subversion and re-engagement—the key elements for a democratic political ethics. In this vision of democratic ethics, freedom does not contrast with equality and solidarity as analytically distinct and conflicting values. The pragmatic spirit of comedy defines freedom in terms of them.

This pragmatic political ethics does not displace liberal values of individual autonomy and dispassionate reason, but embraces and often overrides them. Liberalism sustains negative moral laws of not harming others and otherwise allowing individuals to go their own way. So far, so good. These laws are significant features of the normative landscape. Yet, they neither provide sufficient subversive force against subtle social norms that distort authentic desires nor contribute much toward a positive sense of obligation and connection. A comic ethics of subversion and re-engagement begins from the premise that we are enmeshed in economies, histories, and life-dramas not entirely of our own making. Webs of connection place demands upon us. These demands carry a distinct type of normative force that may extend beyond the narrow range of liberalism's typical moral concerns or the moral discourse that sustains them to broader ethical concerns for equality and solidarity. As we shall discuss in chapter 1, liberal moral obligations are articulated in terms of an "ought," while the libidinally charged obligations of the comic realm appear as those of a "should" and are viewed as a matter less of morals than of what we call an ethics of manners. From the moral view of liberalism, the normative realm of manners may appear to be superficial and conventional and an unlikely source for a political ethics. In fact, as we shall see, the realm of what we might call "social manners" is essential for democracy.

Only a few contemporary philosophers have addressed the realm of manners as a locus of ethical insight and freedom. In an article entitled "The Right to Ridicule," Ronald Dworkin discusses the right of European and U.S. newspapers to reprint the Danish political cartoons ridiculing the Islamic prophet Mohammed.[12] His argument focuses on the central role of free speech for democracy. He insists that multiculturalists are wrong to argue that abusive or insulting speech should ever be censored for the sake of respecting other cultures and religions. Ridicule is an effective means of political speech, he rightly observes, and it cannot be altered into a less offensive rhetorical form without changing its force or meaning. Still, Dworkin does insist that U.S. newspapers should refrain from reprinting the derogatory anti-Islamic cartoons. He points out that these events have been used by Muslim leaders to inflame passions and incite violence among fanatical Islamic groups.

Dworkin's focus on the importance of free speech for democracy obscures equally significant dangers to democracy, including racism and ethnic prejudice. The rhetoric of his argument puts the burden of proof on Islamic peoples disturbed by the cartoons to establish that they are as rational and autonomous as non-Islamic Europeans and Americans. An implication of his conclusion is that rational liberals should protect passionate people (such as the non-rational Islamic people) from themselves (something we've always done so well).

Racist or degrading images can serve to mute and disenfranchise others in ways that preempt free and open discussions. The right to free speech, like any right, must be balanced with other considerations for freedom, including those factors that define the possibility for democratic debate. Concentrated ownership of media is, as we have mentioned, one of these other factors; the impact of racial or ethnic arrogance among those who occupy positions of power over disenfranchised others is another.

It is important to foster social virtues such as civility for a free life.[13] The civil acknowledgment of other persons rests on an appreciation of a degree of commonality and mutual dependence underemphasized in liberal moral theories of autonomy and individual rights. But arguments that focus on civility sometimes portray multiculturalists as policing the correctness of speech and legislating our social manners. In fact, multiculturalists would generally agree that lack of civility cannot and should not be directly addressed through laws. Laws do not serve as the proper vehicle for countering racist habits of movement and manners of speech that can warp social space and preempt democratic speech.[14] Yet racist and other forms of verbal harassment or ridicule are disastrous for democratic societies, and educational institutions should sponsor programs that expose their danger. Ridicule can be an important democratic tool of subversion, but obscene anti-black remarks and images should not appear in the white-dominated public media, nor should rabidly anti-Islamic cartoons appear in the major Western presses at this time.

Some instances of racist humor are relatively minor and require only mild censure. An article in the New York Times Magazine relates the story of 13-year-old boy who, trying to impress comedian Jeff Garlin, tells the joke about an overloaded car: "There's a Mexican, a Russian, an American and a Chinese man in a car. The Russian throws a bottle of vodka out the window and they ask him why and he says, 'There's plenty of that in Russia'. The Chinese man does the same with rice, the Mexican with tacos. . . . Then the American throws the Mexican out the window. Because there are plenty of them in America." Garlin does not respond well. He tells the boy not to tell that joke again. The boy counters, "Carlos Mencia does this kind of joke all the time." "Yeah, but he's Latino," Garlin explains to the boy. If a white guy does it, it's not funny.[15] The same issue of the magazine contains an article by Christopher Caldwell on counterterrorism in the United Kingdom called "After Londonistan." The article contains another reference to humor in the context of the post-9/11 world. After worldwide protests (sometimes violent) over the Danish publication of the caricatures of Mohammed, the United Kingdom proposed a law against incitement to religious hatred. The article mentions that a British comedian opposes the proposed law because it "would make it impossible to crack jokes involving religion."[16]

For historical reasons, the German constitution bans anti-Semitic speech in certain circumstances. The United States is burdened with a troubling history of its own and should, like Germany, understand the parameters for free speech and other classic liberal rights in terms of a larger context of solidarity and social cooperation (on rights to solidarity and the role of education, see chapter 5). Without an appreciation of the power dynamic of types of speech such as ridicule together with the symbolic terrain of politics, we are likely to view oppressed groups as made up of easily deceived and impassioned people who haven't learned as have the rational races the stoic virtues necessary for freedom (or what Nancy Sherman glosses as "sucking it up," and which, by the way, she doesn't fully recommend).[17]

In an interview on National Public Radio, Iranian American comedian Maz Jobrani, who is one of the members of the "Axis of Evil Comedy Tour," responds to a question regarding how the group can manage humor in a time of "terrible news every day coming out of the Middle East." Jobrani's response: "Yeah, we manage to do it. Because . . . we make fun of our own situation and the things we have to go through. We never make fun of the victims. We make fun of the people that say and do things that don't make sense."[18] The use of irony against power's arrogance is central to the meaning of free speech. At the same time, the ridicule of oppressed people only further disenfranchises them. The appropriate expression of the comic virtues, especially the virtue of irony, may be more a matter of social manners than moral (or legal) obligation (much depends upon the degree and nature of the harm), but these virtues are not for that reason any less essential than economic or political elements of freedom. Freedom is just that complex.

In a classic defense of standard liberalism, Isaiah Berlin defines freedom as freedom from external interference, or autonomy.[19] He terms this kind of freedom "negative" and contrasts it with various forms of positive freedom. He points out that negative freedom includes such key liberal rights as freedom of speech, while the various forms of positive freedom broaden out to signify ideals as far-ranging as rational self-control (defended by Appiah) and a sense of honor, status, and citizenship. We will explore these various forms of positive freedom throughout the book. Berlin continues to be important today because he defends the negative freedom that remains at the center of American liberalism and articulates well the conventional American sentiment that the various positive meanings of freedom are dangerous obfuscations of the real thing. Among those who Berlin believes misunderstand the liberal meaning of freedom are colonized people. The apparatus of colonization or imperialism (including, for example, the presence of foreign troops) may incite impassioned people to join nationalist independence and decolonization movements. But because Berlin believes that freedom should be limited to negative liberties, he insists that a foreign government could very well secure such rights better than a government of one's own people. As we shall see, he argues that those colonized people who do not appreciate English liberalism and prefer national independence to the imposition of English-style liberalism confuse freedom with notions of honor or recognition (chapter 5).

One wonders who is confused. The U.S. invasions of Afghanistan and Iraq after the destruction of the World Trade Center towers claimed to bring freedom to foreign people, and yet the invasions can hardly be viewed apart from the motives of reclaiming honor. Social gestures bear a great deal of symbolic force, and they are crucial for political ethics. Insults and other symbolic attacks are perceived as dishonoring (especially on conceptions of manhood) and typically beget violence. Western nations are not immune to these kind of provocations. Proponents of negative freedom have difficulty articulating, indeed even perceiving, what is at stake in the gestures and symbols of power, in particular their arrogance, and yet continue to suffer from their boomeranging effects.

To account for political concerns absent from standard Anglo-American liberal theory, multiculturalists have appropriated the concept of mutual recognition from Hegel. The idea is that individuals derive their sense of identity and self-esteem from the views of them held by others. Drawing upon the Hegelian notion, multiculturalists argue that disempowered groups suffer from lack of recognition by dominant groups. While I shall not further explore Hegel's own contribution to the notion of recognition or the politics of multiculturalism that this notion sustains, it is important for our purposes to note that the original literary source for the Hegelian notion traces back to struggles for honor in classical Greek tragedy. In tragedy, characters such as Antigone and Creon struggle to the death over the failure of each to recognize the honor and authority of the other, for each is drawing from a different tradition of right (*Recht*)—Antigone from the law of the family and Creon from the law of the state.

In contrast with the glimpse into freedom that comes from tragic struggles for honor, genres of comedy turn our focus to the joys of erotic subversion and libidinal connection. In comedy, mutual recognition plays out in contests for friendship and love and not honor or glory. While the tragic shines light on the heroic and, apparently, the highest element of human existence, the leveling impulse of comedy seems well suited for egalitarian democracies. And this is especially true in an age of empire, for what could more effectively unmask the ignorance and hubris of imperialism than comic irony?[20] Accordingly, comedy illustrates that irony is not only an effective tool in the private realm, as Richard Rorty has argued; irony can also play a democratic role in public and political realms. This is on condition, however, that such potent forms of irony as ridicule are used to check rather than add to the arrogance of power. Laughter is, as Nietzsche would suggest, consciousness of power (see chapter 1). Its value for democracy cannot be judged apart from an analysis of power. A political ethics that is aware of the structures that sustain elites does not cancel standard liberal moral and legal entitlements to negative liberties (of property and free speech, for example), but it may trump them.

Multicultural debates conventionally turn on the narrow assumption that to achieve recognition in the public sphere is to win a degree of honor from one's opponent. A comic perspective, in contrast, mocks contests for honor altogether in favor of the pleasures of conviviality instead.[21] These pleasures accompany not the hard-won glory of righteous struggle but the more ordinary joys of an irreverent wisdom and a sympathetic heart.[22] We find these virtues in the Axis of Evil Comedy Tour. When non–Middle Easterners in audiences laugh with (and not at) the Islamic American humorists, the laughter humanizes the "enemy." As one member of the tour has remarked, through humor Islamic people are able "to have a voice" in the West. And, just as importantly, when these same audiences delight in the flagrant ridicule of Operation Iraqi Freedom, the laughter disables power, stymies arrogance, and strikes a blow against the pretend manliness that dominates the political field. After Stanley Cavell, we might call the preference for the social pleasures of comedy over the gloomy games of honor "the pursuit of happiness" (see chapter 4). And as Cavell knew, this pursuit is not just a key element of Hollywood film or our leisurely entertainments. The Declaration of Independence proclaims this pursuit as a right. In this book, we shall identify this pursuit with freedom.

Overview of the Book

The book brings into play philosophical statements on comedy (Cavell on romantic comedy, Bergson on satiric laughter, Bakhtin on carnival, and speculations on Aristotle's missing book on comedy in the *Poetics*) with conceptions of negative and positive freedom (especially, Berlin and liberal theorists, such as Ignatieff, Nussbaum, and Appiah, who are influenced by him). Given that the project aims to discuss comedy and freedom specifically in an American cultural context, it draws as well upon an array of American thinkers (most centrally, Cornel West) who treat emancipatory themes in the comic. While none of these various thinkers asserts the larger thesis of this book, each provides a perspective on comedy and/or freedom that advances an aspect of the larger view that I put forth. This larger thesis challenges the liberal paradigm of freedom (one that opposes freedom to equality and solidarity) and argues for a reinvigorated pragmatist paradigm (one that defines freedom in terms of equality and solidarity). The aim is to replace the cold war–era, tragic discourse on freedom (exemplified by Berlin) with a post–cold war, anti-imperialist vision of freedom as solidarity (as glimpsed in various modes of progressive comedy).

The book begins with chapters 1 and 2 pointing out that while philosophers have given much attention to the relevance of tragedy for reflections on freedom, comparatively little thought has been given to comedy. Chapter 1 opens with the contemporary debate on liberal imperialism in U.S. foreign policy and on the charges of arrogance leveled against the United States. My claim is that while liberal political thought does not have the tools to fully grasp either the potentially tragic implications of hubris or the ways to avoid it, American comedy with its pragmatic spirit does. Comic insights into our libidinal desires and social relationships open up U.S. political thought beyond liberalism's narrow focus on the claims of the abstract individual and attune us to ways to avoid disastrous conflict on the international political scene. Of course, we might have developed the proposed vision of freedom without using comedy at all. However, as I argue in this chapter, comedy may be the exemplary site in U.S. culture to find a libidinal politics of freedom that contrasts sharply with liberalism's valorization of self-ownership. (Think of the comic pleasure that comes of Katharine Hepburn's playful antics with Cary Grant's car and golf ball in contrast with his claim to ownership in the opening scene of *Bringing Up Baby*.)

Chapter 2 turns to Cornel West to anchor our reflections on culture and politics in philosophical pragmatism. Cornel West expands the political horizon beyond the liberal political landscape to register the wounds of racism and imperialism, and to move beyond them, and yet, I argue, his philosophy of hope is not hopeful enough. A more pronounced emphasis on the comic aspect of his tragicomic philosophy would shed light on the value of irony for community building and wound healing, and thus set the frame for a visionary pragmatist approach to freedom as solidarity.

The subsequent two chapters lay out specific elements of irony and satire (chapter 3) and romantic comedy (chapter 4) useful for political thought. These elements of comedy (as found in the three major genres of comedy: carnival, comedy of manners, and romantic comedy) each play a central role in chapter 5. Given my aim of locating a positive social vision, the book focuses on progressive, in contrast with regressive, modes of the comic (e.g., chapter 3 takes up Spike Lee's satire of minstrel shows rather than minstrel shows themselves; chapter 4 highlights egalitarian rather than sexist or classist aspects of *The Philadelphia Story*), while developing an explanation as to what constitutes this difference. As I claim, only those modes of comedy that are consistent with equality and solidarity are genuinely emancipatory. Freedom requires both equality and solidarity.

Preview of the Chapters

Chapter 1, "Laughter against Hubris: A Preemptive Strike": In a unipolar world, how could any political ethics do without the notion of hubris? And yet the tragic implications of hubris slip through the cracks of standard liberal political and moral theories and are typically consigned to fictive narratives and drama. Even such a sophisticated theorist as Michael Ignatieff fails to fully heed its political ramifications, as we shall see in his defense of liberal imperialism. Perhaps no American liberal theorist has engaged tragic literature more than Martha Nussbaum. But while drawing upon comic insights into avoiding tragic conflicts, Nussbaum stops short of proposing a cosmopolitan political ethics through the comic that could preempt acts of imperial hubris. Meanwhile, literary authors, including most prominently Toni Morrison, foreground the tragic consequences of hubris on friendships and communities, and provide comic insights into freedom and solidarity beyond liberalism's constricted focus.

Chapter 2, "Laughing to Keep from Crying: Cornel West, Pragmatism, and Progressive Comedy": As a tragicomic thinker, Cornel West struggles against the sweet truths that veil the tragic ones. West's predecessors in American thought have not always sounded the blue note. The forward-looking optimism of Ralph Waldo Emerson and John Dewey failed to give ample voice to the pathos of American life. West takes from earlier pragmatic thinkers the upbeat experimentalism, the faith in democracy, and the sanctity of the individual as motifs for his thought. Stripped of the tragic sense, however, pragmatism mocks those who know soul-wrenching despair. An intricate balance of optimism with the pessimism that comes from a direct acquaintance with the absurd gives rise to West's own prophetic pragmatism. This is a pragmatism whose vital elements are remixed and recharged in the existential matrix of evangelical Christianity and jazz. But what might we learn if we were to alter the dominant cord of this rendition of American pragmatism from the heavy spirit of Christianity and bluesy jazz to the funk of comedian Richard Pryor? How might the comedian's encounter with the post-soul bottom of American life augment West's bluesy Christian vision? As we shall see in subsequent chapters, an augmented pragmatism, inflected fully by the comic spirit, provides the philosophical basis for reconceptualizing freedom.

Chapter 3, "Authenticity in an Age of Satire: Ellison, Sartre, Bergson, and Spike Lee's *Bamboozled*": Spike Lee's *Bamboozled*, a satiric portrayal of the continuing relevance of blackface stereotypes, provides us with an occasion to ponder the salience of a satiric comedy of manners for an emancipatory political ethics. Ellison's interpretation of American identity through forms of comedy sets the stage for our study of blackface and the quest for authenticity. Sartre's analysis of authenticity provides the initial impetus for understanding the existential force of the Spike Lee film and related cultural debates about what counts as black. However, the individualism of Sartre's existentialism poses some shortcomings for an era in which interdependence and belonging provide the key themes. For this reason, I trace the existential concepts of authenticity and bad faith back to Bergson's theory of social satire. The question then becomes: What if we were to shift the analysis of authenticity from Sartre's World War II–era romance of the solitary individual to an African American satire of manners? Might we use the comic in order to recover what philosophers term "authenticity" and the hip hop generation calls "keeping it real" in the midst of our otherwise cynical and racially mixed postmodern times? The authentic self is not the individual who stands alone but the self in solidarity with others.

Chapter 4, "Engage the Enemy: Cavell, Comedies of Remarriage, and the Politics of Friendship": Radical democracy theorists influenced by deconstruction and liberal imperialists of the Bush administration may not have much in common, but they do agree on one thing: the definitive role of the friend-enemy distinction for politics. However, what if it turns out, as it does in classic plots of comedy no less than tragedy, that we are our own worst enemy? And our enemy is in fact our friend? What might the plot twists of comedy mean for a democratic political ethics? Stanley Cavell's captivating reflections on Hollywood comedies of remarriage in *Pursuits of Happiness,* and in particular, his remarks on George Cukor's *The Philadelphia Story* (1940) prepare us to rethink the relevance of friends and enemies for transnational democracy theory. If freedom lies in solidarity, solidarity is based not on identity but on difference.

Chapter 5, "Three Concepts of Freedom": Isaiah Berlin probed human experience during the cold war period through a tragic perspective and concluded that there was only one true meaning of freedom. The individual is condemned, as he would say, to take responsibility for his own life choices. Freedom lies in individual choice, or "negative liberties." Berlin's view continues to orient much of Anglo-American political discourse, but it does not do justice to the positive meanings of freedom in the American cultural imagination. Through the lens of diverse genres of comedy this climactic final chapter proposes not one but three dimensions of freedom. First, aspects of farce or the carnivalesque (think of queer camp and not minstrel shows) can reorient what liberals celebrate as negative liberty away from individual choice and toward the oftentimes erotic transgression of social norms. Second, social satire and the comedy of manners shed light on the importance of education generally, including the education of character (identified with "positive freedom") for the sake of citizenship in an egalitarian democracy. But while the classic republican ideal of education aims for the rational control of the passions (a view currently defended by Appiah), the comedy of manners offers instead the leveling spirit of irony together with an "understanding heart" (the phrase comes from Cukor's *The Philadelphia Story*). Finally, romantic comedy and comedies of friendship shift the focus of life's contests away from codes of honor toward the more convivial bonds of affiliation and solidarity instead (the third freedom).

The reflection on the erotic politics of comedy leaves us with three central meanings of freedom: freedom *from* repressive social norms, freedom *to* achieve an education (and develop other capabilities as well) through irony, and the freedom *of* securing vital social bonds. Moreover, the erotic politics of our comedy does not ask us to choose among these negative and positive freedoms, as Berlin's forlorn liberalism would require, but to embrace all three as key elements of democracy.

ONE

LAUGHTER AGAINST HUBRIS

A PREEMPTIVE STRIKE

Tragic Beginnings

For twelve years, the United States had stood alone and uncontested as the sole world superpower. Then came the terror of September 11, the crumbling World Trade towers, the damaged face of the Pentagon, and thousands dead. The deaths and destruction prompted much speculation on the reasons for anti-American sentiments and on how the United States might exert its power with a sense of cosmopolitan responsibility. The terror also brought about widespread sympathy for the United States. When French president Jacques Chirac proclaimed that "we are all Americans now," there was a real chance for the United States to exercise global leadership and to lay the groundwork for world peace. But then something went wrong. Instead of seeking world peace, the United States announced a thinly veiled and highly risky strategy for global domination. We were to be engaged in a war against terrorism without definition or end. With plans to invade Iraq, the United States lost the sympathy it had gained from the attack, and France joined with Germany to lead world opinion in the United Nations against American aggression. "When

France is accusing the U.S. of arrogance, and Germany doesn't want to go to war, you know something is wrong," philosopher-at-large Chris Rock quipped and for good reason.[1] To be sure, the U.S. has a sporadic history of imperialist invasion, but the post-9/11 agenda shifted that imperialism into high gear.

The anger unleashed in the 9/11 attacks surprised Americans, who were for the most part genuinely unaware of our long history of imperialist invasion and the hostility that cultural and economic domination, let alone the presence of U.S. troops, can generate abroad. Mainstream historians have preferred to portray the United States as a passive defender of democracy, not as an active imperialist power. Those historians who portray the United States as an active empire typically insist that this imperial role is for the good. Prominent historian John Lewis Gaddis, for example, claims that the politics of the cold war required that the United States assert its power as "a new kind of empire—a democratic empire."[2] Only a few historians have seen through such claims of American innocence as one more romance with American exceptionalism. And yet extensive empirical research demonstrates fairly clearly that, in the words of historian Marilyn Young, "US. foreign policy aims first and foremost for a 'world safe and assessable for the American economic system' " (*GP*, 279). The United States rarely advances pro-democracy programs, and only then when the costs are perceived to be slight. The typical consequence of American imperialism is to subjugate foreign people, viewed as racially or culturally inferior, and to drain their resources. Even the high moral rhetoric commonly used to defend an American empire is hardly exceptional. The French and the British empires also claimed to bestow the rule of law and democracy on inferior populations. Regardless of the rhetoric, imperialism's strategies are sadly the same: to tear down and replace preexisting socioeconomic structures with hitherto unknown systems of dependency.

Whatever we might think about the historical likelihood of a moral empire, the ironies that characterized the surge of patriotism following the 9/11 attack are telling. Stunned by terror in the homeland, citizens who had enjoyed, somewhat cynically perhaps, the stock market bubble of the '90s asked what they might give back to a nation in need. In the mood of shock and mourning that followed the terror, these citizens seemed poised to break out of the exaggerated schedules of work and consumption that had shaped the years before. President Bush, claiming to be, if not our popularly elected leader, at least our "moral leader," did not call out to us to respond to the crisis with a republican ethic of sacrifice. We were not asked for the sake of the nation to ration, buy savings bonds, or trade in the keys to our SUVs for some hybrid model. On the contrary, we were asked to spend, and spend lavishly, as though our lives would depend upon it. In a time of crisis, we peered into the soul of our nation and found it difficult to see past the veneer of materialism that continues to both mesmerize and disturb us. The president's redefinition of duty brought to national consciousness the impact of an economy rooted more in consumption than in production, and even more precariously, in consumer confidence. And so, in the anxiety of post-9/11, we were called upon not to make sacrifices, but to consume and to do so with undaunted confidence. Of course, the call to consume came to constitute an exceedingly pleasant if somewhat unusual embodiment of citizen duty. Many of us were ready to do our part.

The hedonistic embodiment of patriotic duty was, however, definitely going to mess with some basic philosophical distinctions that had emerged in the twelve years of the post–cold war era. In the carnivalized atmosphere of globalization that followed the fall of the Berlin wall, the world-system *seemed* to divide between what German philosopher Cornelia Klinger portrays as the postmodernism of the rich and the communitarianism of the poor.[3] For those who could enjoy the elite postmodern lifestyle, globalization might be experienced as the freeing of the subject from essentializing categories of identity, patriotism among them. This was to be a time for enjoying bodies and their pleasures, the narcissism of unencumbered individualism, the negative freedom of fluid boundaries in a transsexual, transgender, and transnational world. It seemed as though this could be paradise. On the underside of the world-system, disenfranchised populations were left struggling for a sense of belonging or recognition, a positive sense of identity and freedom, and new forms of communitarianism, nationalism, and fundamentalism.

Or so, as I say, it seemed. For, it was never so clear that pomo consumerism, at least the American brand, was not a way after all to write upon the world an American identity—in other words, just one more form of nationalism. The beauty of the first response to 9/11 was that we could have it all. We could be nationalistic citizens and pleasure-loving consumers. We could wave our flags as proud Americans and yet yield to our most hedonistic urges—as long as these urges could be satisfied in the malls and not on the streets. (Buying drugs, according to the ongoing national campaign, finances the terrorists.) What could be more safely delicious?

And yet, as easy as this first response to 9/11 was to be, it was not going to satisfy our nation's conservative moral leadership. Perhaps the emphasis on consumption seemed a bit too feminine—not quite manly enough.[4] In any case, over the next few months, the administration would exploit the sense of national emergency and compensate for any perceived passivity in our nation's identity with a more kick-ass model of citizenship. This second response took the shape of the 2002 National Security Strategy, a project originally laid out by Paul Wolfowitz in 1992, and proposed by Bush as part of his rationale for invading Iraq. The new policy would entitle the United States to so-called preemptive strikes against perceived enemies, indeed, against any power that challenges U.S. global supremacy.[5] This policy turn promised to be full of risk, excitement, and adventure—and manlier, too.

The beefed-up role of patriot as warrior of an active empire (and not merely consumer in a passive empire) may or may not serve to advance the cause of freedom. Much depends on how freedom is defined. Certainly, the double role of consumer and warrior is geared to add overwhelming military force to make the world "safe and assessable for the American economic system" and its ideology of free markets. But the doctrine of preemptive strike would also begin to cast dark shades of meaning on the motto of mall culture, "shop till you drop." If just prior to 9/11, Young could draw the conclusion that the United States aims to be "at once powerful and passive," the National Security Strategy of 2002 changed all of that, and for clear motives. The new get-tough security policy redresses a degree of vulnerability that mainstream America has not known before and compensates for whatever hint of passivity there may be in a service economy—countering any force that threatens to feminize us. After the 1999 film *Fight Club,* I am inclined to view our national evolution to the Wolfowitz doctrine through Brad Pitt's "Project Mayhem."[6] "Let's evolve," Brad Pitt says to the timid Ed Norton. Of course, Paul Wolfowitz is not as cool as Brad Pitt, and George W's Project Mayhem (I take the W as standing for George's alter ego, Wolfowitz) does not target the credit companies; George W's Project Mayhem is aggressively pro-capitalist, capitalist with a vengeance, perhaps even a tragic kind of vengeance—or at least this has been the widespread concern.

It is said that as Americans we lack a sense of the tragic. Certainly, the miscalculations of the Bush administration brought this country more trouble than it was ever able to foresee. The weird mix of consumer capitalism and Project Mayhem militarism, symbolized in the minds of our frightful enemies by the World Trade towers and the Pentagon, profile the dangers of excess and arrogance that we have become. In the ancient logic that defense secretary Donald Rumsfeld dismissed as part of "Old Europe," these twin dangers spell hubris. And the tragic consequences, in political theater as in classic drama, have been clear in advance to all but the doer of the deed. Old Europe's tales warn that it is of the nature of unrivaled power to overstep limits, setting loose the furies that bring it down. Of course, it has been a genuine hope among some that the United States would avoid the usual traps and use its immense power for moral purposes. The liberal philosopher, journalist, and human rights advocate Michael Ignatieff has made perhaps the most thoughtful case for the moral use of our imperial power, and I will examine his arguments more carefully in a moment. But as allies and enemies warn, the imperial logic of the superpower may not allow for the happy ending to which America aspires. Unchecked and unbalanced, power cannot sustain a clear moral path (if there ever was one).[7] Power breeds hubris, and hubris brings about resentment, anger, and doom. The intentions, moral or not, hardly matter.

After 9/11, worldly neoliberal capitalists joined with flag-waving republican patriots to rally behind an active role for an American empire and spread freedom abroad. Ignatieff among others termed this active power "liberal imperialism." Of course, future administrations may lead the United States down a more cautious path of imperialism, one that operates more carefully through economic partnerships with powerful allies. However, this return to pre-Bush-style imperialism does not address the underlying hubris that brought about 9/11 to begin with. One wonders if our country is doomed to repeat a formula of capitalism and militarism, narcissism and nationalism, excess and arrogance—a very old logic of tragic recoil that we cannot even see. Is there an alternative role for a superpower?

Martha Nussbaum contrasts the sense of inevitability one finds in classical tragedy with the comic mindset of the American sensibility (*UT,* 675). If ancient tragedians mourned the blunders that bring about downfall, the comic sensibility acknowledges vulnerability and dependence on others and thereby avoids tragic ruin. Nussbaum does not herself explore the ethics of comedy beyond her brief allusion to its formal character, the avoidance of conflict. But what if we were to play along with Nussbaum's broader claim, and grant that she has steered us toward a truly salutary element of mainstream American identity? Might we find on the surface of American culture some profound comic insight that takes us beyond the blindness to excess and arrogance that the American disavowal of tragedy otherwise implies?

That Awesome Thing: Liberal Empire

In a January 2003 *New York Times Magazine* article, "The Burden," Ignatieff gently urges the United States to wake to its new responsibility as empire.[8] "Ever since George Washington warned his countrymen against foreign entanglements, empire abroad has been seen as the republic's permanent temptation and its potential nemesis. Yet what word but 'empire' describes the awesome thing that America is becoming?" (B, 22). "The 21st century imperium is a new invention in the annals of political science, . . . a global hegemony whose grace notes are free markets, human rights and democracy, enforced by the most awesome military power the world has ever known. . . . In this vein, the president's National Security Strategy . . . commits America to lead other nations toward 'the single sustainable model for national success,' . . . free markets and liberal democracy" (B, 24).

Ignatieff cautions that this mission is not without its danger. "As the United States faces this moment of truth, John Quincy Adams's warning of 1821 remains stark and pertinent," he writes; citing the words of the famous founding father, we have "to ask whether in becoming an empire [America] risks losing its soul as a republic" (B, 24). "What every schoolchild also knows about empires is that they eventually face nemeses. . . . To call America the new Rome is at once to recall Rome's glory and its eventual fate. . . . [T]he city on a hill . . . now has to confront . . . a remote possibility that seems to haunt the history of empire: hubris followed by defeat" (B, 25).

Ignatieff is among a booming chorus of voices that warn the United States of its arrogance. In 1999, before 9/11 alerted the American public to the hostility that imperial power provokes abroad, Thomas Friedman reported on a shift in the discourse of our extreme critics in the Middle East. In 1996, "Iran's mullahs had begun calling America something other than the 'Great Satan.' They had begun calling it 'the capital of global arrogance.'"[9] The shift from the theological language of good and evil to the older language of hubris reflects in part the need to forge a political ethics that translates across cultural boundaries. The Bush administration might take note: the pagan discourse of hubris may indeed garner a transnational appeal that the self-righteous quasi-Christian discourse of good and evil lacks. "Enron embodies Nobel-class hubris," we hear after the corporation's fiasco.[10] This is a deregulated world of out-of-control corporate monopolies; a post-Columbine world of queen bees and out-of-control bullies in the public schools; a global society in which one superpower is no longer balanced by another.[11]

The resentment toward the hubris of the American lifestyle of deregulated power not only resonates at home, it crosses boundaries. The toned-down accusations of the mullahs might not have shifted the brunt of the perception of fanaticism away from the Islamists toward the Americans.

The language does, however, reflect substantial ethical concerns with the single-mindedness of monopolistic capital and unipolar power. Friedman gave us a glimpse into how American zeal is viewed across the world in the same 1999 article: "We Americans are the apostles of the Fast World, the prophets of the free market and high priests of high tech. We want 'enlargement' of both our values and our Pizza Huts. We want the world to follow our lead and become democratic and capitalistic" (*NB*, 43). But if the internationalist agenda of prior administrations made enemies, the Bush sabotage of internationalism and the subsequent bravado of its National Security Strategy seems destined to do more than make enemies; the Bush sabotage, to cite a line from Aristotle's study of tragedy, has made "enemies out of our friends."[12]

The tragic warnings against hubris echo back before the days of Rome. In his genealogical studies of moral terms, Nietzsche contrasts the theological language of good and evil with the pagan ethics of the Greeks.[13] He explains that the common people, or *demos*, of ancient Athens used the category of hubris as a tool for restraining not only tyrants but all kinds of elites. While the Hellenic people encouraged competition (*agon*) for honor and status, they thought to establish restraints on power so that contests would not degenerate into what Nietzsche describes as "a fight of annihilation."[14] We might ponder, Nietzsche writes, "the original meaning of ostracism. . . . 'Among us, no one shall be the best; but if someone is, then let him be elsewhere.' . . . Why should no one be the best? Because then the contest would come to an end and the eternal source of life for the Hellenic state would be endangered" (*HC*, 36). What becomes of those whom the gods behold without a rival? They are "seduce[d by these same gods] to a deed of hubris," madness, and doom (*HC*, 38).

Despite the reference to the gods, Nietzsche's statement coheres with contemporary scholarship. This scholarship corrects the traditional view, which reduces hubris to the attitude of pride or a religious offense against the gods.[15] What liberals explain in terms of the "basic rights of the citizen not to be abused, or exploited or treated violently, Greeks often preferred to express . . . in terms of honour and shame" (*H*, 494). Charges of hubris were directed on behalf of conquered people or lower classes against imperialist states and the rich or ruling classes as "peasant-citizen democracy" grew more effective in Greek states (*H*, 494, 505). An attack on the honor of the individual or group was viewed as a major crime, destabilizing the community and risking social unrest or revolution and war (*H*, 493). Because of the danger of the elites, the people (or *demos*) demanded laws and ethical codes to protect them against hubris as well as to secure some degree of redistribution of the wealth (*H*, 493–94). Those who were the target of hubristic acts or policies were expected to act out in rage and seek revenge. While classic scholarship traces the ethical codes against hubris at least as far as Egypt, Wole Soyinka observes that the codes extend into Sub-Saharan Africa.[16]

Today we understand the logic of nemesis in terms less of the fatal cycles of anger and revenge than of rational decisions and political fact. "Since the beginnings of the state system in the 16th century, international politics has seen one clear pattern—the formation of balances of power against the strong," observes Fareed Zakaria shortly after the invasion of Iraq in his *Newsweek* article "The Arrogant Empire."[17]

It is odd that contemporary defenders of an active American empire invoke the mythos of hubris repeatedly, as though compelled by some force that (after that theorist of madness, Freud) I am tempted to call a death wish. In any case, after invoking the specter of hubris, they do not back down. They prefer instead the bolder move, and demand more, not less, power: "The question, [Ignatieff writes] . . . is not whether America is too powerful but whether it is powerful enough" (*B*, 27). Similarly, citing foreign policy expert Michael Mandelbaum, Friedman writes just before the Iraq invasion, " 'the real threat to world stability is not too much American power. It is too little American power.' "[18] One has to wonder what perverse pleasure comes from tempting the fates.

The decision to invade Iraq is a case in point. Jonathan Schell observes that the global protest against the invasion of Iraq on February 15th of 2003 "will go down in history as the first time that the people of the world expressed their clear and concerted will in regard to a pressing global issue. . . . On that day, history may one day record, global democracy was born."[19] From these multitudes who spoke together against the tyranny of the United States emerged the voice of the *demos* of a global community. Perhaps this proclamation has turned out to be a bit optimistic, but still the irony of imposing democracy from above is clear. Such a politics may give rise to a democratic uprising, but it's not the democracy that the powers-that-be had in mind.

The apologists for the invasion of Iraq continue to claim to fight the forces of evil and to have moral right on their side. It may be that the cold war is over, but the new world system is also bipolar, Thomas Friedman and others insist in order to justify their norm-imposing imperial discourse: "instead of being divided between East and West, it is divided between the World of Order and the World of Disorder" (*PD*, 11). Friedman's imperial discourse may be a toned-down version of Samuel Huntington's 1993 article "The Clash of Civilizations?" As the cold war gave way to the culture wars, Huntington wrote, "[i]t is my hypothesis that the fundamental source of conflict in this new world will not be primarily ideological or primarily economic. The great divisions among humankind . . . will be cultural."[20] But if Friedman lacks the cheap melodrama of the clash of civilizations, his discourse nonetheless disguises a fact: there is a single major actor on the world stage, and that actor refuses all restraint. Given that our days are limited (think China and India), it might be wise to join with other nations to lay down some international rules for restraint. And in fact Ignatieff seems to have something like this in mind.

But for Ignatieff, it is not unrivaled power but the cheap use of power that finally concerns him. "After 1991 and the collapse of the Soviet empire, American presidents thought they could have imperial domination on the cheap, ruling the world without putting in place any new imperial architecture—new military alliances, new legal institutions, new international development organisms—for a postcolonial . . . world," he writes (B, 53). Ignatieff shares the concern for a multilateralism and an internationalism that neopragmatists have carried forward from the cold war days. "Putting the United States at the head of a revitalized United Nations is a huge task. . . . Yet it needs to be understood that the alternative is empire: a muddled, lurching America policing an ever more resistant world alone, with former allies sabotaging it at every turn. . . . Pax Americana must be multilateral, as Franklin Roosevelt realized, or it will not survive," Ignatieff writes in the fall of 2003 as the postwar chaos in Iraq began to threaten greater danger to U.S. hegemony than the ousted tyrant.[21] To be sure, Ignatieff's neopragmatism takes a step in the right direction, but the perception of U.S. arrogance predates the post-9/11 mayhem; in fact it predates the collapse of the Soviet empire. The perception of arrogance has haunted what is called the American century, and Ignatieff's gracious offer for the United States to head the United Nations is not going to make this perception go away, not at least any time soon.

Aristotle contrasted legitimate and illegitimate regimes of power based on whether they aimed for the moderate social life that he termed "friendship."[22] A United States–led alliance of nations with or without the former imperial powers of Old Europe does not constitute the moderate life that he had in mind. He explains ostracism as the banishing of men or cities of outstanding influence (1284a17). Cities of such excellence and ambition may be humbled by other cities "made presumptuous by memories of having once had an empire themselves" (1284a17). One may protect oneself from the politics of leveling that hubris invokes by forming stronger alliances, but it is a misunderstanding to assume that multilateral coalitions serve in themselves to preempt charges of arrogance. As Aristotle makes clear, perverted regimes arise from an "abundance of connections" as well as excesses of wealth or power (1284b22). Only true excellence can serve to legitimate the unbalanced rule of the few. But then who can legitimately claim such unqualified excellence? The assertion of the claim itself provides grounds for the charge of tyranny. When has power ever exerted restraints on itself? It is "better policy," as Aristotle remarks, "to begin by ensuring that there shall be no people of outstanding eminence, than first to allow them to arise and then to attempt a remedy afterwards" (1302b5).

It is a mistake to understand the struggle against Westernism and its arrogance in the terms of the extremists who concocted the terror of September 11th. But the aftermath of 9/11 should sound an alarm for those lured by any new romance with American exceptionalism. The old claim that the United States escaped the class warfare of Europe and its subsequent flirtation with Marxism, reasserted recently by Richard Rorty, downplays the nation's original dependence on slave labor and the violent politics of race.[23] Today as our corporations move their sites of production overseas, our nation continues to depend upon cheap labor and natural resources from disenfranchised populations. Under the conditions of developing countries' neocolonial dependency on rich nations such as the United States, it is difficult to claim for the United States the status of a uniquely moral empire or, as Ignatieff prefers, liberal leadership. A simple return to the multilateralism of the Clinton era does not suffice to foster the kind of friendship that world stability would demand.

This is because any liberal defense of an American empire, with or without its expensive alliances, is in fact not even liberal, at least not if by liberal we mean to include a system of checks and balances that establishes firm limits on power. Ralph Ellison restates and appropriately radicalizes the liberal suspicion of power in the ancient idiom of tragedy as he tracks the psychic and social imbalances of white supremacy in race-torn America: "If the philosopher's observation that absolute power corrupts absolutely was also true, then an absolute power based on mere whiteness made a deification of madness."[24] The tragic echo of the terror of hubris may not be audible in American culture, but it is not absent either.

The romance of America as the moral center of a new world order blinds us to the ambiguity of the moral status of any unbalanced power in a unipolar world. Beware of your enemy, echoes an ancient claim, for your enemy is who you are destined to become. Even before 9/11, dissident voices were asking rather pointedly if "globalization and the political discourse of terrorism [share] a common root in fundamentalism . . . [for they] respectively hegemonize the markets and religion with limited participation from other sources?"[25] As the United States, now armed with the doctrine of preemptive strike, prepares to face off with one evil enemy after another, voices around the world can be overheard pondering how to balance the demands of one kind of tyrant with another. Is there any way out of this uncanny hall of mirrors?

International capitalism penetrates every facet of culture and politics on a scale that is global. Some internationalists speculate that capitalism in one form or another might very well upstage even such a powerful nation-state as the United States. If so, U.S. nationalism no less than religious fundamentalism is doomed to be an ineffective if persistent reassertion of symbolic power against the neoliberal onslaught of capital. The romance of the American empire would be just another defensive shield against the demise of the nation-state, as reactionary as any other identity politics, in the face of the transnational meltdown of global capital.

Still Ignatieff gives us reasons to think that nationalism is not a thing of the past even if it is not the sole force on the world scene. He contrasts the "postmilitary and postnational" identity sought by European countries with the United States, which has remained "a nation in which flag, sacrifice and martial honor are central to national identity" (B, 50). If it seemed as though neoliberalism would render American-style nationalism a relic of the past, "Sept. 11 rubbed in the lesson that global power is still measured by military capability" (B, 50). At this time, only one nation possesses this kind of capability. For Ignatieff this means that the United States alone among nation-states is in the position to write the terms of the new world order.

Ignatieff's profound hope is that the United States will use its power to promote an international legal and economic system that protects a minimal list of basic human rights.[26] Prominent on the list are the classic liberal rights to free expression in speech and religion, property, and due process, or what Ignatieff's teacher Isaiah Berlin clarified as forms of "negative liberty" (HR, 57, 74). Following Berlin, he insists that these liberal rights protect individuals against the tyranny of families, churches, and organic communities. As Ignatieff admits, America's critics challenge the underlying individualism of liberalism as prejudicial against non-Western cultures and proclaim a proposal to universalize a particular conception of right as "arrogant" (HR, 92). But Ignatieff defends the minimal, liberal concept of right, and its underlying individualism, on the basis of its universal moral merit. His claim is that a list of rights that protect individuals from the tyranny of the family or community secures the greatest hope for freedom. He cannot imagine any better moral language for a global community than the liberal vision of negative freedom and the individualism that this vision protects. And he wonders what proposal of moral right could be more free from arrogance than one that grants to each individual the agency to choose the life that is best for him- or herself.

Curiously, the kind of freedom of which Ignatieff speaks, the uprooting of the individual from the family, church, and state, can also be viewed as much as the effects of capitalism as of liberalism. If capitalism together with liberalism liberates individuals from authoritarian codes of meaning, it nonetheless produces its own blind power. In the eyes of the global community, however moral the intentions, an unchecked and unbalanced superpower already entails hubris, and this hubris unravels the social bonds that any minimal system of justice requires. The National Security Strategy pushes the logic of hubris one step further, daring to nihilate (borrowing Nietzsche's language) those who challenge American supremacy. Ignatieff warns against the patent arrogance of the Wolfowitz strategy, and he is right to do so. But he does not always seem to see the hubris that any assertion of a superpower status entails. However moral its intentions, the United States cannot escape the charge of hubris as long as it aims to occupy the position of an unrivaled world power. An unrivaled power constitutes a threat to the multitudes that compose the global community. The ancient democrats referred to any form of unrivaled power as tyranny, and they let it be known that for the sake of the community this kind of power must be brought down.

The Trick of Comedy

In *Upheavals of Thought,* Martha Nussbaum writes of a "characteristically American conjuring trick, turning tragedy into good news. . . . Does this determination to turn bad news into good show that . . . America . . . lack[s] a full-fledged sense of tragedy? If a full-fledged sense of tragedy entails giving up the hope that things can become better in this world, the answer to this question must be yes" (*UT,* 675–76). If Nussbaum is right, then how does this characteristically American conjuring trick work? And could it bring good news today?

Nussbaum refers us to the preface to the revised edition of *Fragility of Goodness* for further discussion.[27] While the preface does not elaborate directly upon the nature of comedy, it does give hints about how tragedy might be avoided. Her claims regarding tragedy in the preface have shifted significantly from the major arguments of the book itself. I shall recount her earlier and later views briefly in order to take them a bit further. Both earlier and later arguments focus on the individual's vulnerability to external circumstances, obscuring the political ethics of hubris and the central role of social relationships for individual well-being.

Consider her early account of the two causes of tragedy. One typical cause of tragedy, Nussbaum explains, is bad luck. External circumstances can bring bad luck upon a basically good character. Her example is the somewhat rash but otherwise basically good character of Oedipus. The second cause of tragedy, according to Nussbaum, is hard choices forced on characters by external circumstances. For example, Antigone and Creon must choose between conflicting duties to family and state. In both kinds of tragedy, the audience feels fear and pity for noble characters who are not wicked and do not deserve to suffer.

Nussbaum's view of the tragic buttresses her modern liberal moral philosophy and neglects the communal context of ancient Greek tragedy. A partial clue to the communal context can be found in Aristotle's observation that tragedy enacts an ironic reversal of plot that turns friends into enemies. Aristotle himself does not develop the meaning of this ironic reversal at all and also indicates no interest in the role of hubris in tragic drama. However, his remarks on the tragic do point to the fact that the destruction of friendships is not incidental; the damage to friendships is part of the essence of tragedy. For a communal culture, the destruction of the web of connections leads to self-ruin. This is the meaning of tragic irony.

Following Aristotle, the early Nussbaum dismisses any claim that the noble protagonist of tragedy is hubristic on grounds that the audience would fail to identify with him or her. For Nussbaum, audience identification is important because it fosters the sympathy that she places at the center of a liberal moral education. A sympathetic response to the fallen characters prepares the audience to acknowledge a universal vulnerability to external circumstances. She consigns friendships to external conditions for individual well-being rather than including friendships as an intrinsic element of individual identity. Bad luck or a difficult decision can alienate friends, and we depend upon friendships and other external conditions for a full and happy life (*FG*, xiv, 387).

Choruses of classic tragedies such as Sophocles' *Oedipus* sing of bad luck, but more poignantly yet they warn of hubris. Listen to the chant of Sophocles' chorus: "Hubris breeds the tyrant, violent hubris, gorging, crammed to bursting with all that is overripe and rich with ruin—clawing up to the height, headlong pride crashes down the abyss—sheer doom! But the healthy strife that makes the city strong—I pray that god will never end that wrestling."[28] These are the lines that motivate the defense of democratic moderation in Nietzsche's early philosophy. Nietzsche interprets this crime correctly as a provocation that disturbs the very friendships that sustain the self. Certainly, flashing forward to the provocations of an American empire, the loss of allies cannot be understood as a simple case of bad luck. The loss of friendships comes about as a direct effect of hubris. The loss of friendships is not a mere secondary effect of a hard life. The consequence of damage to others is a weakening of the self. It is characteristic of liberal theory to obscure this irony of tragic self-ruin.

In the newer preface to *Fragility of Goodness,* Nussbaum shifts the focus of her reading of tragedy from a moral to a political context. Now she argues that an Aristotelian appreciation of our common vulnerability to external conditions (including wealth, friends and family, honor and citizenship) articulates a liberal policy that goes beyond mere moral sympathy for bad luck. Reflections on tragedy support a full-fledged economic argument for the redistribution of wealth (*FG,* xxii).

Moreover, Nussbaum no longer interprets the aristocratic characters in ancient drama as basically good. Our sympathies are now viewed as turning against these characters in favor of the victims of their egregious power. Human tragedy does not come from bad luck per se so much as from "defective political arrangements," and these tragic circumstances are the result of "ignorance, greed, malice, and various other forms of badness" (*FG,* xxx). Her early work, she now believes, was too quick in its criticism of a Hegelian-style "synthesis" that would happily overcome bad political arrangements, including the clash of demands from the private and public spheres. As she explains, conflict between duties to family and career may make life difficult, but social policies might readjust the structure of employment to reflect the facts of family life. The trick of preempting tragedy, say of transforming the struggles of Antigone and Creon into a harmless battle of the sexes, is to set in place good social policies. "We must never forget that tragedies were vehicles of political deliberation and reflection at a sacred civic festival—in a city that held its empire as 'a tyranny' and killed countless innocent people," she writes (*FG,* xxxviii). The comic sensibility, or at least the optimistic mindset, of American life strives against such tragic vices as selfish ambition by cultivating both moral sympathy and structural change.

Nussbaum's new reflections take us far but still fall short of the dialectic of hubris that tragedy portends. This tragic dialectic renders what might otherwise be interpreted as a banal vice, such as vanity or greed, into the terrifying madness that hubris unleashes. Hubris, unlike any simple vice, does not just happen to leave the protagonist alone and without friends. Hubris names an assault on the web of friendships that constitutes who we are. The consequences of destruction on self and others can be horrifying.

Does the logic of hubris carry any force in the contemporary world? No doubt, the dialectic of tragic recoil seems to be of little relevance for a republic that not only takes itself to be immune from the old logic of Europe but also thinks of itself as disconnected from the rest of the world, disconnected even from its own past. But September 11th and its disconcerting aftermath should have changed all that. Our new world should give us some glimmer of awareness that U.S. policies abroad will sooner or later boomerang to have consequences here at home. Moral sympathy and generous American liberal institutions are good, but they are not enough. (We shall return to the virtue of an "understanding heart" in our final chapter in the context of a discussion of irony.) A political ethics for a world that is in fact defined by interdependence and not independence (or what Nussbaum defends as the ontological separatism of liberal individualism) profits from a deeper understanding of the communal context of ancient theater than Nussbaum's liberalism allows.

Nussbaum interprets the demands of social justice entirely within the parameters of liberal individualism. Without an understanding of the social ontology of interdependence, it is difficult to grasp the impact of hubris. Perhaps it is not surprising then that liberals, however well-intentioned, remain vulnerable to charges of arrogance from all over the world. The offer of the stronger to help the weaker by imposing liberal values just does not suffice. Neither nations nor individuals can claim to stand alone, and yet liberalism relegates social interdependence to background conditions for self-flourishing. As a consequence, liberalism misses the symbolic gestures of domination (including forms of cultural imperialism) that can accompany even its most sincere moral claims. Nor does liberalism give serious consideration to the dependencies of strong nations on weaker ones (today we might think of the importance of oil for the over-industrialized nations or the reparations owed by Europe and the United States to the colonized) and the dialectical ironies that these dependencies portend.

The choruses of ancient tragedy represented the communal cry of the *demos* against hubris and the cycles of rage and terror that this crime would provoke. This old language of hubris translates across cultures and nation-states and provides elements of an ethics for a global community, what Schell calls "the will of the world." But then is the United States doomed to be the scapegoat for this re-emerging logic? Is there in American culture any basis for joining our voice with, and not against, the multitudes? Any distinctly American wisdom that might allow us to stand with, and not against, an emerging global community?

A headline in a *New York Times Magazine* article written just after the Iraq invasion reads, "My French neighbors like 'Rugrats' and Tex-Mex. It's our soul they don't want to import."[29] Tex-Mex is delicious, but it is the French fascination with American comedy that is interesting in our context. Nussbaum has claimed that ancient tragedy offers a liberal moral education about liberal virtues, especially generosity. Nietzsche, influenced by the dialectical thought of Hegel, encourages us to extend the lesson beyond liberal virtues to a tale about hubris and the irony of power. Might we not find some corresponding wisdom in mainstream American comedy, a genre that otherwise seems to exhibit nothing more than our passive delight in easy-to-consume pleasures? Might the American preference for the apparent superficialities of the comic demeanor open a deeper perspective on freedom and democracy that could revitalize our sense of who we are, one that could steer us away from the hubris of the flag-waving, honor-seeking nation-state or even of downward-looking liberal sympathy and toward a pleasure-loving social ethic of freedom? The *New York Times* article alludes to what our alienated European allies like and do not like about American culture: "[T]hey don't want to be American, because being American implies to them a willful amnesia, a loss of familial and societal ties," the author writes. Our comedies are popular abroad, while our liberal individualism and our neoliberal values are not. But then do our comedies reveal a larger vision of America, one that unmasks our high-flying moral rhetoric and rigid individualism—preempting tragic hubris through self-humbling laughter?

Rugrats is typical of American comedy, a genre that, Northrop Frye explains, portrays a society controlled by types of bondage transformed to one of "pragmatic freedom."[30] "Comedy usually moves toward a happy ending, and the normal response of the audience to a happy ending is 'this should be,' which sounds like a moral judgment. So it is, except that it is not moral in the restricted sense, but social," Frye observes (*AC*, 167). Comedy does not employ bipolar moral discourse that opposes good and evil, lest it risk its humor. But if American comedy offers a romantic vision of things, not as they are or ought to be, but as they should be, what is the pragmatic freedom that this broader vision portrays? What is this sense of things as they should be?

Two Concepts of Social Freedom, One Tragic, One Comic

The aftermath of September 11th brought conservative and liberal strategists to reconsider John Adams's famous warning whether in becoming an empire the United States risks losing her soul as a republic. As the country comes to terms with its vulnerability to external forces, the model of the enclosed nation-state (with its illusion of separatism and self-sufficiency) has given way to the moral (i.e., naively self-righteous) claims of a liberal empire (needing oil). Of course, any project for American hegemony, even one that works through alliances, is going to be perceived by those who are excluded from its circle of power as hubris and may fuel what the Pentagon now calls "blowback." Hence the need for a third model of the nation-state, one that rests on interdependence in a global community. This third model would avoid imperialism's rhetoric of good and evil and would heed voices wary of arrogance and liberal empires. The comic element of U.S. culture offers us some glimpse into this alternative political ethics, one that deflates the arrogance of moralizing perspectives. The classic liberal conception of freedom as one version or another of independence does not address what a more full-bodied freedom might mean for a partner in the global community. Popular comedy, oddly enough, does.

At the beginning of the cold war, Berlin contrasted two concepts of freedom that continue to frame American moral and political thought and yet fail to capture what is at stake in global politics (*EL*). The first concept, "negative" freedom, anchors standard American liberalism. Berlin locates this freedom as an answer to the question " 'What is the area within which the subject . . . is or should be left to do or be what he is able to do without interference by other persons?' " (*EL*, 121). The second concept, "positive" freedom, "is involved in the answer to the question 'What, or who, is the source of control or interference that can determine someone to do, or be, this rather than that' " (*EL*, 121–22). Berlin traces back this second concept to Kant's notion of rational autonomy. The Kantian notion severs from the empirical self an ideal self. For continental thinkers who came after Kant, including Hegel and Marx, this ideal self could be liberated only in a rational society. Such a society, Berlin warned, may open the door to the dangers of communist, nationalist, authoritarian, or totalitarian creeds.

While Berlin's cold war–era essay is focused on defending liberalism against the authoritarian dangers of this second concept of freedom, he ends the essay with a truncated discussion of a third concept of freedom. Berlin points out that the central aims of anti-colonial and nationalist movements have never been properly addressed by the first and second concepts of freedom. In response to these movements, a third freedom emerges, one that, Berlin insists, is not truly a quest for liberty or even equality, but a struggle for status and honor. More recently, since the culture wars of the 1990s, multiculturalists have reinterpreted this third freedom (via Hegel) in terms of the politics of recognition. Berlin's neglected remarks on the third freedom shed light on these contemporary debates.

Berlin explains that positive and negative conceptions may acknowledge our interaction with others, but "I am a social being in a deeper sense. . . . For am I not what I am, to some degree, in virtue of what others think and feel me to be?" (*EL,* 155). "I desire to be understood and recognized, even if this means to be unpopular and disliked. And the only persons who can so recognize me . . . are the members of the society to which, historically, morally, economically, and perhaps ethnically, I feel that I belong," a society in which I am "recognized as a man and a rival" (*EL,* 156, 157). "It is this desire for reciprocal recognition that leads the most authoritarian democracies to be, at times, consciously preferred by its members to the most enlightened oligarchies"(*EL,* 157). Berlin notes that this third concept, really a hybrid notion, is referred to as "social freedom." It is "akin to what Mill called 'pagan self-assertion'" but extended beyond the individual to the personality of a class, group, or nation (*EL,* 160). Berlin suggests that this concept is involved in the question of "who is to govern us?" and he observes that the focus of this freedom is on assaults on social identity that are experienced as insults. "It is the non-recognition of this psychological and political fact . . . that has, perhaps, blinded some contemporary liberals" (*EL,* 162).

Liberals may aim less to be tragically blind to these social forces than to maintain a degree of autonomy if not anonymity from conventional norms of honor and status. Nussbaum, for example, explicitly warns against the illiberal pursuit of honor and wealth, and she emphasizes the importance of valorizing the individual choice instead.[31] As we have said, she rests her liberalism on an ontological commitment to the existence of separate individuals, and she opposes this liberal ontology rather sharply to any romantic view that subordinates the individual to an organic whole (*SS,* 10). What such a sharp opposition misses is a rich third alternative. However much Nussbaum addresses the importance of friendship for individual flourishing, her characterization of friendships as "external goods" and her portrayal of the social realm as a locus of dependency, neediness, and vulnerability (all forms of the devalued heteronomy) leave individual autonomy as our first and foremost moral and political value. This view fails to bring to the foreground of discussion the intersubjective realm where vital, complex, and troubled dimensions of the social being take root, and where a progressive theory of social freedom might be worked out. Compare Berlin's claim that the aims of nationalist and postcolonial peoples are thoroughly heteronomous and threaten true liberty (*EL*, 156). Excluded from liberal theory is a third possibility for the free life beyond liberalism's autonomy/heteronomy dichotomy.

In an essay called "Home," Toni Morrison writes of concerns for "legitimacy, authenticity, community, and belonging" that motivate many of the narratives of freedom in American slave and post-slavery society. At first glance, these concerns for belonging would seem to recall the struggle for recognition that Berlin finds in nationalist projects, but in fact they diverge. As Morrison reflects upon her own literary project *Paradise*, a novel that juxtaposes two kinds of communities, one that is black nationalist and male-dominated in its inclinations, and the other that is not, she writes of the need to transform the "anxiety of belonging" away from the dangerous moral psychology of honor and revenge to more forgiving "discourses about home" (*HB*, 5). She wonders if "[black] figurations of nationhood and identity are . . . as raced themselves as the [white] racial house that defined them" and if there is not another image of the "world-as-home" (*HB*, 11).

Of course, since Homer's *Odyssey*, finding home has defined the center of comedy. But could the metaphor of home have any significant political value (that is, apart from the nationalist one that Morrison eschews)? Morrison offers another glimpse into the political meaning of the metaphor by drawing our attention to a popular misreading of her novel *Beloved*, one that "works at a level a bit too shallow" (*HB*, 7). The penultimate line of the novel ends with the word "kiss"; it is this word that she suspects may cloud the novel's driving force. She explains: "The driving force of the narrative is not love, or the fulfillment of physical desire. The action is driven by necessity, something that precedes love, follows love, informs love, shapes it, and to which love is subservient. In this case the necessity was for connection, acknowledgment, a paying out of homage still due" (*HB*, 7). The repetition of the word "necessity" indicates a drive that is not a choice because it is not an option. Some vague notion of belonging characterizes a vital human need.

Morrison understands the web of connections that define us in part through a sense of debt to the past, and for an African American writer, this includes unknowable ancestors and their unspeakable pathos. The term "home" names better than love or compassion the sense of connection that is for Morrison both spiritual and selfish and that compels the individual to encounter sources of meaning outside the self that also lie within. In its final pages, *Paradise* turns from bleak tragedy to a vision of "going home" that is almost comedy (and that invites comparisons with Dante's third part of *Divine Comedy*). "There is nothing to beat this solace . . . of reaching age in the company of the other" the narration ends.[32] That is paradise.

Liberalism's individualism makes it difficult to understand the need for connection, acknowledgment, or homage still due as core political concepts. Standard political discourse with its socially minimalist rhetoric too readily flattens these needs to forms of security. In contrast, romantic comedy opens beyond liberal political dichotomies of autonomy versus heteronomy, the individual versus authority, or independence versus dependence, toward a more complex meaning of a free life. To be sure, like liberalism, comedies deflate the conventional values of status and honor and the political battles that ensue. But rather than cultivating a stoic indifference to the heteronomous claims, romantic comedy engages the free life through comedy's presiding genius, Eros (cf. *AC*, 181).

Interestingly, Patricia Hill Collins enlists the term "eros" to characterize the force that is at stake for women in the African American community.[33] In *Fighting Words*, Collins defines as a "visionary pragmatism" a theory of justice that fosters an "intense connectedness," and she cites Morrison's novel *Beloved* as exemplary (*FW*, 188). To develop the novel's central theme, she draws upon the classic essay by Audre Lorde, "The Uses of the Erotic."[34] Oppressive racial systems, Collins writes, "function by controlling the 'permission for desire'—in other words, by harnessing the energy of fully human relationships to the exigencies of domination" (*BFT*, 182). It is this specific concept of oppression that Collins finds in *Beloved*. For the characters of Morrison's novel, "freedom from slavery meant not only the absence of capricious masters . . . but . . . the power to 'love anything you chose' " (*BFT*, 166).

But then how can we conceptualize the novel's vision of freedom? Lorde's essay offers two elements. First, Lorde locates at the core of the person not the cognitive and individual capacity for self-reflection, but a libidinal capacity for creative work and meaningful social bonds. In contrast with the Freudian view of the erotic as fully sexual, Lorde explains, "the very word *erotic* comes from the Greek word *Eros* . . . personifying creative power" (*SO*, 55). A liberal theory typically focuses on the damage that oppression does to the capacity to reflect and make viable choices for oneself; and oppression can and does inflict this kind of harm. But, of course, oppression also sharpens critical insight into fundamental choices. Lorde focuses on assaults on the erotic core of the person. Oppression may render the individual unable to feel properly, and it is this emotional incapacity that defines for Lorde the salient political threat.

A second contrast concerns the direction of the psyche. The liberal view valorizes the capacity to turn inward and reflect upon motives and beliefs. Lorde does not take this capacity lightly, but alters its focus to the growth that begins, and culminates, in relationships. The idea of expanding the self by turning outward appears throughout American visions of individuality, including John Dewey and W. E. B. Du Bois as well as Morrison. In *Beloved*, Morrison describes love through the image of a turtle able to stretch its head outside its shell, or defensive "shield" (*BE*, 105). As Lorde explains, the Greek term "eros" names not a turn inward, but a centrifugal pull of the self outward. The individual grows with, not in reflective distance from, the community.

Lorde's poetic essay on erotic drive takes us some way toward understanding the visionary pragmatism of U.S. culture and its multidimensional quest for freedom. Still, the ethic of eros will strike the liberal defender of autonomy as overly sentimental, and in part for good reason. As we have seen, Morrison herself cautions against overemphasizing the importance of love in her novel. Lorde's essay, written in the cultural climate of the 1970s, articulates libidinal sources of selfhood, but does not lay out in full the sense of connection that defines the center of Morrison's work. The driving force of the narrative is not love, Morrison notes, or at least not the "fulfillment of physical desire" (*BE*, 7). The driving force of the novel is not love but precedes love. In Morrison's *Beloved*, Collins glosses freedom as "the power to 'love anything you chose' "; but Morrison had not written the word "power." Morrison's text reads: "a place where you could love anything you chose . . . *that* was freedom" (*BE, 105*). Instead of power, and indeed, what might be reduced to an individual capacity, she had written of freedom as though it were a place, a haunted but necessary place.

We can understand the connections that Morrison's characters enjoyed and suffered in terms having less to do with the sublimation of libidinal desire, as Lorde's essay would suggest, than with a sense of responsive connection with the past as well as the present and the future. Place as a web of belonging names what a people in diaspora may most of all seek.

A liberal conception of autonomy acknowledges that social relations play a role in individual well-being, but consigns them to the background, as props for the care of the self-reflective subject. The primary focus of the liberal subject is on a first-person narrative of self-ownership. A larger pragmatist vision (pragmatist in Frye's sense) focuses on social entanglements and unfolds in a drama of relationships. Relationships move to the foreground of the plot.

In order to capture the "intense connectedness," we might re-name the force that drives Morrison's narrative "social eros." The term fits with Morrison's reference to ancient Greek and African cultures to articulate the American sensibility that she explores. She explains that a "large part of the satisfaction I have always received from reading Greek tragedy, for example, is in its similarity to Afro-American communal structures (the function of song and chorus, the heroic struggle between the claims of community and individual hubris) and African religion and philosophy."[35]

But if social eros were to replace autonomy on the central axis of normative theory, then what term best names the harm that oppression does? Morrison meditates on the "the concept of racial superiority," and she describes this concept as "a moral outrage within the bounds of man to repair" (*UU*, 39). "Moral outrage" is a common translation for the Greek term "hubris." In "Unspeakable Things Unspoken," she points out that the struggles of the community against hubris often define the plot of tragic drama. In Greek tragedy, it may be the function of the chorus (representing the *demos*, or common people) to warn against hubris. Not surprisingly, Morrison lists as characteristic of black art: "the real presence of a chorus. Meaning the community."[36]

Aristotle defined hubris as an "insult," or "a form of slighting, since it consists in doing and saying things that cause shame to the victim . . . simply for the pleasure involved. . . . The cause of the pleasure thus enjoyed by the insolent man is that he thinks himself greatly superior to others when ill-treating them."[37] Today in the context of both domestic and international politics, we might think of hubris as an act of arrogance, or a crime of humiliation, and understand its perverse pleasure as what those who are morally righteous sometimes seek. The ancient Greek *demos* established codes against hubris and invoked these codes in an effort to control the elites. Morrison returns to ancient sources of democracy through her interest in classical tragedy, but she does not take as central to society the values of honor and status, and the contests in which these stakes were claimed. But if we join with liberal theorists to disparage the culture of honor, we might nonetheless re-engage a vision of the free life that classic comedy relates. Morrison's romantic vision of a home reinvents the meaning of democracy—and of what one might call, after Berlin, a new type of social freedom. The central axis of ethical discourse does not turn around the poles of autonomy and heteronomy. Morrison's focus is on neither liberal independence nor nationalist struggles for honor and recognition. Morrison's central focus is on the acknowledgment of friendships and communities, the outrageous acts that tear these bonds apart, and the comic wisdom that allows for their repair. If the comic mindset frames a prevailing American conception of freedom, then this mindset might be mined for something more than its form alone. From the comic vision, we might find a political ethics of eros and hubris that represents the field of force that Morrison calls home. In the next chapter we anchor this dream called home in the visionary pragmatism of Cornel West.

TWO

LAUGHING TO KEEP FROM CRYING

CORNEL WEST, PRAGMATISM, AND PROGRESSIVE COMEDY

It isn't easy synthesizing the work of the master synthesizer, Cornel West. Cornel West's glimpse into life is as wide and deep as his roots in music and religion. His evangelical message of hope, the syncopated rhythms of unexpected joy against the unyielding absurd, have earned him the title of the blues man of philosophy, jazz king of thought. I may contort the vision of this jazz thinker, this blues preacher, beyond his comprehension, perhaps in the manner of white musicians who, as West remarks, divert the sublime rhythms of the jazz tradition into the easy lyricism of swing.[1] I can only defend myself by stealing a line from that wise councilor (played by West) in *Matrix Reloaded* (Andy Wachowski and Larry Wachowski, 2003): "Comprehension is not requisite for cooperation."[2] And in fact, as you shall see, comprehension turns out to be less important than cooperation in what I have to say.

Now it may sound as though I am mocking Cornel West's fine work, but in fact I take his work quite seriously. As author no less than scholar of wisdom literature, Cornel West struggles against the sweet truths that veil the dark ones. From a melancholic sojourn of thought emerges a voice from the darkness that is as cathartic as it is reflective. West's predecessors in American thought have not always sounded the blue note. The forward-looking optimism of Ralph Waldo Emerson and John Dewey, men who set in motion the pragmatism that lies at the center of American thought, failed to give ample voice to the pathos that rumbles through the dream of a democratic social life.[3] West takes from these pragmatic thinkers the upbeat experimentalism, the faith in democracy, and the sanctity of the individual as motifs for his thought. Stripped of the tragic sense, however, pragmatism mocks those who know terror as well as love, friendship but also soul-wrenching despair—life's full range. An intricate balance of optimism with the pessimism that comes from a direct acquaintance with the absurd gives rise to a new pragmatism, not neopragmatism, but a prophetic pragmatism. This is a pragmatism whose vital elements of fallibilism, voluntarism, and experimentalism are remixed and recharged in the existential matrix of evangelical Christianity and improvisational jazz.[4] In fact, what Cornel West calls a prophetic pragmatism we might rename, just for fun, a pragmatism reloaded.

I do not mean to mock this vital new pragmatism. My intention is instead to acknowledge yet another source of wisdom in American culture. While much of West's work reflects on the tragic soulfulness that black music and religion bring to American philosophy, West insists that the existential matrix of black experience is as much comic as it is tragic. West explains in a recent response to his critics that his "devotion to fun— a word coined in modernity by Americans, is part of my California frontier humor. . . . [S]ome of the aims of professionalism in the academy are to tame the comic . . . and conceal the funk—even as we teach Lucian, Rabelais, Chekhov, Twain, Marx, Morrison, and I hope Richard Pryor."[5] The bluesy vein of black culture may strike the dominant cord of Cornel West's complex thought to date. "To be human is to suffer, shudder and struggle courageously in the face of inevitable death," he intones in a major introduction to his thought (*CWR*, xvi). And indeed "death, dread, despair, disease, and disappointment" are the reoccurring motifs of his tragicomic sensibility (e.g., *CWR*, 101). But what might we learn if we were to alter the dominant cord of prophetic pragmatism from the heavy spirit of evangelical Christianity and bluesy jazz to the funk of the down and low comedian Richard Pryor or Chris Rock? How might the comedian's encounter with the post-soul hip hop street-smart absurd bottom of American life augment or even complement West's bluesy Christian vision? Will we have set free yet a second variation of prophetic pragmatism, one perhaps less Christian and yet no less serious? A pragmatism, if you like, remixed and reloaded?

Let's begin with a more careful look at the tragic element in the tragicomic pragmatism of Cornel West.

The Tragic Element of the Tragicomic

Detached and disconnected from the existential womb of the tragicomic, philosophy may sound, as my students say, as vain and self-important as the monologue of a flat character. Perhaps this is an appropriate concern for that tradition of thought called pragmatism. The tragicomic voice that West encounters in black history modulates the blind optimism of those pragmatists naive to the arrogance of an emerging Anglo-Christian nation. West places pragmatist thinkers, including himself, in a larger tradition of romantic thought, from Jefferson and Rousseau in the eighteenth century, to Emerson and Marx in the nineteenth century, and Dewey and Gramsci in the twentieth. The romantic and revolutionary fervor of these thinkers "unleashed unprecedented human energies and powers, significantly transformed selves and societies and directed immense human desires . . . toward . . . ideals of . . . freedom," West observes (*CWR*, 153). These romantic thinkers diverge in orientation from their progressive counter-parts in the Enlightenment. Their Promethean impulse would transgress the limits imposed by the claims of enlightened reason, self-interest, or the moderate virtues, and dare the risks of untempered thought and deed. In their more powerful moments, these thinkers partake of the evangelical fervor of common folk "out of control, overpowered by something bigger than themselves" (*CWR*, 91). For what is the soul if not a passion for something larger than the self? But while these poetic and political think-ers, these romantic revolutionaries, embrace a giddy sense of possibility that West does not entirely disavow, it is the dissonant rhythms and melan-cholic tones of black music and church rhetoric that give prophetic prag-matism its complex weave. "[T]his new kind of cultural criticism—we can call it prophetic pragmatism—must confront candidly the tragic sense," West writes (*CWR*, 150). Without the tragic sense born of the matrix of black music and religion, pragmatic thought lacks existential dimension-ality. It lacks depth.

What does Cornel West mean by the tragic sense? It is the interplay of "tragic thought and romantic impulse" that captures for prophetic prag-matism the *agon* of "inescapable evils and transformable goods," Dr. West writes (*CWR*, 166). The tragic sense emerges through the struggle against evil. Some evil lies beyond all efforts of comprehension or control, yield-ing the sense of the absurd. It might seem as if the existential problem of evil would be central for any perspective on tragedy, but in fact it does not figure into that classic work, Aristotle's *Poetics*. For an Aristotelian, tragic drama turns less on what a post-Nietzschean Christian might discern as evil than on a simple mistake (*hamartia*), an instance of bad luck, that brings about the downfall of the heroic protagonist. Fate and error, not radical evil, emerges at the center of Greek tragedy. There may have been more to the classical theater than an Aristotelian exegesis allows. It is difficult to encounter a play such as Euripides' *Medea* and not sense something more akin to evil than error of judgment or trick of fate. In any case, the tragic moment that interests West appears—at least at first—to be existential and not classical: "[T]he context of Greek tragedy—in which the action of ruling families generates pity and terror in the audience—is a society that shares a collective experience of common . . . meanings. The context of modern tragedy, on the other hand—in which ordinary individuals struggle against meaninglessness and nothingness—is a fragmented society with collapsing metaphysical meanings" (*CWR*, 165).

The theme of a fragmented society and the irrevocable sense of homelessness that such a society provokes joins with a second theme of moral struggle to give the existential contour to modern tragedy. The tragedy comes from the acknowledgment that struggle is doomed in a world where misery prevails. The moral choice to struggle against the absurd generates the heroism of the agent, be he or she "a person of rank or a retainer, a prince or a pauper," and bestows the cathartic element of the tragic sensibility, West explains (*CWR*, 165). Moral struggle humanizes, generating life-sustaining spirit, in the face of inevitable failure. This existential voice of tragedy reverberated through spirituals in the time of slavery, the blues in the midst of race riots and lynching, the sublime joy of freestyle jazz in the era of Jim and Jane Crow. It fades as the market mentality saturates the streets, struggle is reduced to Darwinian terms, and rewards mean only the material pleasures of bling bling. This contemporary fading of the tragic sense takes us to one of Cornel West's most controversial concerns.

In a culture stripped of visionary struggle, lacking any sense of an *agon* that is communal and spiritual, of a striving that expands the soul outward into expressive connection beyond the self, one finds a flat and pathetic type of desperation that West calls nihilism. Nihilism is the disease of our times. The failure to elevate struggle to moral terms " 'is to admit a strange and particular bankruptcy, which no rhetoric of tragedy can finally hide,' " West explains, drawing upon the words of Raymond Williams (*CWR*, 165). Moral bankruptcy hollows out the urban environment and yields life-defining decisions to external forces. The gangsters who rule the streets in violence claim to have no choice. The global elites who ride roughshod over local communities likewise claim to have no choice. The refusal to take up moral struggle is the central manifestation of nihilism. Without moral struggle, the tragic sense is lost to the brute force of the absurd.

The tragic sense that West invokes echoes through European writers: "My Kierkegaardian attention to death, despair, and disappointment and my Chekhovian concern with icy incongruity and dark absurdity . . . may undercut my Emersonian sense of possibility," West writes (*CR*, 348). Nonetheless "black strivings in a twilight civilization" (to borrow the title of a key essay) inflect prophetic pragmatism with aims and ideals that belong more properly to the African diaspora in the New World than to Europe.[6] "John Coltrane's saxophone solos, . . . Billie Holiday's vocal leaps," and, above all, "Toni Morrison's dissonant novels" guide us through the tragedies and absurdities that define "black modes of being-in-the-world" (*CWR*, 102). Black striving as West understands it is not egocentric or Eurocentric. Such striving does not revolve around the right to own the self, nor does it revolve around the gaze of the other. It is not the search for autonomy or recognition. It is not contained by Anglo or European ideals of freedom. The ur-text of black culture is the "wrenching moan" for spiritual salvation in Coltrane's "A Love Supreme." It is the unanswered search for a sense of home in Morrison's narrative, *Beloved*. What then are these diaspora ideals?

We can discern these diaspora ideals through what is absent in our triumphant times. The United States has no rival power, and yet our culture, Dr. West observes, is nihilistic. American culture is nihilistic not because of the failure to find answers to the ultimate questions of right and wrong, or to conquer once and for all the problem of evil. West does not seek an absolute for a hard times. For what could give meaning to the death of a innocent child, he remarks, as he recalls Dostoevsky's existential reflections on life's absurdities (*CWR*, 92). "Nihilism is to be understood here not as a philosophical doctrine that there are no rational grounds" to comprehend our tragicomic lives; "it is, far more, the lived experience of coping with a life of horrifying meaninglessness, hopelessness, and (most important) lovelessness," West writes.[7] The cure for this disease of the spirit is a politics of faith and conversion in the context of a communal ethic of love. "Black bonds of affection, black networks of support, black ties of empathy and black harmonies of spiritual camaraderie provide the grounds for the fragile existential weaponry with which to combat the namelessness and invisibility of black existence," West insists (*CWR*, 108). Through the black church, these bonds "transformed a prevailing absurd situation into a persistent and present tragic one, a kind of 'Good Friday' state of existence in which one is seemingly forever on the cross . . .—yet sustained . . . by hope against hope" (*CWR,* 427). Communal moral struggle sustains hope against hope that evil—social misery and sin, blind arrogance and blind fate—will be overcome.

These basic human drives for meaning and belonging are easily distorted by an Enlightenment politics of freedom. The Enlightenment thinkers opposed categories such as individual choice and rational autonomy to dogmatic authority, authoritarian traditions, and irrational passions (*CWR,* 93). Around the poles turn conceptions of negative and positive freedom. The underlying dichotomy of inner choice and external force, however formulated, does not speak to the more fundamental need among a diaspora people for a sense of home. West contrasts an authoritarian tradition, rightly attacked by the Enlightenment, with an "enabling tradition" that sustains vision beyond the myopic horizon of the self (*CWR,* 93). Rooted in these sustaining traditions are families and communities that answer to "basic desires for protection, association, and recognition . . . in the face of the horrors of nature, the terrors of history, and the cruelties of fate" (*CR,* 347). The highways and high-rises that tore through neighborhoods denounced as slums left urban America bereft of these sustaining bonds and protected suburbs designed not to know them. Negative and positive conceptions of freedom, freedom *from* and freedom *to,* divide liberals and communists, and may have defined the parameters of cold war ideology. But these parameters do not contain the goals of colonized and racially marked people. From these people, as Isaiah Berlin partly but incompletely explains, emerges the romantic search *for* status and honor that fuels nationalism (*EL,* 118–172). Securing the borders of a national homeland is for people in diaspora the highest form of freedom. Berlin's remarks on what he calls a third and hybrid concept of freedom did not receive much attention during the cold war era, when the ideology of individual choice was sharply set in relief against the command-and-control state-socialism. His casual observations on the rise of nationalism take on a new relevance in the wake of the cold war, as ideological confrontations between East and West yield to ethnic conflict in Europe and Africa, and racial tension and labor unrest smolders in the Americas. As long as unemployed or low-income blacks are treated less as a people than a problem for mainstream America, black nationalist movements in the United States will grow, Cornel West warns.

Yet West does not urge oppressed people to turn to nationalist movements. On the contrary, nationalist movements do not represent the vision of freedom that he has in mind. These predominantly male-led movements reclaim honor and solidify group identity through vindictive attacks on targeted enemies and the ridicule of those perceived as weak. These groups are too often misogynistic and homophobic (*CWR*, 525). West seeks a force of belonging that is cosmopolitan in spirit and inclusive in its rhetoric. He predicts that "[t]he progressive wing of the black elite will split into a vociferous (primarily male-led) black nationalist camp that opts for self-help at the lower and middle levels of the entrepreneurial sectors of the global economy and a visionary (disproportionately woman-led) radical democratic camp that works assiduously to keep alive a hope" (*CWR*, 117).

West is not a nationalist because he understands the more sustaining social bonds grow out of a freedom *of* belonging, a freedom *of*, we might say, achieved not through romantic quests for honor and revenge, but through libidinal pursuits of affection and spirituality. The reach of these bonds transcends the tribe. This is because this freedom of belonging emerges not through struggles that define who has status and who does not, who is in and who is out, in a zero-sum game. This freedom emerges through rituals of acknowledgment that seal friendships, marriages, and communities—in libidinal webs that open outward to all humanity.

Struggles for nationalism are told in the style of epic romance. The romance of nationalism serves not only as a movement for oppressed people. It can serve as well to veil the machinations of what neoconservatives term "liberal imperialism." The genre opposes good and evil in a structure too simple to capture life's drama. On the occasion of the Rodney King riot, West writes, "If we go down, we go down together. The Los Angeles upheaval forced us to see not only that we are not connected in ways we would like to be but also, in a more profound sense, that this failure to connect binds us even more tightly together" (*RM*, 8). Hatred, like love, is a form of passionate attachment, the stuff of tragedy and comedy. To open up a second variation of third freedom and another meaning of home requires a shift of genre. But then what genre of social movement, what tenor of social change, might give us insight into a drive for connection that is not confined by the romance of good and evil, the quest for honor and status, those odysseys that ground old patriarchal communities and new nationalist movements?

The theme of connection sounds more Greek than existential, and West has in fact been viewed as being as much a communitarian as an existentialist. In a significant departure from the standard existentialism of Sartre, West elevates the search for belonging to the highest form of freedom and the most authentic human drive. The absurd is not the metaphysical condition of human consciousness as it is in Sartre's conception of freedom. The African in Africa did not know the black experience of the absurd, not because she did not know freedom, but because she did not know slavery. "The trauma of the slave voyage from Africa to the new world and the Euro-American attempt systematically to strip Africans of their languages, cultures and religions produced a black experience of the absurd" (CWR, 435). But if the ancient Greeks (perhaps as the Africans) centered their communities around male contests for honor and status, West aims to reorient communities around the more tender bonds of affection and spirituality. These bonds begin not in the competitive games of the public arena but in the poignant exchanges of the family, church, and neighborhood. Women-led parenting movements replace male-led nationalists as the visionaries in the struggle for social freedom (CWR, 321). "We have created rootless, dangling people with little link to the supportive networks—family, friends, school—that sustain some sense of purpose in life," West writes (RM, 9). Liberal philosophies fail to address these fundamental needs "because they tend to view people in egoistic and rationalist terms . . . [when people] are also hungry for identity, meaning, and self-worth" (RM, 20). The untempered assertion of Enlightenment conceptions of freedom can collide with, even violate, other conceptions of danger and freedom. For those who struggle daily with the absurd, autonomy understood as either choice or self-mastery does not suffice. Freedom from and freedom to are not enough. Freedom is coming home.

The hubristic assault on social bonds and the sense of homelessness that this assault yields is central to the tragic pathos expressed in Morrison's novels. For West, like Morrison, these social bonds resonate with but do not finally turn on a dialectic for recognition. Morrison's preeminence among African American writers in the context of West's prophetic pragmatism is evident in her remarks: "No African-American writer had ever done what I did . . . —which was to write without the White Gaze. . . . Ralph Ellison: *Invisible Man*. Invisible to whom? Not to me."[8] Hegel's slave seeks from the master the sense of honor and visibility, a search for status that fuels nationalistic struggle. West and Morrison counterpose a vision of home as Eros.

There is one significant difference between Morrison and West. The sense of the tragic in Morrison's novels is resolutely ethical. Evil may not be comprehensible, but it is human in its origin. Like Morrison, West attends to the "wanton destructiveness," the hubris, as the Greeks write, that we bring upon ourselves through a deadly combination of ignorance and arrogance (RM, 10). He shares with Morrison an ethical interest in the Greek language of hubris when he observes the thirst for vengeance and the drive for status and power that captivate gangster mentalities. West complicates the ethical reflections on evil, however, with metaphysical reflections that he finds echoed through the writings of Josiah Royce

(*CWR*, 175). Royce does not view the tragic primarily through the evil agency of human deeds, but as the "capricious irrationality of the world" (*CWR*, 180). " 'The temptation to do evil is indeed a necessity for spirituality. But one's own foolishness, one's ignorance, the cruel accidents of disease, the fatal misunderstandings that part friends and lovers, the chance mistakes that wreck nations:—these things we lament most bitterly, not because they are painful, but because they are farcical, distracting,—not foe-men worthy of the sword of the spirit, not yet mere pangs of our finitude that we can easily learn to face courageously. . . . No, these things do not make life merely painful to us; they make it hideously petty' " (quoted in *CWR*, 181). In Royce West finds a pessimism to correct those Enlightenment philosophers or American thinkers, W. E. B. Du Bois among them, who fail to confront fate's absurd brutality. Du Bois's stubborn rationalism, West observes, prevents him from facing the tragedy of his own child's death. Du Bois writes of this death by natural causes as though its meaning were significantly political, lamenting the loss of his own child as but an abstract symbol for the struggles of the Negro race (*CWR*, 92). The rationalist, West concludes, lacks the tragic sense.

"The painful laughter of blue notes and the terrifying way of the cross . . . constitute the indispensable elements of my Chekhovian Christian mode of thinking," West writes (*CR*, 347). We have not yet, however, found the laughter in the metaphysics of this blues philosopher. West indicates that we might find this laughter if we turn to Chekhov. However, in *The Three Sisters*, the tragicomic play that West takes as the key to Chekhov's work, it is the tragic element that dominates (*CWR*, 555). The play contains moments of compassion and struggle against the pending absurd, but these brief and unsustainable moments do not give much in the way of joy.

Through Royce we can identify a decidedly unromantic genre of the comic through the pure irony of farce. Farce, as the intractable irony of existence, as sheer caprice, accounts for the severe faith of Kierkegaard, the existentialist who holds great sway over West. Royce also prepares for West to incorporate into his tragic Christian sensibility Aristotle's classic reflections on the ironies of mistaken judgment and inscrutable fate. Tragedy is not always the result of blind arrogance or vicious intent. Vigilance against hubris and other human vices does not suffice to hold back the absurd. Spiritual struggle against blind fate and pure chance is also required. Perhaps the implication is that for the post-Freudian, post-Oedipal sensibility of West, drama is part tragedy and part farce. Farce adds shades of the buffoon to the noble tragic character.

Should we conclude then that the comic element that West weaves into his pragmatism signals the farcical character of the absurd, the disorder of the real (*CWR*, 89)? Is the blind foolishness of the buffoon, the farce of fate, the sole element of "fun" that is proper to the comic, that necessary corrective for a pragmatism gone flat? What is the meaning of laughter in the post-soul street-smart urban culture of our postmodern times?

From the Tragicomic to the Comitragic in a Post-Soul Culture

"I would suggest that there are two organic intellectual traditions in African American life: the black Christian tradition of preaching and the black musical tradition of performance. Both . . . are oral, improvisational and histrionic. Both . . . possess precisely what literate forms of black intellectual activity lack: institutional matrices," West observes.[9] And elsewhere: "the prophetic utterance" of black Christianity resembles the "guttural cry and wrenching moan—enacted in Charlie Parker's bebop sound, Dinah Washington's cool voice, Richard Pryor's comic performances" (*CWR*, 16). Black Christianity, guttural cry, and Richard Pryor? Richard Pryor's humor may relieve black angst and sublimate black rage, but the strutting, cursing comedian is neither blues musician nor righteous preacher. Yet the complex racial history of American humor from Uncle Remus's trickster to the blackface buffoon through Pryor's stand-up comedy is sustained no less by matrices of black oral culture. Pryor of course is no slavish blackface buffoon.[10] On the contrary, Pryor's edgy artistry owes much to the tradition of the trickster, the ironic wit who renders evil absurd, the slave who outwits the master at the master's own game.

Pryor's 1970s tough urban humor laid the way for the contemporary multicultural talents of Chris Rock, Margaret Cho, and Paul Rodriguez, among others. But can his comic legacy mitigate if not mend, repair if not preempt, the urban nihilism that prophetic pragmatism discerns behind our wickedly triumphant times? Or does the lewd and ludic element of this licentious wit feed into the nihilistic despair that the jokes, rude insults, and deflating caricature seem to provoke?

Cornel West has weighed in against the proliferation of insult, and in particular the use of the N-word, within the African American community, in his own rap CD.[11] Comic theorists such as the great scholar Mikhail Bakhtin insist, however, that the *ironic* use of insult and bawdy jokes can be liberating and leveling against pretensions to superior status, creating the conditions for the egalitarian social bonds of the kind that West envisions.[12] In his 1978 performance at Long Beach, Pryor mocks "white dudes [who] get mad and [try their best to] cuss," but who just can't make it up to black standards: "[Y]ou all some funny mother fuckers when you cuss. They be saying shit like 'Come on peckerhead. . . . Yea you fuckin' ain't right buddy'. . . . N[ ] be talkin' about buddy this [as he grabs his crotch]. . . . Even Andrew Young be grabbin' his dick as he's talkin' to the President" (AC, 167). This is thumbing your nose (so to speak) to power if ever there was. Is there cathartic value to ironic insult, ridicule, and crude jokes in comedians like Pryor? Or is any redemptive moral value lost in the stigma that the N-word reinvokes?

This is a tricky question. Comedy with a heavy moral lesson is humorless, plainly a contradiction in terms, as Northrop Frye has observed.[13] Comedy does not preach the *ought* of moral imperative; it captivates its audience with the *should* of libidinal fulfillment. Morally and spiritually rigorous characters, the characters not only of romance but also of romantic tragedy, are easy targets of the comic's jokes. Still, as Frye allows, libidinal fulfillment can be more or less ethical, and it is the more ethical that is relevant for West's larger project. When Pryor mocks proper white folks who don't know how to cuss, he does not simply put them down as, say, the suburban straight guy naive to tough urban realities. (The uncool white is the rustic, I suppose, of the postindustrial age; cf. AC, 172.) Irony reverses and disables the meaning of the insult, deconstructing the hierarchies of status and respectability that serious insult reinforces. The ironic insult signals solidarity not hierarchy, displacing stultifying social drives with libidinal drives for affection and expressive pleasure, the core values of progressive comedy.

If not properly moral, progressive comedy may be not only ethical but downright visionary. Tragedy binds the future in the irrevocable deeds of the past, while comedy opens the field of future possibilities (cf. CWR, 177). In situations that are mired in moral ambiguity, progressive comedy alleviates moral tension and diffuses reactive emotions of envy and guilt (and the self-righteous politics that these emotions sustain). In fact, contemporary comedians influenced by Pryor's artistry may on occasion have a more salutary effect than the high moral tone that West finds in the old-style rhetoric of the church. Old church rhetoric may speak effectively and forcefully for "the wretched of the earth," but this rhetoric assumes an uncompromising and elevated posture. It requires the class of the oppressed stand opposed to the class of oppressors as clearly as black is to white. The high moral tone is appropriate in struggles against slavery or legal apartheid, or in the class warfare of global capital: "Society as a whole is more and more splitting up into two hostile camps, into two great classes directly facing each other," Marx writes in the *Communist Manifesto*.[14] In a postmodern situation, however, where social identities yield conflicting advantages and disadvantages, the moral tone of revolutionary tragic Christianity may not resonate—and may even sound arrogant and self-righteous. For the same reason, the expectation for the moral leadership, the epic vision, of a Martin Luther King or Malcolm X may be doomed to meet with disappointment. The post-soul generation of urban life may call for a different kind of leader with a different kind of bravado. One wonders: could it be the bravado of the urban comic wit?

Prophetic pragmatism "acknowledges human . . . conditionedness," West explains, and there are many versions: "My own version . . . is situated within the Christian tradition" (*CWR*, 170). West argues for the Christian version because "it holds at bay the sheer absurdity in life, without erasing or eliding the tragedy of life," and because "the culture of the wretched of the earth is deeply religious," as they are the prey of vicious forces (*CWR*, 171). On a different stage, Pryor mocks the predatory police and vicious dogs trained to hunt black men. These dogs can "catch the average white boy," but they can't outrun black men, he laughs: "By the time they catch a n[], they are too tired to do anything but maybe get petted or some shit like that" (*Richard Pryor—Live in Concert*). The ludic tone of progressive comedians shifts the focus of ethics from tragic empathy for the victims of hubristic white racial politics to the celebration of those who have the wit and luck to outrun enemies. And when outrun, these enemies look more like housepets. The trickster's humor diverts and domesticates the predatory drives that divide us into different species. Its seductive force transforms the predatory drives that Morrison depicts in a tragic vein into the more friendly pleasures that I like to call social eros.

Social eros names the spirit of American comedy that fosters pragmatic freedom (*AC*, 169). The social norms at the heart of laughter are more nuanced and extensive than our abstract moral and legal codes. Progressive laughter shakes up those norms that are absurd, revitalizing the erotic bonds that mold the social sphere. Three classic devices of the comedian correlate with the voluntarism, experimentalism, and fallibilism of a pragmatic progressive culture, liberating from the absurd those who laugh. The first device we have seen already in the wit of the trickster, the tricky slave in classical comedy, and the descendants of Uncle Remus in the United States (*AC*, 173, 174). The trickster, or what Aristotle identifies as the *eiron*, weaves plots to take back power from arrogant masters and staid social norms. Tricksters are not Kantians; they have been known to lie, and they otherwise bend moral codes to bring about the happy endings that everyone secretly desires. They are the thieves who steal from their bosses the emblems of status that prop up false claims to power. As I shall argue, contemporary trickster-style comedians influenced by Pryor,

Paul Rodriguez for example, construct scenarios that reverse social hier-archies. These scenarios enable audiences to reimagine and rekindle the possibilities of agency, augmenting what the old school pragmatist calls voluntarism. A second device of comedy revolves around something or someone out of its proper place. As we shall see, contemporary comedians such as Margaret Cho use the trope of displacement not only as a per-sistent category of Asian American experience but also as a catalyst for what the old school pragmatist terms social experimentalism. Third, the imperfect body and flawed character display in a comic vein what the traditional pragmatist calls fallibilism. This third comic device plays a central role in the bawdy humor of such black female comedians as Adele Givens.

Each of the three comic devices enables those who laugh to take back energy from blocking sources, giving rise to performances as cathartic and uplifting as church but *naturally* but on very different terms. Pryor set the stage for the bawdy humor of contemporary comedy with his irreverent attitude toward the church in such performances as his 1971 *Live and Smokin'*. One skit has him hold up a cross in the face of a vampire, not because Pryor believes in the power of the cross, but because vampires are "allergic to bullshit."[15] I would be tempted to call comic theater the church of the body, but in fact it reaches far deeper into the core of identity, the libidinal core to be sure. As one of Cho's fans remarks after the perfor-mance, with a slight twinkle, "you make me want to be a better person."[16] Of course, we will have to return to the meaning of that twinkle.

Rodriguez, one of the original "Latin Kings of Comedy," exemplifies the use of humor as a force to outwit power. The relevant hierarchies may not allow for the determinant moral judgments that divide oppressor and oppressed. As Rodriguez remarks, prejudices among Chicanos ("more native than the native"), Mexican Americans (first generation who func-tion in English), and Mexicanos (who just speak Spanish) rest uneasily alongside struggles against Anglos who see Latinos as the usurpers of their jobs.[17] Rodriguez tweaks morally self-righteous Anglos with routines in which he points out that the good jobs are not be found among the immigrants who take what Anglos refuse. He suggests that Anglos might stop their whining until they are ready "to strap on the leaf-blower" and start "mowing their own lawns" or nannying their "own kids" (NPR interview). Humor avoids the irritation of direct confrontation, adding sweet "sugar [to] the medicine," Rodriguez says. The sweet truths of com-edy have the effect of displacing and redefining the rough if not brutal racial politics that West finds behind such tragedies as the Rodney King uprising (NPR interview). Comedy is effective in circumstances where the high moral rhetoric of tragedy or epic romance risks polarization, miscommunication, and backlash.

How does the low comic tone accomplish what the high tragic tone of moral discourse cannot? Another of Rodriguez's comic routines gives us a clue. As host of one of Univision's most popular shows aired in Miami to Spanish-speaking audiences, Rodriguez constructs a skit that threatens to cross the line from playful social tweaking to punitive moral reprimand. In the weeks prior to the show, illegal immigrants had been severely beaten in Riverside by police. "If there is justice," Rodriguez muses, "these cops are going to go to jail." He continues, "[W]e might be the minority on the outside, but we are certainly the majority in the prisons"; this means that these cops "are going to become somebody's girlfriend" (NPR interview). Apparently, he was somewhat graphic about what kind of treatment Anglo cops could expect from their "boyfriends" in prison, and was fired in mid-show. Later he found out that most of the phone calls that came in during the show were positive.

A part of the humor of the skit comes from the perspective that accompanies the shift from minority to majority status in prison and the pleasure of the fantasized revenge of the Latinos against self-righteous, moralizing, and uptight Anglos. The simple reversal of power relationships enacted in the prison scene threatens to reestablish the tragic dynamic of honor and revenge that sustains oppressive social systems, if in different hands. The progressive, meliorating force of the humor resides in the very same use of the prison context, which serves to dissuade any easy assumption of superiority by Latinos. By casting the scene between Anglos and Latinos in the confines of prison, and alluding thereby to the heavy Latino presence in this low place, the routine avoids the simple and vindictive reversal of hierarchy, and recovers a degree of honor, paradoxically, through leveling the very social distinctions upon which status is based. The line between the humorous leveling of social distinctions and the vindictive recovery of honor and status is a thin one. It depends much, in this case, on how graphic the skit is. In Rodriguez's retelling of the story, the macho interest in reclaiming lost honor (with its dynamic of condemnation and revenge) is downplayed in favor of deconstructing claims to superiority altogether, replacing such claims with a change in perspective that fosters more the tender bonds of affiliation through humor. In progressive comedy, humor avoids the painful trials that establish honor and status and the hierarchical bonds upon which these trials are based. Chris Rock's retort that gays should be allowed in the military because he surely "doesn't want to fight" reminds us that not only military types, but moralists, militants, or anyone else claiming superior status (moral or otherwise) are comedy's most reliable targets (*Bigger and Blacker,* 1999).

If done well, the ironic use of insult, ridicule, or other forms of real or imagined abuse can render us immune from their more brutal effects in everyday life, leveling social distinctions and establishing friendships based on pleasure. But if the humorous reversal becomes too graphic, and the rhetoric of inclusion gives way to a rhetoric of exclusion, if the arrogant moral tone of good and evil blinds the audience to the humor of the absurd, progressive comedy collapses and we are left with the misunderstandings and violence of tragedy. In progressive comedy, the pleasure of laughter prevails over the drive to recover honor, and sweet happiness wins out over self-righteous claims to perfect justice.

Margaret Cho shares many of the same sentiments and humorous tactics as Rodriguez, while bringing into focus a second element of progressive, pragmatic comedy. Like Rodriguez, she finds that comic ridicule is usefully irreverent in staid, conformist, or oppressive cultures. It offers cathartic release from social tensions and punitive moral demands while avoiding direct confrontation, taking, as she remarks, the "sweet way around politics."[18] She compares her cathartic humor to the meditative practice (*tonglen*) of Tibetan Buddhism: the comedian "breathes in the suffering" of the world, and "breathes out joy"(NPR interview). While the cathartic powers might be somewhat mysterious, she is certain that humor liberates us from exhausting social expectations. Laughter exhales the poisonous social forces.

Bergson speaks of the comic butt of laughter as someone who is absent-minded, unaware, and generally not tuned in with social conventions.[19] The sting of ridicule serves as a prod for eccentrics, wayward individuals, and social misfits to heed social conventions. Cho's progressive humor turns Bergson's insight (as well as his politics) on its head. Laughter liberates the blind perpetrator of the prevailing social norms. It renders our relationships with one another less punitive and more fluid and alive, more attuned to social demands to be sure, but less respectful of conventions that block libidinal energy. Humor that avoids moral reprimand allows audiences to feel "comfortable," as Cho remarks (NPR interview), relaxing moral tension and diffusing the moral drives to condemn and punish. As laughter lets loose the reins of conventional moral judgment, audiences cast off rigid prejudices and punitive moral categories, and experience a revitalized libidinal energy flowing free.

If for Cho as for Rodriguez comedy avoids moral or political confrontation, preferring instead a sweet transformation of our social sensibilities, her queer Asian American sensibility brings into play a different side of progressive comedy. The sly trickster sets up scenarios that threaten to reverse the power dynamic until the target yields to the leveling force of the humor. Cho draws on the humor of displacement. For the Asian American, the racist insinuation that one does not belong to the larger society is cause for perpetual irritation. As Cho explains, her personal failure to measure up to the expectations of gender identity and academic achievement in her own community could only compound the Asian American experience of not belonging, and of being the unassimilable minority (NPR interview with Cho). The experience of being a profilable person of color is like "dying a death of a thousand paper cuts a day," no major assaults, but innumerable minor ones (NPR interview with Cho). At the same time she makes it clear that those in mainstream culture who signal to Asian Americans that they are somehow out of place do not intend to be racist, hold no malice, and do not merit moral blame. Moral discourse is not appropriate, and its use can be socially harmful given the usual misunderstandings of a multicultural society. As Michele Norris remarks in her interview with Cho, the charge of racism is insulting to most people today, and yet social expectations are racially motivated and harmful, and need change. Cho's example is the way white people will come up to her as they will to any Asian American and ask, "Where are you from?" (NPR interview). They don't mean San Francisco, they mean Korea, and they blabber on about whatever Korean comes to mind. She invites her audience to imagine an Asian American walking up to some white person and saying "Hey, are you from France? . . . Well not recently but a couple hundred years ago? . . . I thought so. I love your fries!" The intent of the humor is to draw attention to subconscious racial motivations in social perceptions without the insults and accusations that moral discourse can provoke.

Bergson observed that one does not laugh at vice but at social incongruities, moral rigidity, and other flaws in social bearing that create dissonance in our communities (*L*, 150). Cho uses the humor of not belonging not to recover that sense of propriety that holds together a monocultural society but to set us free from rigid expectations of who does and does not belong. For a postmodernist comic, displacement becomes the norm. Cho opens her 2002 filmed performance in Seattle, *Notorious C.H.O. in Concert,* by praising the heroes and survivors of the tragic event of 9/11. This has been a "tragic time for our country. . . . I have been in New York a lot. . . . at ground zero. . . . I was there day after day giving blow jobs to tragic rescue workers . . . because we all have to do our part. You find out a lot about yourself in times of crisis. And I found out that I lost my gag reflex. I call that a triumph of the human spirit."

Later in the show she mimics a conversation where her Korean mother, trying to deal with suspicions about her daughter's sexual identity, allows that everyone is a "little bit" gay. Cho proceeds to mock marriage except for gays and lesbians. She is not against marriage, she explains, but the world is wrong to think that the single person is somehow "incomplete." The right of gays and lesbians to marriage is "not about romance; it's about equality; and having our relationships regarded in the same way with the same kind of reverence as straight people's relationships. . . . [A] government that would deny a gay man the right to a bridal registry is a fascist state." Progressive comedy augments our capacity for taking delight in social dissonance, surrenders our romantic dreams for the perfect fit, and fosters instead the lively experimentalism (as the pragmatist would say) of a vital democracy.

African American comedians, including *The Queens of Comedy* (dir. Steve Purcell, 2001) Miss Laura Hayes, Adele Givens, Sommore, and Mo'Nique, bring attention to a third element of progressive comedy and a corresponding element of pragmatism. This third comic element is more complex that what is understood reductively as an interest in the body and its polymorphously perverse appetites. Even a casual viewing of the work of black female comedians reveals that central to their comedy is mockery not just of European standards of beauty but of perfectionism of any kind. Images of anorexic white women are juxtaposed with images of fat black women who love their bodies, who love sex, and who love other fat women. Adele Givens opens her *Queens of Comedy* routine with a comic return to the kind of love-your-body sermon that Morrison had cast in a sacred setting in *Beloved*: "[A] flaw ain't shit but a unique identifying mark. . . . If you got a big belly, rub that motherfucker, love it. . . . [N]o matter how fucked up you are, somebody loves your ass."

Compare *Beloved*'s grandmother's sermon as an "unchurched preacher" who "accepts no title of honor before her name . . . allowing a small caress after it"; while the sacred context brings shades of meaning different from those of comedy, the convergence of these two visions is striking. "Let your mother hear you laugh," the old preacher calls out as she begins her sermon (*BE*, 87). On a different stage, Adele walks onstage repeating Miss Laura's introduction that she is a "fucking Lady," using the insult as other comedians use the N-word, not to mock herself or anyone else, but to mock all titles or claims of special status, as she urges the audience to turn that love they show her back around to themselves. And there is laughter. The leveling of titles clears the stage for characters who are flawed and fallible (as the pragmatists like to say) but libidinally rich, or so these comedians insist. If they inspire listeners to be better persons, it is not in the sense of more perfect creatures, but in the sense of getting on with life not despite, but because of, those unique "identifying marks." We could call that a triumph of the human spirit.

The Third Freedom: Comedy and the Politics of the Family

Since the end of the cold war, ethnic tensions and religious extremism have replaced the moral-laden ideologies of communism and capitalism as the major cause of global unrest. Over the same time period, West's prophetic pragmatism has evolved from a revolutionary socialism toward a progressive politics of large-scale, market-friendly reform (cf. *CR*, 357). If Marxism takes as its focus the emasculation of the working class, and the black nationalist, the emasculation of the race, progressive reform extends its reach to the multifaceted concerns of the working family. The concerns of families join together those of diverse racial and class backgrounds, allowing West to construct concrete policy proposals (for public education, parental leave, childcare, child health care, higher wages, a shorter work week, and a shifting of the tax burden away from income and toward consumption) that he regards as of, if not universal interest, at least widespread public appeal. The interest in families, neighborhoods, and communities has always been important for prophetic pragmatism, but only recently have the concerns of families served to anchor the entire political project. *The War against Parents,* co-authored with Sylvia Ann Hewlett in 1998, declares that "in our market-driven society . . . parenting has become a countercultural activity of the first order."[20] Collaborative work with Roberto Unger published the same year argues that "[s]ocial supports for children can serve as the front line in the development of social rights for everyone" (*CWR*, 321).

The shift toward working families allows West to develop a politics of belonging as a cosmopolitan and communitarian rather than an ethnic or nationalist preoccupation, avoiding the pitfalls of Berlin's third freedom. If liberalism grounds cosmopolitanism in the rights of the autonomous individual, prophetic pragmatism grounds global justice in local webs of erotically charged caring. The other-regarding care that the child learns from the devoted parent in what West describes as the "most powerful of human attachments" is the emotive stuff that builds neighborhoods, trade unions, and civil associations; and it does cross ethnic and national borders (*WP*, xiv; cf. *CR*, 24). The web promotes the existential moorings that liberalism neglects, that consumer capitalism threatens, and that nationalism and extreme religion provide with a vengeance (cf. *CWR*, 375–76).

In *The American Evasion of Philosophy* (1989) West had characterized "the praxis of prophetic pragmatism [as] tragic action with revolutionary intent" (cited in *CWR*, 167). His post-'89 turn from revolutionary socialism toward a progressive politics of the family is accompanied by, if I am not mistaken, greater attention toward the comic. West subtitles his afterword to Yancy's *Critical Reader* (2001) "Philosophy and the Funk of Life," gives it an epigram from Chekhov, "To hell with the philosophy of the great men of the world! All great wise men are as despotic as generals," and returns several times in the essay to his interest in the comic. A reference to Chekhov has always served as a balance to his Christianity. West now points specifically to the comic as what the Christian viewpoint lacks. The "Christian viewpoint . . . lacks a strong sense of the comic and the body," he remarks after insisting upon the inadequacy of Jesus as a model for life: "Jesus . . . is for me neither an ethical model (his sense of the comic is too weak), a political model (his failure to condemn slavery or include women in his first-order group of disciples), nor a familial model (his relative lack of eros for intimate or significant others or even philia for relatives)" (*CR*, 353). Given the recent turn to a politics of the family, this inadequacy is striking.

Several years earlier in the introduction to *The Cornel West Reader*, West had written that the sacrificing love of Jesus "puts a premium on death and courage. To be human is to suffer, shudder and struggle courageously in the face of inevitable death. To think deeply and live wisely as a human being is to meditate on and prepare for death" (*CWR*, xvi). West has not yet published extensively on the comic, but one would think that by implication comedy would turn us from death's inevitability to life's mundane duration, taking its pleasure in ever new beginnings. If pragmatic comedy constructs webs of eros, it might also, to borrow phrases from Stanley Cavell's analysis of 1930s and '40s screwball comedy, train us to avoid sacrifice, self-denial, and other ascetic virtues, acknowledging our libidinal drives instead.[21]

If so, then the comic may turn out to be just what West needs to bring existential depth to his politics of the family, while avoiding the charges of his liberal and feminist critics, who view him as nostalgic for the patriarchal Christian family of the 1950s. West claims that his views of the family do not fall neatly into either '50s-style conservativism or post-'50s-style liberalism. He believes that liberals are right to reject the patriarchal structure of the 1950s, but not the nuclear family and its values of discipline, sacrifice, and service. He is critical of the countercultural rebellions from the 1960s, which encourage self-fulfillment at the expense of service to the family and community. As he explains, "narcissistic individualism ran smack into the art and practice of parenting" (*WP*, 134). He insists that "the kind of democratic feminism Hewlett and I promote is hard to discern and detect on the current ideological spectrum" (CR, 359).

Still the Christian rhetoric of servitude and sacrifice continues to confuse feminists and liberals despite their expressed agreement with his concrete proposals.[22] In *Beloved*, Morrison's character Sethe attempts to explain to Paul D the life-giving joy she found when she escaped with her children to freedom. She describes this joy in terms not of sacrifice but of selfishness: "It was a kind of selfishness . . . I was big. . . . And deep and wide and when I stretched out my arms all my children could get in between. I was that wide" (BE, 162). This well-known passage of the novel concludes that "to get to a place where you could love anything you chose—not to need permission for desire—well now, that was freedom" (BE, 162). West's appeal to the virtues of sacrifice may not subjugate women to patriarchal control, but it doesn't sound like the battle cry for liberation that we might desire.

Moreover, it is not clear how West's call for reasserting as the social norm the nuclear family does not relegate gay and other intimate social relationships to the Down-Low or other secret zones of the abnormal, and the family to the secure but boring surface of a libidinally repressed and (hetero)sexually overcharged culture.

His aim, West assures us in his response to Iris Young, is not to return to the repressive family of the 1950s, but also not to give in to the "libertarian feminism that elevates autonomy and choice over social responsibility and commitment" (CR, 359). This type of feminism turns choice into a fetish and plays right into the invisible hands of consumer capitalism. The parent movement escapes the one-dimensionality of left and right, West insists. Perhaps the project would do better with the kind of rhetoric that we find not in old church Christianity but in new school comedy.

Ironically, the values of self-denial that West finds in Christianity may root the conventional American family in the work values of Protestant capitalism that according to Niall Ferguson are not in the end pro-family at all. Ferguson explains: "It was almost a century ago that the German sociologist Max Weber . . . argued that modern capitalism was 'born from the spirit of Christian asceticism' in its specifically Protestant form. . . . [T]he experience of Western Europe in the past quarter century offers an unexpected confirmation of it. To put it bluntly, we are witnessing the decline and fall of the Protestant work ethic in Europe. . . . [I]n the pious industrious United States, the Protestant work ethic [may be] alive and well . . . [but] Northern Europe's declines in working hours coincide almost exactly with steep declines in religious observance."[23] The lower rate of productivity in Europe compared to the United States suits econo-mies that depend less on high rates of consumption and allow more time for families and holidays. Meanwhile in the Atlanta of Maynard Jackson, the old black church of the civil rights era that preaches common cause through service and sacrifice threatens to give way to new church sermons on personal excellence more congenial to the demands of black-owned business than to the family, neighborhood, and community.

The new comedy club scene in cites like Atlanta may in fact be taking over the old church function of relieving angst and rage, but one might wonder if the bawdy jokes do anything more than stimulate the material-ism and narcissism of nihilistic capitalism. West's own brief remarks about comedy focus on Chekhov and his "icy incongruities," not contemporary comedy. Surprisingly, the contemporary club scene may be just the place to find the concerns of family responsibility spelled out in an existential frame.[24] The fact that this same bawdy pro-family comedy is, as Richard Pryor's vampire routine reminds us, just about as far from the religious right as you can get suggests an escape from the one-dimensionality of left-right politics. In *Bigger and Blacker* (HBO, dir. Keith Truesdell, 1999), Chris Rock mocks mothers who abandon their children for a good time ("What the fuck are you doing in the Club at 2 in the fucking morning on a Wednesday night? . . . Is it your Birthday? . . . Go take care of those kids before they rob me in 10 years") or who think they can raise children without men: "You can do it without a man but that don't mean it's to be done. Shoot you can drive a car with your feet if you want to. That don't make it a good fuckin' idea." Of course, some of those women in the club are actually there working a second job to support their families, and others are there for some well-deserved time off. And even while Rock chides irresponsible parents, and emphasizes like West the importance of the father, he denounces sexists, applauds women who enjoy their bodies and their sexuality, and avoids entangling the ethical language of respon-sibility with the religious language of self-sacrifice. Along with *The Bill Cosby Show*, Chris Rock's family routines avoid some of the polarizing, moralizing, stigmatizing dichotomies perpetuated by the old church rhet-oric of sacrifice in a new church age.

Critics accuse *The Bill Cosby Show* of returning to the *Father Knows Best* nostalgia for the patriarchal family because the show centers around the father.[25] The emphasis that black comedians give to the father, how-ever, serves as an important counterweight to the effects of slavery, wel-fare, unemployment, and the prison industry on black families. Each of these social policies targets the role of the father in the black family. *The Bill Cosby Show* may focus episodes around the father and his point of view, but Bill Cosby does not replay the moral role of the stern father of white suburbia circa 1950s. Typically he asserts moral authority only after deflationary humor that reveals that he is not after all better or worse than any one else in the family.

Those comedians who rewrite the language of the family in terms of the pleasure of relationships promote a sense of belonging that avoids the fetishization of choice no less than the ascetic language of sacrifice and service.[26] The family becomes a place of self-fulfillment, not self-less love, a shift that suits a society in which women have reproductive choices, and do not risk their lives in birth, nor men in war—in other words, in a society where servitude and sacrifice are no longer the expectations of citizenship and multiple forms of family-style relationships proliferate. Postmodern feminists might valorize, as does Iris Young, the anonymity in the city over bigoted communities and the right to ground household relationships in choice rather than traditional family structures.[27] But West might also rightly point out that white anonymity and choice, like black invisibility, deny the depth of the drive to belong. Here we do have a choice: we can join struggles for ethnic and racial identity, or we can cultivate these romantic drives in a more comic vein, and redirect the drive for attachment toward the dissonance of families and communities that know how to laugh.

"The interesting question," West writes, "is the relationship between the ethical and the erotic. . . . [T]he erotic without the ethical can become just thoroughly licentious in the most flat hedonistic sense. But the erotic fused with the ethical means there is respect for the other, and that respect for the other also means being attentive to needs of the other given their erotic energies. These kind of issues seem to me fundamental ones because, of course, they affect every relationship. I mean, even in friendships that are nonsexual, there's an erotic dimension" (CWR, 13). Here West is beginning to sound a bit like Margaret Cho's mother, the person, Cho claims, who gave her a sense of humor (NPR interview). We all have friends that we like just a little too much, Cho's mother remarks. Everyone is just a little bit gay. In a nod to the gays and lesbians, we might avoid old church rhetoric and devote ourselves instead to the sweet force that builds friendships, families, and communities. Of course, as the Freudians will remind us, we are hardly ever clear about the meaning of this powerful libidinal force. But then whoever would ever think that comprehension is required for cooperation.

The next chapter will search for this libidinal force of solidarity in the bleak satire of Spike Lee. Only through the sometimes bitter irony of satire can we recuperate a sense of authentic existence through our social bonds.

THREE

AUTHENTICITY IN AN AGE OF SATIRE

ELLISON, SARTRE, BERGSON, AND SPIKE LEE'S *BAMBOOZLED*

Could an age riddled by the ironies of postmodern skepticism find a way of grasping anew the ethics of authenticity? In classic existential terms, authenticity entails recuperating a sense of oneself from the threat of absorption into social roles.[1] After the demise of the 1960s social movements, and the rise of linguistic philosophy, the call for authenticity sounds sentimental and suspect, and in part for good reason. In a highly media-saturated, status-conscious, and techno-powered age it hardly seems possible to extract personal identities from the impact of images or the distracting clamor for status and gain. Nor as social creatures could we conceive of identities uninformed by these social forces and the gendered, ethnic, racialized character they lend us. In life as in theater, we are characters with histories and social identities more deeply than we are bare existential subjects. If character emerges through social meanings, these meanings are problematic less because they insist upon receptivity to unauthored sources than because they are often distorted through stereotypical images with degrading histories. The question is how can we reclaim authenticity at a time when the existential slogan of returning to oneself appears more like a naive escape from, than a sophisticated negotiation of, our complex social lives.

The existential call for authenticity might strike mainstream liberal ears as being of little political relevance. The existential rendition of authenticity appears, however, in more modest form already in classic liberalism. Liberalism rests on moral principles that call upon autonomy, self-determination, or rational decision to guide individuals through webs of images, desires, and relationships.[2] Both liberalism and classic existentialism rest their conceptions of freedom on abstract notions of individualism. Neither is designed first and foremost to negotiate parameters of freedom through the intricate social web that reaches into our libidinal core.

The example of racialized social norms demonstrates some of the difficulties of grounding an ethics of authenticity on individual autonomy or any of its decisionistic and existential variants alone. In our post–civil rights era, no morally sensible person would challenge the principle that individuals are worthy of respect regardless of their race. We agree at least in principle that individuals should be judged on the basis not of their racial (or any other social) identities, but on their merits, decisions, and intentions as agents of self-determination. Freedom lies in this self-determination. Yet the pervasive formal commitment to a respect for individuals is not effective against the racial expectations that circulate in social norms and that inflect judgments of merit and conceptions of who we are. A moral philosophy that foregrounds the self-determined individual relegates the cultural inflections and troubled relationships of civil society to background phenomena, disengaging them from the full impact that they have on our individual lives. It displaces and risks obscuring the significance of various forms of belonging, and the entitlements, responsibilities and participatory practices of citizenship that follow—what, after Berlin, I have been calling our third concept of freedom. With the moral and existential focus on the individual, racial and other social norms remain far from the philosophical center of ethical inquiry, consigned often enough to what liberal moral philosophers perceive to be the less serious realm of social manners. Perhaps then it is to the realm of manners that we should turn if we are to locate the basic tenets for an ethics of authenticity in our satiric postmodern times. Ironically, the critique of social manners takes center stage not in moral philosophy, but in the literary arts of irony and satire.

Spike Lee's 2000 film *Bamboozled* attributes to Mark Twain (falsely, so it seems) the dictum that "satire is the way if we are ever to live side by side in racial peace and harmony." Could satire provide normative concepts and basic strategies for counteracting racialized identities in a post–civil rights, racially divided society? Could satire's ironic and mocking stance toward our social bearing allow us to reclaim what is otherwise in our cynical postmodern times a nostalgic and narcissistic idea of authenticity?

Spike Lee's *Bamboozled*, a satiric portrayal of the continuing relevance of blackface stereotypes, provides us with an occasion to ponder the ethical salience of a comedy of manners in the Information Age. The prevailing theme of the Spike Lee film, the search for authenticity in a charged racialized atmosphere of social masks, unreflective puppets, and stolen identities, invites us to draw upon Ellison, Sartre, and Bergson to locate the vices and follies of our neo-gilded age. Each of these thinkers allows us to recuperate for philosophical reflection important categories of human experience. Ellison's interpretation of American identity through forms of comedy will set the stage for our study of blackface. Sartre's epic romance of authenticity and bad faith in *Being and Nothingness* provides the initial impetus for understanding the existential force of the Spike Lee film and related cultural debates about what counts as black.[3] Given that the individualism of Sartre's existentialism poses some shortcomings for an era in which interdependence, belonging, and solidarity provide the key themes, we shall trace the concept of bad faith back to its possible origins in Bergson's social theory of the ridiculous. Our question then becomes: What if we were to shift the analysis of authenticity and bad faith from Sartre's World War II romance of the solitary individual to a social satire on manners? Might we use satire in order to recover the romantic possibility of what the hip hop generation calls "keeping it real" in the midst of our otherwise cynical postmodern times?[4]

Before we begin to examine the salience of satire as a critical social tool in our age, we shall take a quick glance back at standard claims regarding a very narrow American identity as put forth by one of classic liberalism's conservative defenders, Harvard professor Samuel Huntington. Professor Huntington's romantic quest for the roots of American liberalism in the manners and mores of a specifically Anglo-Protestant identity translates anachronistic biological racism into cultural racism, and constitutes a frighteningly powerful assault on both multiculturalism and cosmopolitanism. Postmodern skepticism may provoke an ironic detachment from such dangerous romantic claims, but the ironic stance can also leave a vacuum that disorients subjective agency and progressive social change. Huntington's cultural racism requires a response, one that recovers the classic existential question "What constitutes authenticity?" for our post-soul, hip hop, image-saturated American culture—this time through the dark, edgy, but ultimately redemptive perspective of tragic black satire. As we shall see, if self-deception and the denial of history distort our identities, then the test of authenticity is not individual or communal (in Huntington's culturally exclusionary sense) but social.[5] Owning up to oneself entails owning up as well to the demands of history, friendship, and family.

Who Are We? Mainstream American Culture and Blackface Humor

In *Who Are We? The Challenges to America's National Identity,* Huntington views the United States as united by not only a liberal political creed but also a "core or mainstream culture."[6] More provocatively, he claims that the tragic events of September 11th served the enabling function of revitalizing a national culture worn thin by multiculturalism and globalization. Citing founding father John Jay, Huntington lists six basic elements that have defined American identity: customs and manners, language, religion, principles of government, war experience, and common ancestry. Only common ancestry, Huntington remarks, has lost its relevance. The ethnic-racial roots of the Anglo-Saxon settlers have been rightfully challenged by immigrants and ex-slaves, he acknowledges. But if citizenship no longer turns on English ancestry, Huntington insists that our customs, manners, and core values do: "Throughout American history, people who were not white Anglo-Saxon protestants have become Americans by adopting America's Anglo-protestant culture and political values," Huntington writes (*WE,* 61). Those liberal elites who would propose a culturally rootless cosmopolitan creed against a race-based nationalism have missed what he takes to be a third option: "[T]here is no validity to the claim that Americans have to choose between a white, WASPish ethnic identity, on the one hand, and an abstract, shallow civic identity dependent on . . . political principles, on the other. The core of the identity is the [Anglo-protestant] culture that the settlers created" (*WE,* 62).

To be sure, it is appropriate in our multiculturally rich times to inquire about the relevance of a culturally rooted third option.[7] The social norms that define much of who we are emerge through our cultures, and these norms compose, as Huntington suggests, the substance that sustains such abstractions as our moral principles. Let us assume then that the interpretation, justification, and application of historically situated liberal principles does indeed rest upon the customs and mores embedded in a culture. Various liberals across the spectrum believe that the liberal creed thrives in what is often understood to be a culture of democracy, and Anglo-Protestant culture plays a significant role in the American national culture and moral philosophy, along with, we must add, doctrines of white supremacy.[8]

What then would this Anglo-Protestant element be that sustains, according to the argument, our liberal creed? Huntington writes: "In the absence of rigid social hierarchies, one is what one achieves. The horizons are open, the opportunities boundless, and the realization of them depends on an individual's energy, system and perseverance, in short the capability for and willingness to work. . . . In other societies, heredity, class, social status, ethnicity and family are the principal sources of status and legitimacy" (WE, 71). On behalf of Huntington, one must say that our national culture is not just an ethic of work. That we find perhaps far more exemplary among struggling immigrants. Ours is an ethic of individualism that locates our core identity through our work and imbues even our contemporary neoliberal individualism with a quasi-religious if not downright arrogant moral mission. As Huntington writes, "Protestantism in America generally involves a belief in the fundamental opposition of good and evil" (WE, 69).

Yet, given the cultural significance of the blues, jazz, hip hop, and, as we shall see, our original American comedy, how could anyone today seriously argue that our national culture owes its character and values entirely to a highly moral Anglo-Protestant work ethic? Even Huntington allows that our culture includes not only our somewhat moralizing missionary work ethic but also our "entertainment and leisure-time pursuits" (cf. WE, 60). It is difficult to argue that our entertainment and leisure-time pursuits are now or ever have been Anglo-Protestant—at least in any straightforward or morally justifiable form.

In the 1985 essay "An Extravagance of Laughter," Ralph Ellison explores American mores and morals through the dialectic of Anglo-Saxon culture and its Jim Crow–era antithesis. Recalling the grueling racial customs of the 1930s, he observes that the "challenge [of black Americans] was to endure while imposing their claims upon America's conscience and consciousness, just as they had imposed their style upon its culture."[9] We will return to the extravagant role of laughter for American identity shortly. For now it is important to acknowledge the centrality of African American culture to American culture.

Still, this impact of the African American presence on the core culture has not always occurred in what one might describe as authentic terms. If American identity as measured through our mainstream culture is to a significant degree black, the images, creations, and values produced by African Americans are often warped and misappropriated through the bad faith of a white-dominated socioeconomic system. "Every Nigger is an entertainer," says the old comedian father Junebug in Spike Lee's *Bamboozled*. Junebug is played by Paul Mooney, a former writer for Richard Pryor, who is the recognized genius behind the contemporary renaissance of African American satiric comedy. The Spike Lee film recalls the black-face origins of American comic theater, where blackened minstrels play the fool for white amusement. The film questions whether blackface stereotypes do not still warp our racialized identities. In a satiric comedy set to insist upon the relevance of the past and to locate our typically American blindness for our historical situation as a form of bad faith, Junebug, the old comedian father, represents less the patriarchal obstacle to youthful ambitions (romantic comedy's standard fare) than an ironic commentator, an imperfect moral center, and, most centrally for the film, a call for authenticity beyond what he himself, as comic entertainer, can claim.

For indeed whatever it is that Spike Lee aims to achieve with his own satiric film, it is not entertainment. On the contrary, the film's satire painfully and decisively pulls back as far as it can from the cheap ease and casual repugnance of an all-too-typical form of American comedy—the minstrel show. Perhaps the film's failure as entertainment is the price to be paid for an uncompromising demand for black authenticity in compromising circumstances. Certainly, the film's labored satire parts company not only from the minstrel show but also from the pleasures of mainstream American romantic comedies. While chapter 4 returns to those romantic comedies, we cannot find what is progressive in their libidinal pursuits without the prior philosophical awakening that this bleak satire demands.

The plot focuses around the decision of the comedian's ambitious black son to write a minstrel show for a big television network. The young, hip, white, and vaguely Irish executive who signs on the show to boost network ratings and the black father who refuses to sell out to such commercial enterprises represent opposing forces on the conscience of the son. The white executive defends blackface minstrelsy on the basis of a claim that at once raises and throws into question the possibility of authenticity in the United States. The minstrel show, the white executive insists, "allows us to laugh and to cry and to feel like real Americans." In the context of the film, the irony is clear: without blackface as an occasion of cathartic engagement and emotional revitalization, the assimilated American whom Huntington locates as culturally definitive, and whom Stanley Crouch redescribes as the "artificial white guy," may be at risk for an existential malaise of a distinctly WASP variety.[10] Spike Lee, however, is less concerned with the bleached white soul than with the existential well-being of

African Americans. In the era of gangsta rap and "Timmi Hillnigger jeans" (term from the film), the drive to "keep it real" through minstrel performances of identities affects not only whites devoid of depth but also African Americans, Latinos, Asians—it reaches to the roots of our expansive American culture. America in the largest sense may very well be gangsta rap with its avarice and rapacity. In any case, the minstrel mask serves as an appealingly hip route through which African Americans no less than assimilated Americans might feel fully alive, real, and most authentically themselves.[11] The disguised insult of minstrelsy played out in the style of the gangsters and whores of mainstream hip hop culture may emerge too often as the essence of the hip, the beat of the cool, and a lesson on the allure of bad faith.

In his essay on laughter, Ellison traces the history of the peculiar interdependence of white, or mainstream, cultural identity and blackface. He remarks that in the Jim Crow era, Negroes were "perceived as barely controllable creatures of untamed instincts. . . . Negroes were considered guilty of all the seven deadly sins except the sin of pride, and were seen as sometimes comic but nevertheless threatening negative to the whites' idealized image of themselves" (*GT*, 174). Only the Christian sin of pride, that vice of arrogance, is set aside.[12] Ellison explains further: "For I knew that from the days of the minstrel shows to the musical and movies then current, many non-Negro outsiders had reaped fame and fortune by assuming the stereotype of blackness. I knew also that our forms of popular culture, from movies to comic strips, were a source of national mythology in which Negroes were the chief scapegoats, and that the function of that mythology was to allow whites a more secure place . . . in American society" (*GT*, 162).

Sometimes Americans have engaged in blackface ridicule to secure a superior social status. Such downward-looking mockery targets a permanent outsider or inferior and sustains patterns of social arrogance by exaggerating features of others. The stereotypes objectify and dehumanize. More significant yet, however, are the specific types of images and characters (the sins, as Ellison remarks) that are projected. The black man can be viewed through fear as the sexually aggressive and violent buck or through more or less disguised contempt as a natural servant or Uncle Tom. The contemporary popularity of gangsta rap in suburbs draws attention to other uses of blackface as well. Individuals who, regardless of race, do not meld seamlessly with the righteous work-oriented WASP culture may identify with a hip buck style from popular culture to express sexual passions and aggressive drives or to cultivate an aura of coolness.

Bamboozled ridicules the latter types of attraction to blackness through its own mockery of the multicultural audience for the minstrel show. From the minstrel show to elements of hip hop culture, blackness serves as the existential symbol of the hip, the uniform of the cool, a facade of authenticity—a faux claim, as it goes, to keeping it real. When the black writer, the old comedian's son, presents the wigger VP with the idea for a minstrel series guaranteed to revive the network's ratings, the VP jumps for it. The VP knows the idea is going to work because, as he says, he gets a boner. For the enthusiastic executive, his boner is an element of blackface, the vital juice that registers an apparent upsurge of identity. No boner, no show. No show, no American identity. Blackness lies at the libidinal core of American identity. As has been often noted, it seems that Americans typically require some racial crossings, a little gangsta rap, a dash of blackface here and there, to be able to laugh and to cry, and to become authentically themselves. It is this use of blackness that the film ridicules most.

If blackness can be a false mask of the real, can our American preoccupation with racial difference also emerge as the place to reclaim a genuine conception of an American cultural identity? Is it possible for blackness as the ultimate racial difference to emerge as a cultural force, even a trope for authenticity, apart from its faux primitivist associations with the irrational, existential man, the liberating black id to the uptight white superego? A response will turn in part on the role we grant to styles of comedy, with their uneasy racial undercurrent. As it turns out, Ellison and Spike Lee are not the only ones to look behind our exaggerated, missionary work ethic, with its overstated moral tone, to a no less unyielding need for comedy to fathom the intricacies of our libidinal core. Historian Daniel Wickberg argues that our "Anglo-American exceptionalism" rests upon "a link between political liberty and humor."[13]

What is this sense of humor, this vital anchor of what we fancy to be our American exceptionalism, this missing counterbalance to Huntington's morally upright conception of American identity? We may indeed, as I shall claim, find in American comedy our saving grace, but it is not going to be as easy as one might think. Wickberg clarifies what has become a common distinction between modern English humor, which is bourgeois in origin, and continental forms of comedy known as ridicule, associated often with an elitist French culture. Aristotle explained ridicule as laughter at those who are naturally inferior, and he believed that it was only appropriate for the socially inferior to play such buffoons at the theater. The modern French form of ridicule developed as a game of the wit played for pleasure and social status. English humor, in contrast with ridicule, asserts itself as "a term of both a sympathy and laughter . . . allowing for the possibility of nonderisive laughter *with* rather than *at* another person, and [places] an altogether novel value on the capacity of a person to laugh at himself" (*SH*, 8). This capacity for humor is said to sustain "the liberty and racial diversity," and "prevalence of odd and eccentric types in English society" (*SH*, 43). The culture of humor allows Wickberg to acknowledge the social significance of the eccentric individual and of racial diversity, whereas Huntington focuses exclusively on the Anglo-Protestant culture of the boorish worker. As Wickberg explains, pre-modern forms of ridicule portray entire characters in terms of their foibles, that is, laughing not at individuals but at types of the ridiculous. Humor valorizes the character as a unique individual, laughing at that range of foibles and eccentricities that liberty permits, while blunting the sharply critical edges of satire with the sentimental appreciation for difference (*SH*, 8). Foibles can be, in other words, a sign of authenticity. None of us, after all, should aspire to be perfect. The very goal converts readily (as we shall see in chapter 4) into a self-defeating project of hubris.

By the time of Mark Twain and the gilded age, humor becomes a defining virtue for the American middle class. Franklin Roosevelt would declare that there is an invigorating "connection between the sense of humor and American democracy" (*SH*, 203). Recall that twentieth-century continental philosophers from Adorno and the Frankfurt School to Sartre and Derrida have emphasized the disavowal of structural ambiguity as the locus of bad faith.[14] In contrast, from the U.S. perspective, authoritarian figures such as Hitler and Stalin were said to have "lacked the fundamental and necessary attribute of a sense of humor"; cultural critics envisioned that the "American sense of humor could be exported to countries suffering under the yoke of dictatorship, thus preparing for democratization" (*SH*, 203). If both continental and American calls to authenticity hinge on valorizing irony or aporia, the forms of ambiguity may differ. Humor, as a comic formula of laughing with while laughing at—not the dark angst-ridden aporia of the continent—was America's unique weapon for world peace, and Hollywood was the celebrated vehicle.

Our attention to *Bamboozled*, however, should already signal trouble for any uncomplicated appeal to humor as the ultimate American virtue, even if we end up reclaiming the comic virtue through Spike Lee's edgy satire. For trouble surely lurks behind any simple and non-satiric view of humor's contribution via Hollywood to "liberty and racial diversity." If the export of American culture, and in particular our contagious American humor, was thought to set the stage for the spread of democracy, this very same humor has served as well as a vehicle to export our brand of racism. After all, the very origin of American humor lies in the blackface minstrel show (*SH*, 124).

The American minstrel show, our original form of comedy, was performed in the 1830s and '40s among working-class Irish immigrants, who like African Americans were viewed as either slavish buffoons and entertainers or servile workers. Interestingly, the Irish brought an element of ridicule to original American humor, much as they did for British culture. Just as the Irish ridiculed their superiors in England, they donned blackface masks to ridicule the middle-class elites, and perhaps on rare occasion indicate solidarity with black Americans. Toward the Civil War and into the era of Jim Crow, however, minstrel entertainers are said to have switched loyalties, and ridiculed blacks with the aim of gaining insider status. At the same time, blackface images became more vicious. As the minstrel show reaches mainstream audiences in the twentieth century, Hollywood softens the images, and minstrelsy takes on that sentimental (and highly entertaining!) mix of ridicule and sympathy, of laughing with and laughing at, known as bourgeois American humor (*SH*, 34). It is this peculiar kind of sympathy of whites for blacks that *Bamboozled* mocks in the new minstrel show produced by the network and devoured by a melting-pot audience of new immigrants and old, all in blackface. Spike Lee is no fan of entertainment.

The enduring strength of this seductive weave of insult and sympathy, of ignorance and arrogance, in American comedy appears through its hold on even our most critical and sophisticated cultural observers. Consider for example Stanley Cavell's admiration for Fred Astaire's invigorating tap-dance routine with a black shoeshine man in *The Band Wagon* (dir. Vincente Minnelli, 1953). In the routine, the aging white entertainer prepares for a comeback by once again appropriating without full acknowledgment the African American arts of dancing and singing that were the source of his youthful success. Robert Gooding-Williams demonstrates that Cavell's otherwise rich remarks on the film inadvertently reduce African Americans and their culture to serving as an "instrument for redeeming melancholic, white subjectivity."[15] Blackface is one of our characteristically American temptations for finding authenticity (signaled in the case of the tap-dancing Fred Astaire by his renewed vigor and redeemed subjectivity) through inauthentic means. The film explicitly contrasts the tragic, European high art with a distinctly American popular culture portrayed as comic, entertaining, and rooted in blackface minstrelsy. Wickberg encourages us to contrast continental and American styles of the comic instead. Traditional European styles of ridicule distance the laugher from the object of amusement, whereas in sentimental middle-class American culture, the narrowing of distance between subject and object of laughter is said to have "resulted in a recognition of self in the other" (*AR,* 34). The aging Astaire, along with his sympathetic viewer in the film audience, reclaims lost vigor through the reflective vehicle of black Americans who, like the black tap dancer in the Fred Astaire film, fail to appear as subjects in their own right. The admiring appropriation of blackness (in this case black styles of singing and dancing) for an illusion of white authenticity may be naive and well-intentioned, but it is also blind hubris.

Lawrence Blum has classified the emotive forces of racialized systems in terms of the drive for superiority and hatred of others.[16] In blackface, the clarifying Jim Crow passions of superiority and either hatred or abjection of the other yield to confusing patterns of envy and fear. This libidinal shift is significant, and we will return to it below. The humor that is valorized by our democratic sentiments is said to bring us a greater awareness of ourselves, along with our foibles and vices. As we have seen, the prevalence of blackface images demonstrates that such awareness does not always happen. Humor may as well allow one to play with disavowed parts of oneself at a safe distance—indeed, to hover in the duplicitous frame of mind that the existentialists term "bad faith." While Wickberg leaves the sentimental element of blackface humor in the foreground of his scholarship, Eric Lott uncovers in the moment of recognition darker shades of white identity. Blackface displays "a white obsession with black (male) bodies . . . , [even as] it ruthlessly [disavows] its fleshly investments through ridicule and racist lampoon."[17] From the white male–dark male dyads in Hollywood film to the "racial crossings" of white hip hop, "you are in the presence of blackface's unconscious return," he writes (*LT,* 5). The strangely pleasing aesthetic of identity and disavowal entangled in their opposites defines blackface's continuing relevance for our post–civil rights hip hop American culture.

As Gooding-Williams argues, the other viewed through the medium of the self may not be a genuine other at all. The other self may turn out to be a false mask, a second self as imagined blackness. But this second self, this blackness, is also the apparent source of increased vitality for ever incompletely assimilated Americans. The enervated, alienated, assimilated "individual" of liberal lore is often enough compelled to reclaim authenticity through an inauthentic encounter with otherness as blackness. This is the standard paradox of American identity, object of Huntington's romantic quest.

As the existential philosopher of authenticity, Sartre warns that the path toward authenticity is riddled with angst. And indeed, this second blackened self is threatening, to be kept under lock and key as the controlled, enjoyed, and punished id, source of renewal perhaps, but of destruction and violence as well, the black core of a mainstream if increasingly multicultural American identity. So we are not surprised that if the appropriation of black libido rejuvenates a historically WASP American identity, there are as well more disastrous consequences. The police violence against the black "revolutionary" group (the Mau Maus) in the Spike Lee film, sparing only the white member, provides an occasion to consider the link between blackface as mock source of authenticity and the consequences of the punitive instinct that blackface imagery solicits. We are the prison nation. Before the industrial-prison system, the lynchings of the Jim Crow era exhibited most clearly the primitive rage to punish under civilization's mask of moral righteousness. The old entertainer in the Lee film exposes through ridicule the white envy of big black lips as well as the fear and violence that lurks underneath: in one of his routines, Junebug goes on about whites who will pull off the highway when they spy victims of a car accident. The whites want to grab up those big black lips for themselves—those big lips that one finds in minstrel shows. We'll know who's really white when they start lynching us again, he quips. Envy of projected black primitivism easily converts to the habits of fear and punishment. There are two main types of black men for mainstream audiences: the cool hipster and the criminal, and there is not a whole lot of difference between them.

The old entertainer's routines solicit that mix of laughter and tears that Ellison terms "Black humor," and describes as a useful if imperfect counterstrategy to racism (GT, 178). Black humor can diminish the impact of white hubris, mocking at once its vanity and ignorance, easing fear and potentially self-destructive rage, all the while strengthening the bonds among those who laugh together. Like its racist blackface counterpart, black humor secures community at the expense of ridiculed targets. Unlike blackface, it targets the vices, most centrally the arrogance and ignorance, of dominant groups. While racist ridicule creates or sustains stereotypes that marginalize, segregate, and dehumanize, antiracist humor uses mockery to break audiences free from such stereotypes. It mocks not only the mockers but also those who have been bamboozled by inauthentic images of their identity. African Americans have devised elaborate forms of black humor to salvage sanity and shield pride in the face of the insults and provocations of those bent on egging them on. Ellison experienced the surreal rites of bloodletting firsthand.

In his essay on laughter, Ellison acknowledges the ancestral wisdom of black humor, but he finds that there is something more in the racial encounter that the bare comic element cannot capture. Underneath the laughter of black humor lurks a fully tragic moment that Ellison strives in the essay to understand. " '[T]he wise man never laughs but that he trembles,' " Ellison writes, borrowing his words from French poet Baudelaire (*GT*, 145). Toward the end of his essay, Ellison discerns this tragic underpinning of American racial humor in terms of what he calls the American Joke. Of African Americans and their humor, he writes, "Their challenge was to endure while imposing their claims, . . . just as they had imposed their style upon its culture," and then he adds, "Forced to be wary observers, they recognized that American life is of a whole, and that what happens to blacks will accrue eventually, one way or another, to the nation as a whole. This is their dark-visioned version of the broader 'American Joke' " (*GT*, 185–86). The racial encounter that defines America is predicated on a classic tragic irony: it is inevitable that self-destructive arrogance, the sin of any class that knows no boundaries on its power, boomerangs, returning the terror inflicted upon the other. As Ellison explains, "if the philosopher's observation that absolute power corrupts absolutely was also true, then an absolute power based on mere whiteness made for a deification of madness. Depending on the circumstance, whiteness might well be a sign of evil, of a 'motiveless malignancy' which was to be avoided as strange dogs in rabid weather" (*GT*, 172).

"Keep 'em laughing" are the final words of advice, the ancestral wisdom, that Junebug offers to his son. Behind the fool's mask of the entertainer, we glimpse more than one possible identity: the humorist who diffuses the destructive impulses of black rage and restores black community through the ridicule of hubris, or the dark ironist whose bleak vision of hubris and self-destruction can make one tremble. A long line of characters, from the original blackface minstrels to *Bamboozled*'s White Negro VP and some of those would-be revolutionaries, find a mock authenticity in blackface, that insurgence of insensitive desire, that boner that Ellison glosses in terms of the primitive instincts. When this energizing drive expresses itself without restraint, it unleashes a force that can be as tragic as it is surreal. But then might we find in comedy styles of authenticity, modes of renewal and revitalization of our identities that do not boomerang with savage revenge? Do we find moments of redemption that do not collapse into dark satire or pathetic tragedy?

Ellison on the Absurd as the Source of Humanity and Why It Is Somewhat Anachronistic

In his essay, Ellison proposes a route to authenticity through an encounter with the absurdity underneath bourgeois social manners. Laughter, he suggests, can "pierce the veil of conventions that guard us from the basic absurdity of the human condition" and open the possibility for the mutual recognition of a common humanity (*GT,* 146). His reflection upon the role of the absurd follows his viewing of a play authored by the Southern playwright Erskine Caldwell. The play portrays poor whites indulging in the primitive vices typically attributed to blacks. Here we have whites acting as though they appeared in blackface, and yet fully white. By avoiding moral judgment against white sexuality and sadism, he experiences a shock of self-recognition that is cathartic: "[W]asn't . . . [the] horsing all over the stage . . . embarrassingly symbolic of my own frustration as a healthy young man whose sexual outlet was limited (for the most part) to 'belly-rubbing' with girls met casually at public dances? It was and it wasn't, depending upon my willingness to make or withhold a human identification. Actually, I had no choice but to identify" (*GT,* 196). The authenticity of the perspective is signaled by the cathartic calm of, as he writes, "my divided selves . . . made one again" (*GT,* 193).

Perhaps, in some situations, an encounter with the absurd underneath the social plane of conventional manners may establish the cathartic regrounding that Ellison envisions. The Freudian unmasking of human nature as savage, the Sartrean insight into man as a useless passion, the tragic-comedy of the absurd—these have been the terms to define a century of terror lurking behind the masks of the so-called civilized races. The new millennium should not leave behind an awareness of that primitivism that lurks underneath our moral masks. It is not clear, however, that the primitivism of the absurd suffices to form the basis for a new humanism, as Ellison intends. In any case, the convoluted social plane of the post–cold war era spins the question of authenticity, the longing for an identity that is real, around a different axis.

The images, roles, and relationships of our globalizing civil society do not operate centrally along the metaphysical divides that characterize other eras, those vertical divides between the individual and the masses, the civilized and the uncivilized, the superego and the id, reason and passion, city and nature, or subject and object. In variants of the vertical axis, questions of identity and authenticity turn on the primitive that lies underneath rationality, the boner as it were. The questions of identity and authenticity in the information age arise instead from the manners and mores of the social infrastructure within and across cultures. The troubled social terrain upon which we forge our identities has shifted attention from the vertical axis of reason versus passion to the horizontal network of "information" and the social relations that this media-saturated information sustains. The artificial American, Norman Mailer's White Negro, who would seek authenticity through the appropriation of violent black libido appears ridiculous in the context of Spike Lee's film. The boner is not real; it is but another social mask. The African American rapper (Big Black Africa) who seeks the real through proud ignorant black primitivism appears equally ridiculous. Metaphysical speculation regarding a primitive libidinal drive toward death and destruction may for good reason underlie the twentieth-century conception of the individual. In the age of interdependence, however, the irrational is too reductive to address the strains on our troubled social bonds. The question of our image-saturated, status-driven age is not how we break through all images and conventions to find the primitive real. There is no real underneath the images and social histories. This question is how we can maintain a sense of social belonging, one that acknowledges thick histories of racial and ethnic identity and what these histories contribute to our self-images, while becoming authentically the individuals that we are.

Spike Lee's satiric portrayal of blackface raises the possibility that we might reclaim our authenticity through the ridicule of ethnic and racial stereotypes that distort our individual identities. At the same time, for the characters of the film, there is no individuality except as a social being with a developed sense of belonging to histories, communities, and cultures larger than ourselves. How do we theorize authenticity for a social being? Before Sartre's austere epic of solitude, *Being and Nothingness*, Bergson combated the ridiculous through the social function of laughter. "The high comic vision of life is . . . an achievement of man as a social being," explains one Bergson scholar.[18] What does this comic vision have to teach us about authenticity in our time?

From Sartre's Metaphysics of Bad Faith to Bergson's Social Satire of the Ridiculous

Bergson has written that "[a]ll that is serious in life comes from our freedom" (L, 111). If so, then we might expect that the denial of our freedom, what Sartre terms bad faith, could bear some significant relationship to the ridiculous. Bergson continues: "The feelings we have matured, the passions we have brooded over . . . in short, all that comes from us and is our very own, these are the things that give life its ofttimes dramatic and generally grave aspect. What, then, is requisite to transform all this into a comedy? Merely to fancy that our seeming freedom conceals the strings of a dancing-jack, and that we are . . . humble marionettes" (L, 111–12).

The possibility that the terrain of the ridiculous might on significant occasion overlap with that of existential bad faith is posed by the Spike Lee film. The anomalous existence of Pierre Delacroix, the black Harvard-educated writer for the Continental Network System, appears to have simultaneously the characteristics of bad faith and the ridiculous. So too does the network's white senior executive, Dunwitty, the hipster who, with a hint of Irish background, seeks a mock authenticity by absorbing the style of black stars (black male athletes, not serious writers) contained within picture frames and displayed like trophies on his office walls. Dunwitty's and Delacroix's contrasting styles of inauthenticity turn on racial differences. Dunwitty can appropriate totemic elements of black masculinity to augment his position in the entertainment industry. His power lies in the fact that he can take off the mask of blackness as easily has he can put it on. He controls blackness; blackness does not control him. It's true that other races sometimes take on a black style to indicate solidarity with African Americans, and this solidarity can at times be authentic. Dunwitty, however, uses blackness at the expense of African Americans and African American culture.

Delacroix likewise appropriates aspects of a racial identity that he was not born into, and again, in such a way as to lack authenticity. Authenticity does not require that Delacroix adopt a fixed monolithic racial identity of blackness as his own; on the contrary, any unquestioning assumption of predetermined meaning or rigid stereotypes leads to inauthenticity. Authenticity requires that one deal squarely and critically with sources of meaning and value that one cannot just shrug off. Delacroix avoids aspects of his blackness apparently for individual gain, and is indifferent to claims from a culture, community, or history that are not simply matters of choice. He assumes a French name, greets the film viewer with a "Bonjour," and seeks to be recognized at the network as, to borrow an existential phrase from Sartre, "a man like all other men."[19] In the white-dominated culture, Delacroix's continental strategy for appropriating whiteness, in contrast with Dunwitty's hip American appropriation of blackness, does not succeed. He does not control blackness; blackness controls him. His white peers fail to return his greetings, and he is overlooked for an important meeting. He cannot belong to the white network by choosing to avoid a racial identity. After the meeting, Dunwitty commands Delacroix to stop writing inauthentic "white-bread" scripts about blacks, scripts not likely to boost the network's ratings, and to reconnect with his black roots. In other words, he is ordered to get authentic. So-called black authenticity sells. Eventually, Delacroix does reconnect to blackness in just the terribly inauthentic terms required by the network. As he yields to the network, the images of blackness in his office, in contrast with the well-contained images in Dunwitty's office, take on surreal proportions. These are not framed flat images but antique blackface dolls and puppets, including a Jolly Negro money bank. Over the course of the film, the mechanical dolls conjure primitive forces beyond anyone's control. We have the feeling that De-lacroix is (as his name would indicate) about to become the object of a sacrifice.

Delacroix does not immediately yield himself to the demands of the info-tainment network. He attempts instead to take control of his own life. Properly offended, he stages a dramatic exit. He presents to the white executive a project for a new minstrel show. The aim is to offer the net-work entertaining caricatures of blackness that are so exaggerated that they will boomerang with a vengeance. The series is to be so outrageously racist that he will be released from his contract, while the show's biting satire will generate public censorship of the network. As it turns out, his ambition to single-handedly fight the system in his own terms is unrealis-tic. He is, in a classic Sartrean formulation of bad faith, blind to the exigencies of a situation. To define oneself in the terms of the white net-work, whether as its passive servant or as reactive nay-sayer (in its pseudo-cool or criminal varieties), is to fall victim to its needs. It is to become the scapegoat. Indeed, it is very hard to find any other way out.

The satiric edges anticipated by Delacroix are reabsorbed into an affirmation of the very caricatures they are meant to subvert by the team of white writers.[20] This reabsorption translates into popular entertainment for the multicultural masses and profits for the investors (cf. *PM*, 134). The first change is to set the show not in the projects (as Delacroix orig-inally intended) but safely and sentimentally in the apparently discon-nected past of the old plantation's watermelon patch. The show's senti-mentalized ridicule of blacks as "niggers," a nostalgic look at the kind of clowns we like to be in our time off from work, presents the formula of American humor from minstrelsy to Hollywood—the chief object of Spike Lee's critical scorn. Laughter, unlike Spike Lee's intellectual scorn, is con-tagious. Delacroix cannot resist the audience's laughter, and he gets sucked into his own success. The fact that laughter sweeps away Delacroix along with the others in the mixed-race audience of the film does not bode well for any utopian vision of a racially mixed harmonious society.

Still, the major stars of the minstrel show, the former street artists, Manray and Womack, who are slated to play the coons Mantan and Sleep 'n Eat, wisen up, regain a sense of self, and refuse to play along with the Continental Network. It is too late for Mantan. He has already been tar-geted as a sellout by the Black Revolutionary Mau Maus (named after those who revolted against British colonialism in 1950s Kenya), and their leader Big Blak Afrika (played by rap star Mos Def).[21] The Mau Maus kidnap Mantan after he has been thrown back into the streets by the network, and execute him on live webcast. Delacroix's assistant Sloan confronts Delacroix with his Uncle Tomism (she documents for him the history of the grateful Negro, among other minstrel roles), and its tragically ridiculous consequences. Her gun goes off, and we see a Delacroix falling, followed by a montage of reoccurring blackface images from a documentary (Marlon Riggs's *Ethnic Notions*) on racism in Hollywood films and television. As Delacroix lies dying, his voice repeats the words of his father, "Keep 'em laughing." The viewers of the film, however, should not be laughing—not anymore than they should be crying. The film is not fun. Its not even cathartic. And it certainly provides no easy formula for authenticity.

Spike Lee's satiric film contains dimensions of Hollywood comedy as well as classic tragic drama. The fact that the film takes a tragic turn for Delacroix, and most of the major black characters, while the white network prospers, exposes a genre apartheid of tragic black world and happy white world. What I would call genre apartheid—the segregation of the races within separate genres and character types (serious hero versus comic buffoon, etc.) within a single film—are common enough in American film history. From classic films such as *Gone with the Wind* and *Showboat* to the contemporary film *The Green Mile*, racialized characters inhabit distinct social spheres divided into comic, tragic, or romantic subplots, with happy, sacrificial, or inconsequential endings accordingly. We view ourselves and others through genres.

Bamboozled, however, is not to be viewed from the point of view of the pathos of sacrificed or inconsequential black lives, not any more than from the happy-ever-after oblivion of standard Hollywood comedy. The film aims instead to satirize the stereotypes that perpetuate such racialized genre divisions. It must resist its own value as entertainment to maintain its critical edge. Satire is the first word spoken in the film, defined in Delacroix's voice-over narration as a form of ridicule of vice or folly, or as a form of irony. Of course, tragedy, too, contains irony, and the film does have its grave aspect. But Delacroix's detached and somewhat pedantic voice narrating the film as a retrospective view from a dead man dressed as a puppet—a dehumanized blackface puppet, but a puppet nonetheless— invites tragic pathos or even the laughter of an audience toward an external object of ridicule, from the larger intellectual perspective of a kind of satirist. This narrating voice does not satirize some external other. The object of ridicule is the narrator's unsympathetic inauthentic self as well as those viewers who might acknowledge aspects of themselves reflected in the characters of the film. Bergson's theory emphasizes the corrective function of laughter on those portrayed as out of tune, not just with themselves, but with their communities. The fact that Spike Lee's satire turns the focus of laughter around to the narrator suggests authenticity as the central theme of the film. The satire functions as a genre of self-critique, but one that stages the existential moment of self-recognition very differently than does Sartre.

The targets of the film's satire include not only the narrator but also other African Americans, Jews, and certainly the whites and other non-blacks who condemn and/or envy, fear and/or love, appropriate and/or deny blackness. Along with most of the characters, Delacroix and Big Blak Afrika are mocked for their exaggerated styles of either identifying with or denying blackness. Both characters have re-named themselves in relation to the question of their racial identity. Big Blak Afrika tells his sister Sloan he has rejected his slave name—the name his parents gave him, his sister corrects him—and has chosen instead his own identity. If Delacroix and Big Blak Afrika take on self-chosen identities, what one would think to be an existentially serious endeavor, both men appear in the film as ridiculous, even "embarrassing," as Sloan tells her brother.[22] Neither character portrays for the viewer a man who is free. Womack and Manray, unlike either Delacroix or Big Blak Afrika, are in fact able to reclaim authenticity. They do so precisely by breaking out of their blackface roles, without, as Manray's final unmasked tap dance at the minstrel show indicates, leaving behind their roots and identity in black history. On the contrary, through their understanding of blackface, both as abhorrent stereotyping and as a highly skilled and after all quite impressive art on the part of black actors, they recover that history, good and bad, but with a critical eye. In contrast, Delacroix and Big Blak Afrika struggle to assert serious identities against ridiculous stereotypes, only to end up blind fools of the system they would revolt against. That existential formula for authenticity, to choose the self, easily reduces to a formula for bad faith.[23] One does not choose the self—not any more than one can give birth to oneself. The self is tied to a larger racialized world; authenticity emerges from acknowledging and working through a troubled sense of belonging.

The character of Sloan originally appears free from stereotypical roles, and perhaps as a tentative voice of authenticity through remembrance of history but also through family and community as well. However, as she well knows, no character's identity is ever solely his or her own. Characters are inherently vulnerable to the definitions placed upon them by others, and, indeed, Delacroix maliciously succeeds in framing Sloan as a jezebel. Once cast into a blackface role, his little "lamb" (as he calls her) becomes one more victim of the network ready for the sacrifice. At the same time, Delacroix unwittingly sets the stage for his own downfall. In the final act, a disheveled Sloan aims her gun, and Delacroix falls like a puppet whose strings have at last been cut.

In his 1945 *Anti-Semite and Jew,* Sartre explains bad faith as a type of duplicity, or ignorance of oneself. Authenticity requires, he writes, "a true and lucid consciousness of the situation, in assuming the responsibilities and risks that it involves" (*S,* 90). Sartre lays out the metaphysics of freedom and bad faith around a complicated axis of subject and object. In classic Sartrean terms, the man of bad faith refuses to live with the ambiguity of a situated freedom. He may conceal from himself the truth regarding his situation, or he may abdicate his responsibility for choice in it. Typically, in classic male-centered existentialism, the subject who surrenders to bad faith takes the latter path. He allows himself to become the passive object of the look of the other, yielding perhaps as some men do to roles or stereotypes or other external frames that are imposed upon him. "He tries to think of himself as an inanimate thing, thereby to abdicate his responsibilities" (*S,* 108). There is, however, a second path to bad faith. The man of bad faith may disconnect himself from his situatedness in society and claim for himself the status of a pure and unattached subject. In either case, Sartre observes, he deceives himself.[24]

Interestingly, the theme of duplicity—the lack of self-knowledge—plays as central a role in Bergson's theory of the ridiculous as it does for Sartrean bad faith. No less than bad faith, the ridiculous is the result of self-ignorance: "it is really a kind of automatism that makes us laugh—an automatism . . . closely akin to mere absent-mindedness. To realize this more fully, it need only be noted that a comic character is generally comic in proportion to his ignorance of himself," Bergson explains (*L,* 71). It will not be surprising, then, that the discussion of duplicity and bad faith in *Being and Nothingness* touches upon the idea of the comic, perhaps with Bergson in mind. Of the homosexual in denial of who he is, Sartre writes: "Here is assuredly a man in bad faith who borders on the comic since, acknowledging all the facts which are imputed to him, he refuses to draw from them the conclusion which they impose" (*BN,* 107).

The parallels between Bergson's object of ridicule and Sartre's bad faith are more extensive yet. Sartre explains that bad faith yields our inner subjectivity to the external frame provided by the look of the other. Similarly, Bergson explains that the comic vice appears as "the momentary transformation of the person into a thing" through the imposition of an external "frame" (*L,* 97). "Doubtless there are vices into which the soul plunges deeply with all its pregnant potency. . . . Those are tragic vices. But the vice capable of making us comic is, on the contrary, that which is brought from without, like a ready-made frame into which we are to step. It lends us its own rigidity instead of borrowing from us our flexibility" (*L*, 70).

It is not easy to step out of such a frame, not when that frame is maintained by what Spike Lee would have us call the "network." Neither the morally sincere nor the ironically detached subject corresponds readily for Sartre or Bergson with the authentic. A passage from *Being and Nothingness* touches upon the ironist in order to prepare for a discussion of inauthenticity: "In irony a man annihilates what he posits within one and same act . . . permit[ting] us to raise a new question: What are we to say is the being of man who has the possibility of denying himself?" (*BN*, 87). There are shades of the ironist in the famous scene of the waiter in the café who would transcend his role through its exaggerated performance. Sartre writes: "His movement is . . . a little too precise. . . . [T]here he returns, trying to imitate in his walk the inflexible stiffness of some kind of automaton while carrying his tray with the recklessness of a tight-rope-walker. . . . [H]is gestures and even his voice seem to be mechanisms. . . . Society demands that he limit himself to his function" (*BN*, 101–102). In this comic scenario, the waiter plays at performing a social role that does not absorb his whole identity, and yet he appears to us to be one more of Bergson's mechanical fools. The refusal to acknowledge the role one cannot not play is a form of bad faith. Elsewhere, Sartre describes the Jew who suffers the illusion that he can rise above the situation created by the anti-Semite through self-irony: "Thus we may explain that particular quality of Jewish irony which exercises itself most often at the expense of the Jew himself and which is a perpetual attempt to see himself from the outside. . . . This is another ruse of inauthenticity" (*S*, 97).

If Sartre portrays the self-ironic, self-conscious puppet as a type of fool, moral sincerity fares hardly better. For Sartre, as for Bergson, the virtue of earnestness does not guarantee authenticity, let alone racial peace and harmony; on the contrary, it leads readily to the ridicule ever in wait for the humorless boor. Bergson's example is Moliere's ridiculously earnest Alceste. "[T]he comic is not always an indication of a fault, in the moral meaning of the word," Bergson observes (*L*, 149). Sartre's example is the pupil who "so exhausts himself in playing the attentive role that he ends up by no longer hearing anything" (*BN*, 103). Neither the social vices mocked by Bergson's laughter nor the Sartrean phenomenon of bad faith operates on the moral plane, but prior to it. "We may . . . admit, as a general rule, that it is the faults of others that make us laugh, provided we add that they make us laugh by reason of their *unsociability* rather than of their *immorality*," Bergson explains (*L*, 150). Replace "unsociability" with "inauthenticity" and we have a fair interpretation of Sartre. In either case, we are in the normative realm—not of the earnest moral "ought" but of the comedian and dramatist's situation-savvy "should."

Yet Bergson's keen interest in the social graces signals a difference from Sartre that is significant for Spike Lee's satiric film. One never laughs alone, Bergson insists, as laughter performs a social function. He explains, "Society will . . . be suspicious of all *inelasticity* of character, of mind and even of body, because it is the possible sign of a slumbering activity as well as of an activity with separatist tendencies, that inclines to swerve from the common centre round which society gravitates. . . . And yet, society . . . is confronted with something that [is] . . . scarcely a threat, at the very most a gesture. A gesture, therefore, will be its reply. Laughter must be something of this kind, a sort of *social gesture*. By the fear which it inspires, it restrains eccentricity" (*L*, 73). Ridicule aims to make one aware of habits, attitudes, or even aspects of our speech that are not conscious acts. We do not become aware of them until those around us call attention to them. On the significance of the social mediation of the self, Sartre could not be more different. Consider Bergson's diagnosis of separatism as a problem, and Sartre's view of the inauthentic person as the one who conforms to the conventions of mass society. Of the inauthentic consciousness, Sartre writes: "This man fears every kind of solitariness. . . . [H]e is the man of the crowd" who dares not think on his own (*S*, 22). For Bergson laughter rudely awakens the man who is out of tune with himself, his companions, and the claims of an open, flexible, and vital community. Laughter's function is "to correct men's manners" through cultivating a social sense akin to the appreciation of music (*L*, 71). In contrast, Sartre sees the reduction of the subject to the status of a function in the social plane as bad faith. Separatism is not the problem. In classical existentialism, it's the answer.[25] This is because for Sartre, there is no gesture that is not the result of a conscious intention. The dialectical claim that "I . . . know myself only through the mediation of the other" is, as he writes, an ontological impossibility (*BN*, 91).[26]

The potential differences between classic existentialism and a social comedy of manners on the role of the other in the recovery of the self carry significant political implications.[27] A comic vision of the self coheres with dialectical views of the self as constituted through social, historical, or psychological forces that one could hardly be expected to ever fully know. Certainly one depends upon the other in order to gain a sense of oneself. Part of maturity requires acknowledging debts to external sources of value and meaning. The classic existential position views such ties as anathema to individual freedom as self-choice.[28] Even as Sartre comes to view the situatedness of racial identity as central to the question of freedom, as he does in *Anti-Semite and Jew*, he takes such a social identity as of mere strategic relevance. Never does he view social identities such a race as positive sources of meaning that one inherits without choice. Only alone and in a silence of an empty space does one find the sheer spontaneity of the existential self.

In the book on the Jews, Sartre observes that the primary concern of the Jew in anti-Semitic Europe is not the loss of self in the social sphere, but alienation from it. Sartre believes that this Jewish preoccupation with the need to belong stems from the failure to reach the loftier plane of human existence. The Jew is "haunted by that impalpable and humiliating image" that anti-Semites have of him, Sartre writes (S, 132). "However, it should not be thought that Jewish uneasiness is metaphysical. It would be an error to identify it with the anxiety that moves us to a consideration of the condition of man. I should say rather that metaphysical uneasiness is a condition that the Jew . . . cannot allow himself today. One must be sure of one's rights and firmly rooted in the world, one must be freed of the fears that each day assail oppressed minorities or classes, before one dare raise questions about the place of man in the world and his ultimate destiny. In a word, metaphysics is the special privilege of the Aryan governing classes. . . . The disquietude of the Jew is not metaphysical; it is social. . . . He cannot perceive the loneliness of each man in the midst of a silent universe. . . . He is the social man *par excellence,* because his torment is social" (S, 133–34).

Sartre's metaphysics of subject and object has not held up well in the postmodern era. Michael Walzer observes, in his preface to Sartre's *Anti-Semite and Jew,* that the Jew emerges from a historical culture and that even Jewish irony, that apparent resort to unsituated subjectivity, may be less a symptom of bad faith or anti-Semitic prejudice than an authentic sign of belonging to an intellectual Jewish culture, one that prizes irony.[29] So too other Jewish stereotypes may not have their origin totally in anti-Semitic cultures; these stereotypes may have authentic counterparts in Jewish cultures. In a multicultural society, social groups free from rigid stereotypes and deadening group identities recover histories of meaning and value to revitalize living cultures.

What if we were to salvage the philosophical significance of the quest for authenticity by shifting the existential analysis of identity and freedom from the austere World War II metaphysics of the solitary individual to the social terrain of satire as interpreted through Spike Lee? Might a genre shift from the epic romance of Sartrean metaphysics, the adventure of the individual who chooses his self, to satire's study of troubled social relationships and complex histories of belonging recuperate the value of authenticity for our cynical age?

"Bamboozled," or Bad Faith as Reinterpreted through Satire

The paradigmatic act of bad faith is for Sartre the refusal to make a decision and the passive acceptance of oneself as an object defined by the other. Spike Lee alters the primary focus of bad faith from the refusal to choose the self to ignorance of one's situation. This gestalt switch has significant consequences for our neoliberal valorization of choice at the expense of historical and social responsibility. By emphasizing the salience of the situation over the drama of self-choice, the Spike Lee film transposes the core meaning of authenticity along with its opposite, bad faith.

Consider the nature of inauthenticity as we find it in the main character, Delacroix. In an attempt to fit in, Delacroix adopts an accent and precise gestures that are a bit too studied, excessively cultivated, one might say almost continental, but not otherwise locatable. Indeed, he attempts an identity that cannot be situated. In his aim to belong he allows himself to be deceived and cheated, serving as puppet for a system.

Let us redefine the notion of bad faith as it emerges from the film in terms of *having been bamboozled*. The dynamic of the bamboozled diverges from a classic existential model of bad faith. For while the type of bad faith named by the title of the film involves self-deception, and in particular the denial of a historically embedded situation, the significance of this denial is not wholly Sartrean. Delacroix thinks he is self-determined and therefore free. In 1950, Anatole Broyard, drawing upon Sartre's study of the inauthentic Jew, pinpoints "minstrelization" as the inauthentic Negro's main avenue of flight (*PIN*, 59). "Keep Smiling" is, as Broyard observes, the minstrel's motto. Delacroix does not smile. And yet Delacroix is also a puppet, doomed as are the other types of inauthentic souls to being bamboozled out of a true self. Delacroix's goal is familiar; it is to be the successful and self-made man—that man who invents his own identity. Sam Huntington claims that this American variant of the existential dream is of Anglo-Protestant origin. The paradox is that the more Delacroix clings to the romance of the self, the more he exemplifies the flight of inauthenticity. The film brings us close to Sartrean themes of authenticity and self-deception, only to turn us away from existential self-choice toward satire's critical examination and acknowledgment of vital social bonds.

Extreme times reveal stark choices, described by Sartre as the ontological possibilities of fight or flight: "In periods of crisis and of persecution, . . . [the Jew] is a hundred times more unhappy, but at least he can revolt"

(*S*, 79). We do not live, however, in this kind of times. The texture of relationships and social identities during our neoliberal era renders occasions for decision making less amenable to slogans and principles, more nuanced and, as Sartre argues, easily evaded: "But when all is calm, against whom is he to revolt? He accepts the society around him, he joins the game and he conforms to all the ceremonies, dancing with the others the dance of respectability" (*S*, 79). We have seen that Big Blak Afrika does not understand the subtleties of revolt in the post–civil rights era—the age of hip hop that he aims to represent. He takes on the earnest resolve of the warrior, Malcolm X. Borrowing from Malcolm X's words, he insists that he "will not be bamboozled," but he does not understand how to translate these words into the contemporary situation. In Sartrean terms, he is the "man of resentment," for whom "social reality is uniquely that of the No" (*BN*, 87). This spirit of negativity, this reactive man, perpetuates a situation he does not understand. Consequently, he is easy prey to such exaggerated stereotypes as the big buck, exhibited and framed already in the white VP's office—framed, that is, by the network. The scene of the rappers putting together a "black album," in an out-of-date reaction to the Beatles' *White Album*, but spelled b-l-a-k, without the "c" of the white man's language, signifies the dulled awareness of a group that revolts but does not see. The uneducated revolutionaries caught in the past do not challenge stereotypical blackness; in their vanity and ignorance, they just repeat it. The once earnest dream of a nationalistic revolution has become, in the age of the network, embarrassing. Social freedom, that is, the freedom that signifies a sense of belonging, should not be defined in terms of membership in a monolithic culture, religion, or race.[30] The pseudorevolutionary crew plays right into racist fantasies, fueling a charged atmosphere of fear and anger. This racialized atmosphere sets the stage for the tragic scapegoating to come.

But then, is authentic revolt possible in an age not of revolution, but of satire? Delacroix awakens from his dream of accommodation, and resolves to attack the network through the media-savvy weapon of ridicule. The aim of Delacroix's projected series is to mock the minstrel show and those who, through ignorance or greed, perpetuate the blackface roles. This is no doubt the aim of Spike Lee's film as well. We might debate whether Spike Lee's satire of blackface succeeds, but Delacroix's attempt is doomed from the start. Delacroix quickly loses control of his project to the white writers. All intended satire is reabsorbed into the sentimental mix of insult and humor that profits the white-dominated network and amuses to no end its mixed-race audience. The question is, can we discern why

Delacroix's satiric project is so easily bamboozled, whereas Spike Lee's mockery of the same exaggerated stereotypes—the buck in Big Blak Afrika, the coons in Manray and Womack, and the Uncle Tom in Delacroix—can make a claim to succeed?

Bergson presents us with a clue toward understanding the difference between the resentful writer of the minstrel show and Spike Lee's project. In his theory of laughter, Bergson observes that "the line to take for creating an ideally comic type of character, invisible to its actual owner . . . but visible to everybody else, . . . inseparable from social life, although insufferable to society, . . . this mixture is vanity [and ignorance]" (L, 171). Delacroix's ambition to break free from the system does not break free from those debilitating comic vices. His intent to break down the system is compromised by his vain desire to be recognized through the system and his ignorance of the history that Spike Lee (through Sloan's use of the Marlon Riggs documentary) provides. Much like the warrior Big Blak Afrika, Delacroix misses the constitutive claims of friendships, family, community, and history—the various social bonds that compose who we are. Delacroix, whom we first see as unsituated man seeking recognition from the network, and then as the man of resentment in revolt against the network, finally yields to the passivity of the grateful Negro. Each scenario presents a distinct formula for bad faith. In each case, the independent man is revealed to be nothing more than a puppet. Delacroix does not see what Sloan tries to tell him and the audience already knows. Sloan reaches Delacroix only in the final scene of the film, as he lies dying before the images of the documentary. The larger social forces that can constitute vital claims do not originate in ourselves, and therefore they are not available to us without the assistance of others. In other words, we do not know ourselves except through others. Delacroix finally accepts this assistance and acknowledges Sloan's redemptive friendship, as indicated in his death scene. In that final scene, as he realizes he is dying of the wound she inflicted, he takes the gun from her hands and wipes clean her incriminating prints.

Spike Lee translates the stark existential choice of fight or flight through alternatives of producing entertainment for the network or satire for an African American audience as an independent film director. This call for authenticity appears through the character of the old comedian, who prefers his smaller audiences over the lure of Hollywood. Spike Lee no doubt aligns *Bamboozled* in a similar tradition of film, one that includes Robert Townsend's 1987 satire *Hollywood Shuffle*. But if Hollywood sometimes plays the bad guy, it is also the case that resisting the temptations of power is itself a frequent theme of Hollywood. Think of the sentimental and very entertaining Frank Capra film *It's a Wonderful Life* (1946). One has to wonder if Spike Lee's satiric film makes good on what turns out to be a rather standard anti-capitalist populist theme in a way that Hollywood's corporate-sponsored comedies do not?

In order to answer this question, we need to look more carefully at the diverse styles of comedy recalled through the film. The peril of blackface ridicule is clear. The virtues of black humor are represented in Junebug's ridicule of the exaggerated objects of white fantasies. His display of the counter-insults of black wit brings cathartic pleasure to the black community, and may serve as well to correct white vanity in his mixed audiences. Spike Lee's film engages some of the elements of black humor; however, the intellectual form of satire that the film engages may be less cathartic than illuminating. By posing the black humorist as a character named Junebug dressed in a clownish bright orange suit, last seen fallen into a stupor, the film signals some doubt regarding his reliability as a figure of authenticity. It is as though the film warns that the entertainer, whose profession is to amuse more so than to enlighten, risks perpetuating the exaggerated minstrel images of blackness—the enviable if feared black libido—through the big black lips and other figments of white fantasy that he provokes. Junebug's ridicule mocks the mockers, targeting uneducable outsiders in order to sustain black community. Spike Lee's existential project of self-ridicule struggles for authenticity through critical reflection among its predominantly African American viewers. Like Delacroix, Spike Lee aims to trouble our culture's proliferation of blackface. Neither Delacroix nor Spike Lee aims for his satire to be in the least bit entertaining.

However, if the film, through its independent production, achieves what Delacroix's strategy of working for the network fails to do, this is because the film, unlike the projected minstrel show, stems from motivations and causes that are not fully reactive, not, that is, just dark ironic satire. Clearly the film poses the question as to whether such gangster rappers as Big Blak Afrika and the Mau Maus succumb to minstrelsy, but it also raises the romantic possibility of authentic African American identity through the use of such genuine artists as Mos Def and writer Paul Mooney, among others. For the savvy viewer of the film, these authentic and after all highly skilled artists exceed the frame of the blackface roles they play and recall the capacity to express racially or ethnically rich, historically informed characters for who they perhaps should be. These are characters who have decisively not been bamboozled.

Humor as Subverting Inauthenticity through the Force of Friendship

A moment of decisive existential awakening within the film itself occurs in the scene where Womack confronts his friend Manray, or Mantan, with what he has become. The film stages this climactic scene not as a metaphysical journey of existential self-discovery, but as a romantic element in what is otherwise bleak satire. In so doing, the film shifts the project of authenticity from an individual's quest for self-identity to the social achievement of becoming oneself through the force of a friendship.[31] In this central scene of the film, Womack enters into the dance studio as Manray has lost his patience with his students and dismisses them with contempt. Womack, who comes to report that he is leaving the network, confronts his friend on what one might call the matter of his manners. Of course, for social comedy, this is no trivial concern. Moreover, in a racist society, it is a serious threat. Manray backs away from his friend and does not respond. Womack does not immediately leave, but instead goes in and out of blackface, and then calls out, "Do you recognize me? Do you recognize me?" This remembrance of friendship serves as a catalyst for breaking Manray out of the role that has enframed him and bringing him back from his vanity to himself. Bergson explains that "we are never ridiculous except in some point that remains hidden from our own consciousness. It is on others, then that such observation must perforce be practiced" (L, 169).[32]

The other is the vital mediator of the self.[33] Yet Spike Lee's image of the masked audience at the minstrel show serves as a reminder against any naive romance of the People. While modern democracies require ties across culturally diverse, polyglot peoples, large-scale consumer-oriented networks of culture and consumption constitute persistent threats to authenticating bonds of friendships, families, communities, and historical memories. This is what Delacroix learns, though tragically too late, through his friend, his father, and his assistant.

Sartre has argued that our existence is an open question. Perhaps, but much is presupposed in the style or genre in which we ask a question. The stark metaphysics of *Being and Nothingness* takes its cue from a time of wartime crisis, when options could be as simple as fight or flight. In more ordinary times of turmoil, the classic existential poles of subject and object appear as endpoints on a horizontal axis in a social field. Such simple choices as subject or object, alone or assimilated, revolutionary or sell-out, are not nuanced enough to navigate the social terrain. In the Spike Lee film, these simple choices reproduce the stereotypes that the characters had aimed to overturn. African American existentialism is not in the end Sartrean.[34]

Delacroix's final words are from the writer James Baldwin: one pays for one's mistakes with the kind of life one lives. The authentic life is contrasted with the life of a puppet, a dancing fool, and a machine. The themes of the satiric film are almost, but not quite, European. If African American writers borrow from European sources, as Ellison's biographer Lawrence Jackson claims, they do not yield to any "inherent weaknesses of the Continental culture, . . . compared to the vigor of American Negro life."[35] For the classic French existentialist, the climactic turn of authenticity is found in the solitude of the individual. In the African American context, solitude may signify not metaphysical freedom but a kind of social death. The lone writer detached from friendship, family, and history, the numbed individual who would aim for an "invented life," cannot overcome the exhaustion of an inauthentic existence, not at least in Spike Lee's bleak satire.[36] Ridicule targets the rigidity of the mechanical—the opposite, Bergson observes, not of the beautiful (as Aristotle had thought), but of the gracious. In the film, the son who turns his back on friends, family, and the past is left to die alone, while the old comedian aims to grace those same bonds with his humor. Similarly, Womack pulls Manray out of a menacing role in the network through the grace of his friendship.

Spike Lee's pessimistic portrayal of racialized America fails to locate a clear basis for the common humanity that Ellison envisions. There is in the film no shared laughter across racial boundaries, none at least that is authentic. No Irish, Jewish, or white person awakens from their role to gain self-knowledge—unless one counts those viewers of the film who find themselves enlightened by the film's satiric gaze.

In a society striving for checks and balances against the social vices, ridicule can serve as a corrective. Such laughter, however, must be properly aimed. There is the laughter that mocks the weak. This laughter fuels the arrogance and ignorance of the strong. Blackface is one such art. But there is as well the laughter that unmasks racial and ethnic vanities through its ironic sting. Spike Lee's satiric tale of blackface does not leave us hovering above the artifice of our social roles. Nor does it allow for any easy romance of a common humanity. Spike Lee's film offers glimpses into a vision of authenticity through the grace of social bonds. It is in the mix of satire and sentiment that Spike Lee rewrites the formula for an emancipatory, multicultural identity—an identity that may indeed be real.[37] In the next chapter, we turn from satire to romantic comedy to flesh out a comic vision of solidarity for a democratic political ethics.

FOUR

ENGAGE THE ENEMY

CAVELL, COMEDIES OF REMARRIAGE, AND

THE POLITICS OF FRIENDSHIP

Contemporary Democratic Theory and the Friend-Enemy Distinction

Life, liberty, and, not property per se, but the pursuit of happiness name our fundamental sense of rights in this country. But are we at all clear on what happiness, or at least its pursuit, entails? Certainly we might say that of all the good things that lead to individual happiness, few are as important as friendship. This is not only true on a personal level. As Aristotle argues, cooperative bonds in the household and among citizens ground thriving political communities. Of course, modern-day liberals rightly reject Aristotle's tight, conflict-free communitarianism for a more fluid, egalitarian, and multicultural society, but it is difficult to envision the ideals of politics, including citizenship and justice, apart from some strong sense of solidarity that comes from social bonds. The ontologically detached and excessively rational agent proposed by some liberal theorists obscures the attachments that bind us to others. These attachments give us our depth as persons. It would be hard to live without them.

But then it's also hard to live with them. As any casual study of politics reminds us, passionate attachments can fuel fierce alliances and tragic conflicts. Post–cold war tensions in Eastern Europe, Africa, and the Middle East have led to the downfall of states and the rise of global terror. The relentless tensions of the post–cold war era may have divided the world along unpredictable lines, but they have also given rise to a curious convergence among otherwise opposed political perspectives. Leftist democracy theorists influenced by deconstruction and democratic imperialists of the Bush administration may not have much in common, but they do agree on at least one thing: the vital role of the friend-enemy distinction for democratic politics.[1]

Mouffe and LaClau argue that rationalists such as Habermas who aim to eliminate conflict as the basis for democracy ignore the subtle forms of coercion behind any appearance of consensus.[2] These radical democrats lack faith not only in reason but also in the old left's revolutionary fervor for a perfect utopian world. Instead of reaching out for a romanticized world beyond conflict and politics, Mouffe and LaClau call upon new left movements to form alliances (what they term "equivalences") to displace the hegemony of neoliberal capitalism. This forging of a leftist hegemony would entail (via the logic of deconstruction) the exclusion of those who do not share equivalent ideas of freedom and equality. There is no politics without the potential for enemies.

The radical democracy theorists may be right to point out as part of their political realism the persistence of irrational conflict, and to expose the usual appeals for resolving conflict through common reason as the ploy of some emerging hegemon. But these deconstructive democrats have difficulty locating any clear way out of political tensions that are potentially deadly. Mouffe is fully aware of the problem. As she explains, once we accept the necessity of the political and the impossibility of a world without exclusion and antagonism, what needs to be envisaged is how a pluralistic democratic order is possible.[3] Such an order could be based only, she argues, on a distinction between an "enemy" and an "adversary" whose existence is legitimate and must be tolerated. A pluralistic democracy would transform a deadly and antagonistic politics based on enemies to an agonistic politics, which allows opponents to be treated as tolerable adversaries who belong to a "common symbolic space" in a "multipolar" world. The question she leaves us with is what kind of political ethics could define this common symbolic space and restrain conflict in a multipolar world so that inevitable conflict does not turn deadly.

The conservative liberal theorist Michael Ignatieff puts forth claims on behalf of spreading American-style freedom and democracy that are arguably even more bereft of sound ethical limits. Ignatieff defends the moral idealism in the foreign policy goals of the Bush administration against the relativism of leftists.[4] He acknowledges that such imperial intervention might very well entail the tragic logic of self-deception and hubris, but he argues that Jeffersonian democracy is well worth the risk. He writes:

> What is exceptional about the Jefferson dream is that it is the last imperial ideology left standing in the world, the sole survivor of national claims to universal significance. All the others—the Soviet, the French and the British—have been consigned to the ash heap of history. This may explain why what so many Americans regard as simply an exercise in good intentions strikes even their allies as a delusive piece of hubris.
>
> The problem here is that while no one wants imperialism to win, no one in his right mind can want liberty to fail either. If the American project of encouraging freedom fails, there may be no one else available with the resourcefulness and energy, even the self-deception, necessary for the task. (45)

But if to the rest of the world the U.S. policy of democratic imperialism sounds less like a noble contest of ideals and more like just plain old hypocrisy, then perhaps this is because avoiding the dangers of hubris and self-deception is not incidental to what democracy should mean. Contemporary democracy theorists left and right who have brought from classical drama the notion of *agon,* or contest and struggle, back to the center of the political stage fail to face up to its dramatic structure, its narrative nodal points, or even, for what I would call an authentic democratic politics, the vital play of *irony* against hubris. For as we shall see, the successful use of irony against the self-deceived arrogance averts the tragic, and it allows for the imperfect friendships known through that literary genre that opposes the tragic, namely, the comic. In what follows, I shall explore the relevance of the comic for contemporary democracy theory through a reflection on nothing less profound than Hollywood comedies of remarriage as defined by Stanley Cavell. But let's first take a brief glance at what the Western philosophical tradition has had to say on friendship through the eyes of one of its more ambivalent friends.

Derrida, the Politics of Friendship, and the Democracy to Come

In an extensive study of friendship, published as *The Politics of Friendship,* Derrida draws the general conclusion that the prevailing philosophical model of friendship in the Western canon is based on one single type of relationship—the relationship between brothers. As he writes: "[F]rom

Plato to Montaigne, Aristotle to Kant, Cicero to Hegel, the great philosophical and canonical discourses on friendship will have explicitly tied the friend-brother to virtue and justice, to moral reason and political reason."[5]

The prominence of the friend-brother relation especially for our contemporary interest in democracy is clear already in classical Greek philosophy. Aristotle, as Derrida points out, suggests that while the bond between husband and wife illustrates the virtue of aristocracy, and monarchy grows out of the natural relationship between father and child, a well-founded democracy is like the friendship among brothers (*PF*, 197–98). Of course, Aristotle had an ambivalent attitude toward democracy, but the favorable characterization of social bonds in terms of a friendship among brothers stuck. We might think of the motto of the French Republic, "liberty, equality, fraternity," or of Philadelphia (which is incidentally the setting of that classic Hollywood remarriage comedy, *The Philadelphia Story*, but more on this later) as the cradle of liberty and city of brotherly love. In an essay elaborating upon Derrida's claims, John Caputo suggests that "[w]hen the 'Society of Friends,' the Quakers, named their polity Philadelphia, the city of 'brotherly love', . . . this was surely only a figure for loving all humanity, all our friends. But that is the very thing Derrida is questioning."[6]

Derrida's concern is the way in which this single prevailing model of friendship overemphasizes the importance of similarity for our ethical relationships, and doesn't account for how we might approach on a friendly basis those who are different from ourselves. He observes that the typical focus on brothers in conceptualizing our ethical identities leaves out or distorts the type of friendships that women cultivate either among themselves or with men. He questions Aristotle's dismissal of the relevance of eros, or sexual tension, for some of the best friendships. And he wonders how the dynamic of these alternative relationships might alter or expand our notions of virtue and justice, perhaps for the better. After all, Aristotle's elaborate account of the friend as another self continues to strike many scholars as narcissistic, elitist, and male-centered. This is because the Aristotelian account evolves around the superiority of two men who are fairly much alike in what the Greeks called *arete*—what Caputo loosely translates as "virile stuff." Assuming the concerns are more or less well-founded, the Aristotelian model of friendship cannot serve very well for pluralistic democrats. There must be better models for understanding exemplary types of friendship in democracies than those based on nearly perfect citizens who are just about the same in every way.

Derrida concludes his extensive study with an appeal for just such an alternative model of friendship and politics. Oddly, though, while Derrida had argued for the importance of women throughout his study, he rests his final appeal not on behalf of friendships between women and men, or among women themselves, but upon the otherwise friendless stranger. This appeal draws us toward the refugee uprooted from family and community, without a history or even a clear future, and of course lacking any of the protective rights of citizenship. I am not going to insist that this radically detachable stranger vaguely fits some kind of liberal archetype of pre-political man (man in the state of nature), although it is tempting to do so. I do want to return, however, to Derrida's neglect of women.

My alternative focus on more down-to-earth ethical realism (or at least the kind of realism we get in romantic comedies) should not be read as a gesture of dismissal for Derrida's high-minded insights. On the contrary, an ethical-religious modality of hospitality of the type that he suggests opens generously toward strangers, and should supplement any progressive liberal politics and its accompanying theory of justice, even if only on a quasi-religious plane. Note that while Derrida may critique the rationalism and universalism of Enlightenment ideals, and resist any temptation to offer for democracy theory a utopian blueprint for the future, he is no left-leaning political realist of the kind that neoconservatives love to hate. On the contrary, while they may not be friends, Derrida and the neoconservatives hold one thing in common: along with the neoconservatives, Derrida shares the Enlightenment's hope and what after Ignatieff we could call a moral idealism for a democracy that is "indefinitely perfectible" (PF, 306). His "prayer" on behalf of the stranger in a "democracy to come" provides a deeply ethical contrast with the aristocratic model of rule by the excellent ones, the elite men of virtue, which is how Aristotle defines his own version of a "city of prayer."[7] If for Derrida democracy remains more a prayer than a definable goal or rational principle, this is because of his concern first and foremost for those who fall outside of any hegemonic plan (even those radical democracies of the kind offered by LaClau and Mouffe). Of course, Derrida's hyperbolic ethical concern is necessarily riddled with the classical aporia of deconstruction. No doubt, we might find lurking behind the mask of the stranger the face of the deadly terrorist! Still, the possibility of extending friendship toward someone who is not in any ordinary sense our friend, who may indeed be our worst enemy, is for Derrida a prayer for happiness too.

In *Deconstruction and Pragmatism*, Richard Rorty accuses Derrida of being sentimental and even romantic, and Derrida does not shy away from these charges: "I am very sentimental and I believe in happiness," he acknowledges.[8] And with this turn toward the quasi-religious plane of friendship and justice, the arch deconstructionist no longer sounds like the postmodern ironist, or the Parisian Puck, as he was once known. In his later writings, Derrida has turned quite dramatically away from such earlier skeptical poses to embrace in his work on friendship what he calls *"aimance"* (*PF,* 66). It is not exactly clear what Derrida means by this strange new word. *Aimance* can be partly translated as love. It also suggests, as Caputo remarks, the English word "romance" (*DZ,* 190). "For friendship is 'such stuff as dreams are made on,'" Caputo adds in his comments, as he draws his line from Shakespearean romantic comedy (*DZ,* 190).

Now this shift back and forth between comedy and the sublime— between sentimental romance on the one hand and hospitality for the stranger on the other—is not only confusing, it seems to be pulling us in two quite different directions at once. The plea for a democracy of strangers points toward the most sobering act of generosity we might ever encounter. On the other hand, sentimental love, or *aimance,* draws its sensibility from the ironic, sometimes even zany, playfulness embedded in romantic comedy, as the allusion to Shakespeare's *Midsummer Night's Dream* suggests. Both forms of friendship threaten autonomy or self-rule with a heteronomy that Derrida, following another Jewish philosopher, Levinas, uses to decenter traditional subject-centered ethics. Either form can liberate, unleash, or otherwise disorient passions away from the self-interested practical self or calm rational rule-following individual, and toward the disruptive force of our entanglements with others. But then while Derrida dwells on a highly serious quasi-religious mode of hospitality for his ethics, as he does in his later writings, he leaves us wondering if comic romance might provide some alternative, perhaps more pragmatic, ethics for contemporary democracy theory.

Romantic Comedy and Pragmatism

It is not surprising that Derrida teases us with the possibilities of romantic comedy, only to leave the genre neglected in an otherwise exhaustive study of friendship. Romantic comedy emerged and just as quickly disappeared from the modern stage with Shakespeare, and hardly does it enter into anything remotely resembling what might be called the Western philosophical canon. And yet, romantic comedy characteristically centers dramatic tension around conflict-ridden relationships, often enough erotic relationships between men and women. Interestingly too, while romantic comedy disappeared for centuries, only recently did it make a comeback, this time in Hollywood film. Stanley Cavell examines this return in those classic 1930s and '40s Hollywood films that he defines as comedies of remarriage in his *Pursuits of Happiness*.[9]

Cavell focuses on the emerging egalitarianism between men and women and the implications of this equality for democracy. The genre turns around contests, not just between men, but rather more centrally, between a man and a woman, neither of whom is content to allow the other to gain the upper hand. In introducing the genre, Cavell provides a hint of historical background, suggesting that the films address the daughters of the generation who fought for and won the suffrage. These daughters shifted the struggle toward the spheres of family and civil society. The setting of such a prominent film as George Cukor's 1940 film *The Philadelphia Story* in Philadelphia, the cradle of liberty, points toward a generation's attempt to rethink the meaning of a free society, not we might say (having read Derrida) through brotherly love, but through romantic comedy's focus on remarriage.

Cavell's study of comedies of remarriage takes us some steps forward in understanding models of friendship relevant for both virtue and justice, models that subdue the narcissistic, aristocratic, or patriarchal vices that most concern Derrida. The friendships in these films exhibit some of these tendencies, to be sure; but the friendships also work against such forces, which are portrayed as blocks on human happiness. Hence we shall find in the comic *agon* a model of democratic conflict that falls to this side of the messianic moment of Derrida's perfect democracy to come, and yet avoids the tragic fury of forces that may follow the friend-enemy model of politics. For as we shall see, the lesson of remarriage comedy turns out to be similar to what Oedipus learns in the deadly encounter with the stranger at the crossroads in the Sophoclean tragedy: beware lest that person whom you took as your enemy turns out to have been your friend. This is a core ethical lesson for both comedy and tragic drama. Indeed, often enough one turns out to be one's own worst enemy. But if romantic comedy and tragedy are in some ways the same, they are also in some ways different. While tragic dialectic can romanticize lethal conflict as an inevitable ground of the human condition, comedy offers clues for its pragmatic limits.

Cavell's remarks on the difference between Dewey's pragmatic moderation and the nineteenth-century tragic romanticism as found in Hegel provide some philosophical backdrop before we launch into a full-scale discussion of film comedy. Cavell explains that "even though anyone could say he began his life as a Hegelian, really the Hegel that Dewey uses consists of two or three moves. They are very important moves. They are moves that exist by trying to find the middle way of two extremes, but they are not moves that sense the spiritual negation—the mutual negation—of these extremes. So that to find a way out of the mutual negation is itself a kind of spiritual torture. In Dewey you don't have spiritual torture."[10] The contrast between the mild optimism of twentieth-century social pragmatism and the tortuous perfectionism of tragic thinkers, along with their post-Nietzschean counterparts, opens a path toward better understanding the contributions of Hollywood comedy to contemporary ideas of equality, freedom, and democracy.

The Comedy of Remarriage

The comedies of remarriage, perhaps best exemplified by Cukor's *The Philadelphia Story,* but also including such films as *The Lady Eve* (Preston Sturges, 1941), *It Happened One Night* (Frank Capra, 1934), *Bringing Up Baby* (Howard Hawks, 1938), *His Girl Friday* (Howard Hawks, 1940), *Adam's Rib* (George Cukor, 1949), and *The Awful Truth* (Leo McCarey, 1937), emerged as central to Hollywood film from 1934 to 1949, and then reappeared in the 1990s.[11] I view Cavell's interpretation of the genre's major literary themes as revolving around two political elements.

First, as mentioned earlier, Cavell's depiction of the films as comedies of equality between men and women locates the basis for what we can identify as a democratic element. Cavell argues that democracies require a spirited relationship among equals, beginning with what has been one of democracy's basic institutions, namely, marriage. He elaborates upon the role of marriage through the classic social-contract image of autonomous individuals leaving a state of nature and yielding some of their natural freedom to accept the bonds of society and the happiness these bonds secure.

The second political element of the comedy, what Cavell locates as an aristocratic tendency in these films, seems, at least for Cavell, to balance the first element without contradicting it. He locates the aristocratic element primarily in the pursuit of perfection. According to this view, the films portray the ethical or spiritual education of character. Cavell's attention to the tension of democratic and aristocratic elements produces a rich reading of the films.

Cavell's own intellectual roots in nineteenth-century transcendentalism lead him, however, to overvalue perfectionist themes that romantic comedy's mishaps more often than not tend to undermine. And in fact, the rowdy upheavals of the sexually vibrant '20s and the socioeconomic crisis of the Depression prepare for these films to mock a range of pretensions of personality and society, both aristocratic and Victorian.[12] Let's look again at the key themes of one of the major films as we shift the parameters of the genre from classic liberal contract theory and aristocratic perfectionism to the social pragmatism of 1930s American political culture.[13]

Let's start with Cavell's discussion of the democratic element. In the essay on *The Philadelphia Story*, Cavell draws arguments from John Milton's tract on divorce to explain the importance of happiness in a marriage for democracy. It has less to do with the traditional emphasis on raising children than one would expect. Milton writes: "[N]o effect of tyranny can sit more heavily on the commonwealth than . . . household unhappiness on the family. And farewell all hope of true reformation in the state, while such an evil as this lies undiscerned or unregarded in the house: on the redress whereof depends not only the spiritful and orderly life of our grown men, but the willing and careful education of our children" (*PH*, 150–51). Milton goes on to describe "unhappiness in the marriage [as] bondage to 'a mute and spiritless mate.'" After citing these remarks, Cavell elaborates: "It seems to me accordingly to be implied that a certain happiness, anyway a certain spirited and orderly participation, is owed to the commonwealth by those who have sworn allegiance to it—that if the covenant of marriage is a miniature of the covenant of the commonwealth, then one may be said to owe the commonwealth participation that takes the form of a meet and cheerful conversation" (*PH*, 151). While it is said that a spirited marriage is good for children, Cavell takes the main point to be that a good marriage, as a good commonwealth, turns not on reproducing the population but on lively conversation.

Cavell draws out the theme of conversation in a discussion of two scenes in *The Philadelphia Story*. In the first of the scenes Cary Grant and Katharine Hepburn blame each other for the failure of their marriage. (I use the actor's instead of the character's names in cases where the actor's presence is striking in the film. As Cavell notes, the genre plays on this presence with allusions and puns, as in the line I am about to quote from Cary Grant's character in the film.) Hepburn reminds her ex-husband of the vice, his weakness for alcohol, that led to their divorce. His reply: "Granted. But you took on that problem when you married me. You were no helpmeet there, Red. You were a scold." Cavell takes up Cary Grant's claim here. It not the vice per se but the lack of a certain kind of conversation that marred their relationship. He writes: "This . . . is once more exactly a brief for his divorce from her, based on Milton's . . . perception that 'a meet and happy conversation is the chiefest and noblest end of marriage.' The conjunction of being a helpmeet with being willing to converse . . . comes out again in a late exchange . . . [after she realizes that she has some problems of her own]. . . . 'I'm such an unholy mess of a girl,' [she laments, seeming to agree with his accusations], to which he responds, 'Why that's no good, that's not even conversation' " (*PH*, 146).

Now any feminist critic of Cavell has to smile after reading his comments, because it is fairly clear in the film that the brief for divorce comes from the woman, not the man. The film emphasizes the fact that she could not live with his drinking problem. This slip on Cavell's part alerts us to be on the lookout for ways he tilts the reading of the genre in favor of a male perspective. It is this tilt that I want to contest, along with some of the traditional biases of narcissism, elitism, and patriarchy that, as Derrida suggests, any good democrat might want to deconstruct. As long as we are looking to the genre, most of the films that Cavell picks out in fact favor the woman's perspective over the man's. Now *The Philadelphia Story* is an exception to this tendency, but exceptions, as Cavell likes to remind us, do not necessarily undermine general rules.

Still, Cavell is right that the films often enough do center marriage around a spirited conversation, driven by an ever-illusive difference. This comic dynamic perpetuates what is colloquially called the battle of the sexes. But, as we shall later see, the comic dynamic reoccurs among partners and friends of the same sex, and wherever it occurs it produces an erotic basis for some of our friendships—friendships that may well be, as Cavell writes of marriage, "a miniature of the covenant of the commonwealth." The question is whether the conversations have any kind of determinate structure or recurring themes and images that might lend a hand in deconstructing the undemocratic forces of elitism, narcissism, and patriarchy.

Among the several connected themes of the genre of remarriage comedies, Cavell notes the absence of the woman's mother. Again, this is not true for every single film, and as Cavell notes, happens not to be true for *The Philadelphia Story.* (But as we have said, exceptions do prove rules.) And so for good reason Cavell interprets a recurring dismissal of what all the traditional (somewhat Victorian) mother can stand for as further evidence in favor of the spirited pleasures of conversation and the erotic tensions upon which these pleasures may be based. My only concern here is again with Cavell's one-sided focus; for the traditional father is equally a problem in these films, as we shall see clearly in *The Philadelphia Story.* Marriage is not to be taken as having some staid moral purpose such as obedience, property, or good reputation, let alone some old-fashioned devotion to nurturing and care that renders the self mute.

On the contrary, the major characters reject such unpleasant Victorian values along with their happy-ever-after promise of a peaceful and secure home life. Another prevalent image, the presence of a boat or other vehicle set for adventure, turns the marriage around a more stimulating and less Victorian axis. In *The Philadephia Story* this boat is called the *True Love,* and the boat is associated not only with the marriage of Hepburn and Grant, but also with the fiery redhead Hepburn herself. (In *The Awful Truth,* the vehicle is a motorcycle.) To expand upon Cavell's thought a bit here, we could contrast the themes of security, dependency, and morality that defined the earlier respectable marriage, themes that reappear in the cold war period, with the themes of adventure, freedom, and contest in the comedies of remarriage. This is important because even if the female characters occasionally yield to submissive poses of bondage, poses that should make a contemporary audience wince (as when Hepburn parrots Cary Grant's words in announcing the change of plans at the final wedding scene), the women in the films are the equal to the men in style, personality, in short, the comic virtues.

Aristotle consigned what must be one of the primary comic virtues, wit, to an inferior mode of friendship; but he understood the highest type of friendship to center around a limited number of very close friends held together through the pleasure of conversation. If we allow for the fact that these friends might not all share the same perspective, that they might be as different as the fantasized difference between the sexes, then we might also allow for a little more playful conflict in the highest form of philosophical conversation among some intimate friends. Indeed, we might say that without comic play, including the incongruities of perspective or meaning displayed in wit, there is none of the fiery red spirit that Milton and Cavell agree are necessary for democracy. Democracy requires the comic virtues practiced among couples and clusters of friends.

These comic virtues contrast sharply with the vices of the boor, but also with the pedant or any other type who drains the spirit of "gaiety and social wisdom"(here I do repeat Cavell's phrase, *PH,* 238). Even at the wedding scene in *The Philadelphia Society,* where Hepburn nods to Grant's fatherly authority, and offers to be "yar," like their boat the *True Love,* meaning "easy to handle," Grant responds, "Be whatever you want. You're my redhead." The association of the female characters and relationships with a boat or some such vehicle of adventure rather than, say, with oceanic figures of (s)mothering love reinforces the spirited quality of marriage and society, with the usual difficulties in tow.

Cavell teases out Nietzschean themes in the films to underscore the point that marriage is not in these films and should not ever be about a happy ending where conflict is resolved. The claim is perhaps most clear in his discussion of *The Awful Truth.* Marriage aims not for the goal of a tame, domesticated, and dully secure life. It is a daily festival of contest, or, to use the Nietzschean theme, the "repetition" of playfully erotic conversation. In comedy, to say "yes" to this festive existence manifests itself through perpetual conflict. For while these romantic comedies incorporate the element of adventure (usually, the chief element of romance), they avoid romance's typical gesture of consigning the woman to the role of trophy, the hero's prize. In these comedies of remarriage the woman is the man's prime contestant. "The love impulse manifests itself as conflict" is not only the sage advice of an otherwise ludicrous psychiatrist in *Bringing Up Baby*, but also what I think we could identify, again expanding only a bit from Cavell's own suggestions, as an underlying theme of all these films. Of course, Milton does talk about restraint, or orderliness as well, and these contests do have certain very necessary limits that we need to fully consider. Let's turn to Cavell's locus of the major themes or images of the genre and see how far we can follow him.

As we have said, the first two images, the untamable vehicle of adventure and freedom and the absence of the nurturing mother, pose the woman less as a prize and a promise for the end of conflict than as a permanent enemy combatant. In the more egalitarian moments of the films, each partner in the couple becomes the vehicle for the other's freedom. In other moments, one of the two serves as the vehicle for liberating the other from what might otherwise be a mute and dispiriting life. In any case, this liberated desire, this spirited expression of erotic tension, gives us the meaning of freedom in these films. If marriage is about bondage, there is in this bondage not less but greater freedom. Marriage liberates these characters from the enervating bonds of the old society.

A third image of the films important for Cavell is the allusion to the pair as so much alike as to be sister and brother. Now while it is true that this image is there, Cavell's particular interpretation takes us down a path that I do not wish to go. On the contrary, as I shall suggest, reexamination of the image of the pair as sister and brother points to where the two political elements (liberal democratic and aristocratic) that Cavell lays out begin to unravel, and alternative, pragmatic parameters for the necessary checks and balances of different types of people in an egalitarian society begin to appear.

The difference between our interpretations turns on the central question that Cavell poses at the beginning of the essay on *The Philadelphia Story*. How is it that of Hepburn's three suitors in the film, the former husband (Cary Grant), a lower-middle-class journalist (played by Jimmy Stewart), and a wealthy ex–coal miner named George, with whom she is engaged until the end of the film, she ends up back with her former husband? For Cavell, the answer turns on sameness, on the couple being like sister and brother; while I shall argue that on the contrary, the erotic tension that holds the couple together turns on their differences.

Clearly, George is not the right partner for Hepburn, but is there a simple reason why? If the film does not invite us to like his character, this is not for any moral failing. On the contrary, George represents a very high form of moral rectitude, too high if anything, at least for comic romance. We could say he's just the kind of moral idealist that neoconservatives praise. The problem with his character is not his moral stance but his less than inviting social manners. These are boorish manners that are hardly conducive to the gay and sociable wisdom upon which the comic vision depends. Hepburn's decision against George (and it is a woman's decision here that is at stake) is also a rejection of a type of marriage based on work and moral rectitude. Marriage is not in this film primarily those values of a conservative life, economic wealth, and upright morals. Comedy points toward a social ethics of manners that tempers moral concerns and holds together society.

But then why reject Stewart? Stewart's character is also drawn from the less-privileged classes, but unlike George he has some of the comic virtues. He certainly brings the pleasure of contest and spirited engagement. Hepburn remarks after reading his book of short stories that underneath that veneer of cynicism, he has the magical gift of the poet. While the poetic gift does go hand in hand with a narcissistic tendency, at least in Stewart, the gift of transformative vision is real nonetheless. Near the end of the film, after the transformative scene at the pool, the formerly cynical Stewart tells Hepburn she is like a queen, and even proposes to her, but this changed woman turns him down. Cavell does not give us anything like a full answer as to why this happens, but he does give us some enticing hints. He raises the question of whether class differences between Stewart and Hepburn keep them apart. This is also when he turns his focus to the sibling-like relation between Hepburn and Grant. As he writes, "[h]aving grown up together, or anyway having created a childhood past together, remains a law for the happiness of the pair in the universe of remarriage comedies" (*PH*, 136).

The childhood theme comes up in the films in different ways, and it serves among other things to bring out the playful intimacy and equality between the couple. In a film purporting to be about the Philadelphia story, we might understand the theme as well on analogy with the needs of the nation-state. The nation requires an imagined or otherwise quasi-mythical sense of a common past or collective memory, lest it collapse. This is one problem for failed states. So too marital happiness requires creating a sense of a past together. Cavell, however, chooses instead to emphasize the sibling-like sameness of the couple, to the point that Susan Bordo in her own reflections on the genre even goes so far as to call the relationship "slightly incestuous."[14]

Now this allusion to incest, or marriage within kinship lines, points further down the aristocratic path of remarriage comedies than I want to go. If the growing-up-together theme underscores the similarity between two superior characters who are enough the same that they might has well be siblings, the genre is not going to provide so much a substantial alternative to the canonical model of friendship that Derrida rightly aims to deconstruct as an interesting variation of it. Cavell often counterposes the sameness of the couple with an allusion to importance of sexual difference. But what does that difference amount to?

Before, however, we can look for a way out of the aristocratic democracy that Cavell reads into remarriage comedies, we need to understand it. Remarriage comedies at least as Cavell sees them turn on the education of manners. It is Cavell's concern with a proper education, or what he calls the perfection of character, that prepares him to respond to the question of what kind of companionship provides the best foundation for democracy.

The perfectionist theme takes in a couple more images from remarriage plays. Cavell argues that remarriage comedy, like old comedy, focuses typically on the heroine, who undergoes a symbolic death and rebirth (think of the subplot of *Much Ado about Nothing*). As in older comedy, this death and rebirth have something to do with the heroine's virginity. In traditional Shakespearean comedy, the father attempts to protect his daughter's virginity; its apparent soiling signifies her death, and the recovery of innocence, her rebirth. In the remarriage comedies the theme of virginity comes up in a new way. The issue is no longer one of protecting physical virginity; instead the theme alludes to the heroine's original sense of being intact as an autonomous person, or so Cavell insists. Her symbolic death (as in Hepburn's venture at the pool with Stewart) signifies her willingness to yield her virginal autonomy, through a kind of education (symbolically a "rebirth") that is also an emancipation. This emancipation is, Cavell argues, provided by men who bear something of a paternal authority as well as magical powers.

If this sounds somewhat patriarchal, it is, and it doesn't always fit the films. In *Bringing Up Baby, The Awful Truth,* and *The Lady Eve,* it is primarily the woman who is "educating" the man, usually about his own desires. As I have said, this education counts as a kind of liberation, the kind that comedy provides, and tilts the entire film somewhat toward the female point of view. Cavell is right, however, to note that in *The Philadelphia Story* Hepburn is lectured to about her imperfections by a variety of men, including not only her own patriarchal father but also the somewhat paternalistic Grant. Whatever the paternal role in her education, we can see clearly that the change amounts to her learning to reconnect with herself and these men.

Cavell is cautious about how we might interpret this paternal authority in what are after all comedies of equality. Certainly, there is a clear distinction between the kind of paternal authority that we see in Cary Grant and that of her old-fashioned, patriarchal father. As Cavell explains, Cary Grant's "authoritativeness, or charisma, may poorly or prejudicially be interpreted as a power to control events. Maybe it is a power not to interfere in them but rather to let them happen. (The association of an explicitly magical person with a power of letting others find their way . . .)" (*PH*, 139). Cavell alludes to the wise man as magus, magician, teacher, therapist, and perhaps philosopher, too, given that Cavell does pose himself through his style in these essays as something of a similar paternal/ironic figure. The Socratic role of the teacher is pivotal for the creation of the woman, or Cavell's "new woman," against the norms of obedience or respectability. Cavell does not mention any complementary metamorphosis for men, although he does acknowledge in passing that women in the films can liberate men. And so one wonders if there is not more back and forth between the two characters than Cavell's definition of the genre allows. In any case, as we have said, whether this midwifery role for the central male character is generally true, it does appear to operate in *The Philadelphia Story*. In fact various men tell Hepburn that she is like a virginal Greek goddess, a "married maiden" Grant says, and that she cannot be a full woman until she gives up that high-and-mighty pose. Cavell interprets this virginity as yielding her natural autonomy for the sake of the Lockean-style contract, one which marks her pathway from natural autonomy into social bonds.

Now let's return to our initial puzzle, namely the question of why Hepburn should end up with the seemingly paternalistic upper-class Grant rather than the less paternalistic and just as magical Stewart, especially in an egalitarian comedy. As we have said, Cavell claims that the pairs to be re-wedded in the genre have in some sense grown up together. True enough. Grant does characterize his relation to Hepburn in this way; but still by the end of the film this requirement could apply as much if not more to Stewart and Hepburn, taken together as a couple, as to Hepburn and Grant. In fact, within the bounds of the film, Grant's character does not undergo any great change at all, and certainly not in relation to Hepburn. Grant has mastered his excessive drinking, but that was pointedly not with Hepburn's assistance. Even more, the paternalistic Grant insists that his companion's task is not so much to change him as to accept him with vices and all. So much for his education by her. Meanwhile, the film shows both Stewart and Hepburn coming to terms with their mutual arrogance and general snobbishness. Why not say that Hepburn and Stewart are with respect to this vice like sister and brother, and that they both have some growing up to do? After all, as mentioned earlier, in the climactic moment of the film, both undergo a metamorphosis from a compromising rendezvous the night before Hepburn's planned wedding to George. Stewart learns to be less of a snob toward the rich. And the social embarrassment of the incident prompts Hepburn into acknowledging her own mishaps and accepting vices in others as well. Her virginal goddess-like character does not have to do with her refusal to surrender her natural autonomy for the sake of marriage. It has much to do with her queenly arrogance and the very vital need to repair an already existing social fabric. It is this altered focus that shifts the parameters away from that Cavellian weave of classic liberal autonomy and aristocratic perfectionism, and toward the emerging social pragmatism of the 1930s.

Let's return to the question of Stewart and Hepburn. The magic of the late-night rendezvous brings greater self-awareness to a humbled Hepburn. It also leaves Stewart so mesmerized by Hepburn that he returns from the encounter with some of his intellectual snobbery against the upper class in check. In this sense that we could say that the film turns around both Hepburn and Stewart "growing up," and doing so together like sister and brother. But this mutually transformative education apparently does not set them up as the appropriate pair to marry, and we need to understand why. Are we left with class difference as the only plausible block to their further relationship? If so, this would underscore the film's aristocratic themes, and in one of the most snobbish ways possible. Let's look more carefully at what Cavell thinks is aristocratic about the film, and why he judges this to be a good thing.

His argument for an aristocratic element in a comedy of equality is actually quite complicated. It begins with a consideration of what the film depicts as appealing in inherited wealth. Cavell is not interested in elements of the film legitimating artificial class pretensions or rigid class definitions, at least not in any obvious way, and he sees Hepburn as undermining class pretensions in her appreciation of characters such as Stewart. What Cavell views as salutary about the upper class is their leisure for the cultivation of what he calls the "genuine individual" (*PH*, 155). Cavell writes that "a 'first-class human being,' an otherwise dark notion . . . [does not have] to do with a hierarchy of social classes, or with some idea that there are different kinds of human beings. . . . [T]he difference I see . . . may be expressed this way: the natural aristocrat, better in degree but not in kind than his fellows, is not inherently superior to others, but . . . further along a spiritual path anyone might take and appreciate. . . . This is dangerous moral territory . . . under surveillance most explicitly with George's defeat and departure. . . . This danger must be run in [comic] romance, which wishes the promise of union and renewal, not expulsion" (*PH*, 156).

It might help for focus if we think of the cultivation less of the genuine individual per se than of intimate companionship, to avoid what I take to be a possible misreading of Cavell's text, as well as to correct Cavell's, dare I say, characteristic tilt toward a one-sidedly male perspective. It is odd after all that Cavell places a photo of a radiant Cary Grant at the opening of a book that is supposed to be about the (re)creation of the modern woman, or egalitarian marriage, rather than any kind of male narcissism. Comic romance, unlike the genre called romance, assures that perfection is not pursued by the separate individual who seeks self-knowledge in the reflective sphere of nature, as Thoreau might be said to have done at Walden's pond. This path to self-knowledge is presumably traveled through what in an account of such romantic comedies as *Midsummer Night's Dream* Northrop Frye terms a "green world" and what, as we have emphasized, for these couples is a erotic sphere of adventure, metamorphosis, and contest.[15] The nineteenth-century transcendental motif of self-knowledge reoccurs in a narrative of romantic comedy, where I think we can say it is a bit more down-to-earth. The couple grows through an intimate encounter, as Stewart and Hepburn might be said to have done together at a pool, not alone in the more sublime dimensions of thought, but in their pleasure together.

Cavell offers his version of what such a path of self-knowledge for a couple might entail through an argument drawn from Matthew Arnold's *Culture and Anarchy*. According to Arnold, a flourishing society requires the correct balance of Hebrew conscience and pagan Greek spontaneity. Cavell views Hepburn's self-righteousness as an instance of Hebrew conscience that can be properly balanced only by Grant's spontaneity. The result of this balance in marriage as in a nation is the perfect union. Marriage requires that Grant and Hepburn correct their individual flaws and advance spiritually toward a cultivation of the virtues. Cavell emphasizes that this path toward perfection does not entail any artificial classist assumptions regarding different kinds of human beings, but only that humanness comes in degrees, and that a metamorphosis along this path makes possible a more perfect individual. So George is not as good a human being as Hepburn and Grant, and this is not because of an inherent class difference, but because of shades of self-deception that Hepburn and Grant have overcome. Comedy leaves as exiles those melancholy spirits that threaten social ruin with their envy and jealousy, and George is apparently just such an overly flawed character. Hepburn on the other hand overcomes the worst parts of her queenly presence, retaining the virtues of her Hebraic conscience while yielding to the compassion, desire, and vulnerability of a flesh-and-blood human being.

But does Cavell's perfectionist sensibility and the aristocracy of character it sustains really cohere with the zany pleasures and screwball mishaps of comedies of remarriage? Admittedly there are lingering aristocratic themes in a film in which George declares, as he marches off in the end, that class, along with the whole aristocratic lifestyle that Hepburn and Grant represent, is on its way out. But is also true that in these films even the ridiculous characters utter truths that need to be heard. And in a democracy that is as it should be.

Indeed, Cavell's aristocratic focus on perfectionist themes might be persuasive except for one overwhelming fact. The whole point of the film is *not* that Hepburn learns to become a more perfect person. This is important. What Hepburn learns first and foremost is not to strive toward some grand image of herself. On the contrary Hepburn must come to accept human *imperfection.* It is true she does become a better human being because of this insight, but crucially what she most needs to learn is that she is not that pagan goddess of strength, that superior creature that she had tried to be, and that attempting to play such a role is destructive, both to herself and to those around her. One is often enough one's own worst enemy. The situation at the pool serves as a kind of social leveler between Hepburn and the others in her life, prompting her to strip off her goddess pretensions along with a Greek robe, and acknowledge human frailties. But then we should see as well that this morally uptight goddess blurs the images of pagan and Hebrew that Cavell aims to separate. Arnold's theory of culture is just not going to work for this film. In fact, Red, as Hepburn's character is called, is much more spontaneous and spirited, and in this sense "pagan," than the coolly ironic Cary Grant. In any case, as far as I can see, the film does not aim primarily to open a romantic path toward perfection, a rather narcissistic if not snobbish quality for a genre that turns on the prevalence of comic error and unexpected irony, but instead to point out that acknowledging ordinary vices is part of what allows friendships to thrive.

Cavell's perfectionist themes drawn from such nineteenth-century transcendentalists as Thoreau and his pond seem heavy-handed, if not a tad bit narcissistic, in this Depression-era Hollywood film. Interestingly, the theme of narcissism does come up in the film. Hepburn alludes rather mysteriously to the beauty of Narcissus in a gesture of some kind toward the poet, Jimmy Stewart. She does this after having left George at the party, and before the event at the pool with Stewart. While she seems on the one hand to use the comparison in appreciation of Stewart's poetic gifts, she adds rather oddly that Narcissus drowns as he tries to kiss a reflection of the moon, who was also a goddess.

I think it is this mysterious comparison that gives us our most important clue as to why Stewart's proposal is to be rejected. Stewart's desire for Hepburn may in part be based, as is Grant's, on the solid ground of friendship, but unlike the latter it is way too tinged by the kind of narcissistic fantasies that accompany what may be called romantic love. These fantasies are narcissistic inasmuch as they come less from knowing the other person, with their vices and all, than idolizing them. And for this film it's the wrong kind of love. Stewart may be the immediate vehicle for Hepburn's self-knowledge, but the encounter at the pool leads him to view her less as she is than as a queen. It is finally Grant and not Stewart who both understands and balances her limitations, and promises a more salutary relationship.

But if this balance is not because of some dialectic between his spontaneity and her rigid conscience, then what kind of balance does he offer? Let's go back to see if we can see the pattern to the characters who finally pair up in remarriage comedies, some pattern that further rules out Hepburn and Stewart becoming a couple. Cavell provides us a strong clue when he points toward the ways in which many of the themes of *The Philadelphia Story* come straight out of *Midsummer Night's Dream*. Taking the parallels between the two plots, we can see Grant as spurned by the uppity Hepburn just as Oberon is by Titania, queen of the fairies. In the Shakespeare play, Oberon plays the role of deflationary ironist to Titania's overinflated arrogance. The ironist sets the stage for metamorphosis and steps back to watch the plot unfold. The roles of Grant and Hepburn are similar.

Comic plots often enough set up characters of contrasting vices on an Aristotelian scale of the virtues. In other comedies, the characters may balance one another along the lines of pagan spontaneity and Hebraic conscience, but this is no rigid rule. In the case of this film, Grant and Hepburn play the parts of what Aristotle terms the *eiron* and the *alazon*, with deflationary ironist set against the overinflated boaster, someone whom we might otherwise call an arrogant snob. Much of the *agon* of comedy would be generated by the contest between characters who may be richly drawn and yet embody such contrasting vices.

In *The Philadelphia Story* we see the *agon* between the deflationary ironist and the uppity snob not only in the main plot, in the characters of Grant and Hepburn, but in the dynamic as well between Stewart and Ruth Hussey's character, the photographer and would-be artist Liz. Ruth Hussey's character serves as a useful and witty deflator to Stewart's pretensions in much the same way as Grant does for Hepburn. When Stewart loses the ironic skepticism that usually defines him, and falls into the trap of idolizing Hepburn as a queen, he is no longer useful in the same way. This poet's gift of transformative perception recalls the narcissistic projections of romantic love; it does not make for the egalitarian marriage of contest and conversation (or "spirited conversation," as Cavell writes) that give us pleasure in the films. The egalitarian contests play lovers against one another in, as Cavell says, the perpetual festival of contest. Hepburn may be held in bounds by Grant's cool irony; but without her fiery boldness there would be no spirit in the relationship.

In this genre of companion-style marriage, we do not have the romanticization of separate spheres of gender identity from the Victorian era, or any complementary doctrines of male and female perfection as these spheres presumed. On the contrary, here we have marriage as friendship, but in the state of perpetual conflict, relentless sibling rivalry we might say, but without the sameness that should concern deconstructionists such as Derrida. If Grant is the magus/educator in this story, as Cavell suggests, it is less because he embodies some perfect pagan principle of spontaneity than because of his role as ironist. Of course, in relation to George, the boor, Grant does reveal as well a spontaneous side. And in fact rich characters have multiple aspects to their identity, and so too thrive in multiple relationships. Marriage does not suffice to complete one, and only the romantic lover would think it could. Still, in this film marriage is central, and Grant's persona is most apparent in contrast with the self-deceptive arrogance of the virginal goddess that he helps to expose. As the teacher or philosopher, a paternal yet not patriarchal Grant steps back from direct control, lending the hand of the ironist to the plot here and there, but allowing those around him to unravel and rediscover who they are for themselves. This is not to say that the characters accomplish this task by themselves; it's just to say that pedantic moralizing lectures of the type given by Hepburn's father are likely less to educate than to harden their intended target. This film ends with less equality than, say, Shakespeare's Beatrice and Benedict, because whatever spirit Red adds to the marriage, Grant's ironic role takes the upper hand. This film is for that reason less egalitarian than one might want. Still the film serves well to show that needed most in a democracy threatening to become an imperial hegemon is not another moral lecture, but the mocking tone of the comic ironist. No wonder Stephen Colbert, Dave Chapelle, Chris Rock, and Jon Stewart are among our most salutary political voices today.

Romantic comedy tries as best it can to include everyone in the new society, lest the play darken. The pleasure at the end comes from a festive celebration of imperfect souls. So why must the film expel the imperfect George, the self-made man and exemplar of one contending view of what it means to be American? Cavell argues that it is his envy and resentment of his betters, which is to say that George is not in that class of better people. If we are to avoid the more aristocratic side of Cavell's interpretation, however, we might focus less on George's occasional envy and more on the unyielding sense of superiority that his quickness to condemn betrays. This same kind of moral arrogance mars Hepburn's own character, and George is not going to help her keep this vice in check. The film doesn't finally exclude him from all society, just this one.

This is not to say that the film constitutes any unproblematic endorsement of democracy either. The film makes clear through the uninvited appearance of *Spy Magazine* at the wedding that "the people" are not immune from their own types of overreaching. The tyranny of majorities, and the necessity for preserving some sense of the private life against this kind of public surveillance, is signaled by the antics of Sidney Kidd, the magazine's editor. Still these tyrannical forces are perhaps never so lethal as when the masses unite with the wealthy under the imperial banner of moral self-righteousness, and it is in the figure of George and not Sidney Kidd that we find the latter tendency.

Remarriage comedy depends not upon the cultivation of individual perfection but upon the balance of our different vices and the incomplete virtues they enable through our social bonds. Throughout the comedies of remarriage, marriage is envisioned not as a perfect union of superior characters, but instead as the conflict-ridden romance based on the playing off of vice against vice, vices that become disastrous, as tragedy demonstrates, when they are not reined in. Of course, this play of vices doesn't necessarily divide up between characters quite as happens in *The Philadelphia Story* or *Midsummer Night's Dream*. Shakespeare's *Much Ado about Nothing*'s central couple, Beatrice and Benedict, each take turns playing the role of ironist against overinflated tendencies in the other. (In contrast, romantic love pulls together the couple of *Much Ado*'s subplot). Other comedies of remarriage show different comic vices. In *Bringing Up Baby,* a screwball Katharine Hepburn falls for the boorish Cary Grant. Not even in comedy is the boor—that enemy of comedy—once and for all dismissed from social relevance. Rather, the genre of remarriage comedy illustrates in the realm of character and marriage what Madisonian liber-alism recommends for the machinery of government, and the pragmatist expands to the larger democratic society, a necessary balance of counter-vailing powers, without too much investment of authority in any one place over time.[16] This kind of pragmatic liberalism does not encourage us to target enemies as do our radical democratic friends, but instead, picking up on the subtitle of a more recent remarriage comedy, to engage them.

Indeed, this play of checks and balances in romantic comedies disap-peared in the security-oriented 1950s and its aftermath, only to once again emerge in the post–cold war era. In the Coen brothers' comedy of remar-riage alluded to above, *Intolerable Cruelty: Engage the Enemy* (2003), George Clooney and Catherine Zeta-Jones play their arrogance off one another just like Shakespeare's Beatrice and Benedict. In another Coen brothers film, *The Big Lebowski* (1998), Jeff Bridges plays the ironist slacker to a self-righteous Vietnam veteran played by John Goodman. This is a buddy film, not a comedy of remarriage, but their friendship rests similarly on the constant friction between them, and that friction too stems from the difference of perspective their respective vices lend them. In *The Big Lebowski* it is even more clear than in the older films that the characters are not ever going to correct their vices, and they do not expect anything different of one another. Instead, as is typical of this kind of buddy film, the play of their vices against one another sustains the friend-ship. It is the friendship of the buddy films, and not romantic love or morally and economically defined gender roles, that defines 1930s roman-tic comedies and allows what otherwise might seem like a traditional defense of marriage to open up a path for understanding a broader con-ception of the many kinds of friendship that ground a democratic society.

We have said that the social ethos of remarriage comedy coheres less with a classic liberal contract theory than the social pragmatism of 1930s U.S. culture and shows some signs of re-emerging in the post-cold-war-era romantic film comedy. Let's see if we can now be clear on what these different genres of democratic politics entail.

Contract theory rests on the decision of the individual to yield natural autonomy for the security of a union. Cavell draws upon contract theory when he argues that remarriage comedy centers around yielding indepen-dence (or symbolically, one's virginity) in the pursuit of happiness through marriage.

These films, however, are about not marriage but remarriage. The remarriage theme centers around revitalization of friendships that are already there rather than their original creation from some virginal state of nature. Accordingly, the films do not revolve around the need to yield some degree of independence for the security marriage can bring; this picture of domestic life as a threat to one's freedom may dominate the so-called matriarchal comedies of the 1950s, as has been argued.[17] Susan Bordo points out the sardonic quality of Rock Hudson's speech in the 1959 film *Pillow Talk:* "Before a man gets married, he's like a tree in the forest. He stands there, independent, an entity unto himself. And then he's chopped down" (*MB,* 117). A situation of what one scholar describes as "female *hubris* and male *angst*" leads, as Bordo writes, to "male rebellion against domesticity" in James Dean–style existential films of the 1960s and Clint Eastwood action figures of the next several decades (*SM,* 250; *MB,* 119). In these contexts, women are sex goddesses or trophies, but not real friends.

Long-standing friendships repair the disruption that our ordinary vices cause in a social life. The classic liberal tension between autonomy and dependence does not bear on Hepburn's decision to remarry Grant. It comes up only in her lecture to her mother. Hepburn urges her mother to give up on her philandering husband and save her self-respect, to which her mother expresses fears of abandonment. While the mother's options leave the simple choice of self-respect or a dependent kind of love, Hepburn's decision is posed by more complex parameters. Her choice revolves around three suitors, and three types of relationship: the romantic love projected by the poet, Jimmy Stewart, the status-oriented marriage of the upright George, or unending contest with Cary Grant. Remarriage to Grant promises not only restraint but also emancipation, the freedom that one experiences in, as Cavell would have it, a conversation with a friend. And if this is freedom, it is not what liberal theory posits as autonomy, but what romantic comedy unfolds as the liberation of eros of a predominantly social kind. It assumes human imperfection, social interdependence, and the vital play of checks and balances that a spirited exchange provides. It in this social vision of friendship in adventure and contest that we find a microcosm for democracy.

Conclusion

Democracy, like friendship, is based not on virtue but on vice, and on the spirited conflicts that our ordinary vices sustain. But if these vices are to enable our virtues, then they must act as restraints on one another. Blind arrogance is one of the more dangerous vices in politics as it is in friendship, and often the basis for tragedy. It is as well the ready target of laughter in comic romance. Let us assume that the companionships of romantic comedy serve as a miniature form of democracy. If so, then we might say that democracy thrives through conversation and contest as well as through dialogue's comic structure. The balance of irony against arrogance is not incidental to democracy but essential to its basic meaning. Solidarity presupposes not unity but difference. Indeed, it thrives upon it. In the final chapter, we shall propose a threefold definition of freedom that does not oppose freedom to solidarity or equality but instead demonstrates their mutual interdependence. While the threefold definition constitutes a strong challenge to Anglo-American liberalism, its appeal in our culture is apparent in our progressive comedy.

FIVE

THREE CONCEPTS OF FREEDOM

The practices of comedy provide terribly effective tools, strategies, and tactics for reinforcing social patterns of domination and exclusion. Oppressive communities, for example, may generate internal unity by using ridicule to target social outcasts and threaten any member who dares not conform. However, the practices of comedy can also provide weapons for emancipation from oppressive communities and their rigid norms. Think of the Guerrilla Girls, an anonymous group of feminist artists who, masked in gorilla heads, use outrageous wit to expose sexism and racism. One of their art posters proclaims, "The Guerrilla Girls think the world needs a new weapon: THE ESTROGEN BOMB. Drop it on Washington and the guys in government will throw down their guns, hug each other, say it was all their fault, and finally start to work on human rights, education, health-care and an end to world poverty. Got leftover estrogen pills? Send them to Bush, Cheney, and Rumsfeld, 1600 Pennsylvania Avenue, Washington DC 20500, USA."[1] Or consider how sexual and gender differences can implode altogether in drag-queen shows. Queer communities have long parodied gender and sex roles, as well as rites such as marriage that are practiced in

[116]

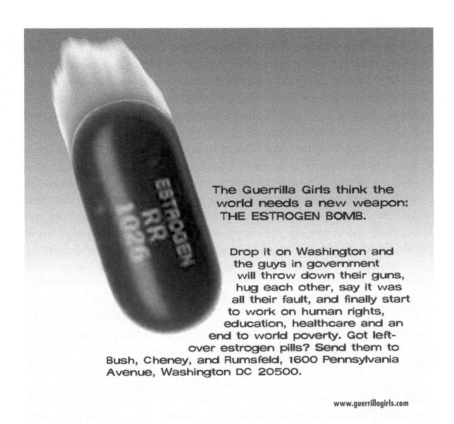

The Guerrilla Girls think the world needs a new weapon: THE ESTROGEN BOMB.

Drop it on Washington and the guys in government will throw down their guns, hug each other, say it was all their fault, and finally start to work on human rights, education, healthcare and an end to world poverty. Got left-over estrogen pills? Send them to Bush, Cheney, and Rumsfeld, 1600 Pennsylvania Avenue, Washington DC 20500.

www.guerrillagirls.com

earnest by straight communities, to gain distance from oppressive norms and invent new sources of identity and alliance.[2]

Clearly practices of comedy ranging from ridicule to romantic comedies enable and constrain our identities and relationships, and therefore affect our experience of freedom. In this book, however, I have been arguing for an even stronger connection between freedom and comedy. Comedy not only offers counter-tactics against oppression and visions of less oppressive identities. Comedy also offers insights into the very meaning of freedom, and these insights augment and even alter our standard philosophical conceptions of freedom.

It may seem surprising to treat comedy as such a rich source of philosophical wisdom, given that, in contrast with tragedy, comedy is generally thought to be more entertaining than enlightening. While philosophers may view tragedy as a reliable source of wisdom, they have been more likely to neglect comedy altogether. The classic defense of liberalism, Isaiah Berlin's post–World War II essay "Two Concepts of Liberty," exemplifies this typical prejudice (*EL*, 118–72). Berlin draws upon a broad range of human experience to clarify the meaning of freedom. And while tragedy features a prominent role in the discussion, no mention at all is made of the comic. It strikes me as puzzling that tragedy has so often served as a respectable source for philosophical reflection, while comedy has not. Could it be that the neglect of comedy might betray, to use a locution from tragedy, a certain "blindness" in our usual patterns of thinking, and that this neglect is due in part to the fact that occasions for comedy typically focus attention on our bodies, affects, and intimate and social relationships—topics that have also been neglected by philosophers? If so, then the emerging philosophical interest in these topics should garner greater interest in comedy as well. Of course, the insights that we gain through comedy into our libidinal lives might emerge from other practices as well. But comedy, like tragedy, is a significant feature of our lives, and I doubt that we can fully understand the many aspects of freedom apart from it. Some of our experiences and understanding of those experiences are tied into specific genres or styles and methods of approach. Comedy reveals aspects of our libidinal lives in ways not apparent anywhere else.

In this final chapter, I aim to put forth a general philosophical statement on the nature of freedom by drawing from the various insights regarding comedy developed in earlier chapters of the book. However, rather than begin directly with this larger statement, I shall use Berlin's beautiful cold war–era essay on liberty as both a foil and a launching pad. As I lay out Berlin's analysis, we should keep in mind the question for this final chapter. That question is, What would happen if we revisited the parameters of our most sublime political value, namely freedom, from some ordinary forms of comedy rather than from tragedy? While no simple formula can convert a tragic perspective on freedom to a comic one, the example of the Guerrilla Girls provides as good a place to begin as any. A thought experiment of the type philosophers especially enjoy might go something like this: What would be the impact of dropping the estrogen bomb on an otherwise sober philosophical statement on freedom?[3] I attempt to avoid essentializing gender differences as well as any easy, untroubled view regarding our potential for social harmony by understanding this project somewhat ironically, as one of demasculinizing, and not feminizing, freedom, and by taking the capacity for ironic critique as central to cultivating freedom.

My major claim is that freedom can be understood only by incorporating into its core concept the important social values of equality and solidarity. In other words, there is no authentic freedom, including what Berlin terms negative freedom, without the other two dimensions of freedom as well. If any of these dimensions is analytically severed from the other two, then that dimension loses part of its meaning. Moreover, my comic perspective on freedom offers an interpretation of these three dimensions of freedom that is unapologetically feminist, queer, and multiracial. The consequence is to shift the focus of negative freedom from private choice to transgressing norms of identity, positive freedom from rational autonomy to egalitarian styles of social attunement, and solidarity from claims of universal recognition to inclusive rites of affiliation and belonging.

Cold War Liberalism and Freedom

We are now ready to develop the discussion begun in earlier chapters on the distinction between "negative freedom," central to the Anglo-Saxon liberalism of Locke, Hobbes, and Mill, and "positive freedom," which branches off into continental political traditions associated with Kant, Rousseau, Hegel, and Marx. Berlin lays out these two traditions of freedom against the background of the cold war confrontation between first-world liberal democracies and second-world socialism and communism. He touches upon a third tradition of freedom as well—one that he locates in the drive for solidarity among third-world anti-colonial movements, and does not think highly of. While liberal moral and political theorists influenced by Berlin, including Kwame Anthony Appiah and Martha Nussbaum, have since reclaimed aspects of positive freedom, there continues to be much less interest among liberal theorists in the third freedom, or what Berlin calls "social freedom." This third freedom, however, is no less important than the other two freedoms, and its key role in our lives becomes all the more evident once we take our cues from comedy.

Berlin's major claim is that negative freedom is both the core concept of classical political liberalism and the sole legitimate notion of freedom. Classical Anglo-Saxon liberalism, as he explains, rests on securing for the individual a realm of freedom to make choices for his or her own life apart from external authority or social control. To be free is to be *free from* external interference, including even subtle and non-coercive forms of paternalism. The primary source of anxiety for liberals is the coercive power of the state. Liberal political systems are supposed to govern with checks and balances, the rule of law, and basic rights. The ultimate aim is to guarantee sovereign individuals a range of options for exercising choice in their private affairs.[4] While democracy or self-government may better serve to guarantee individual rights than other forms of government, there is, Berlin observes, "no necessary connection between individual liberty and democratic rule" (EL, 130). A "liberal-minded despot" might allow his subjects more personal freedom than an illiberal democracy (EL, 130). Liberalism's emphasis on individual self-ownership at the expense of social modes of alienation and engagement continues to undergird the meaning of liberal freedom in its contemporary guises, even if theorists take more care to insist upon the resources that individuals require to live well (especially Nussbaum) and to make the right choices (Appiah).

This liberal concept of freedom as negative freedom supports a specific concept of human rights currently referred to as "negative rights." Negative rights, also called "first-generation rights," emerged as central political demands during the bourgeois revolutions in the United States and France. These rights include, for example, the right to free speech, expression, and religion, participation in elections, and ownership of property. Liberal thinkers have "compiled different catalogues of individual liberties," but they agree that "we must preserve a minimum area of personal freedom if we are not to 'degrade or deny our nature'" (EL, 126). What this nature is has been and will remain "a matter of infinite debate" (EL, 126). (As I shall later argue, the fact that our "nature" remains an endless topic of debate especially among queer theorists and Foucauldians suggests that we need a much more subversive notion of negative freedom than liberal theorists put forth, one that we can find in various genres of comedy.)

Positive freedom has a longer and more convoluted history than negative freedom, dating back to Plato and Aristotle as well as Kant and Hegel, but dramatically re-emerging in demands for social and economic equality within the socialist revolutions and workers' movements of the early twentieth century. More recently, positive freedom is understood in terms of "positive rights," including rights to basic necessities, public education, fair labor conditions, social security, health insurance, and the like. Because of their central role in early-twentieth-century politics, these rights have also been called "second-generation rights." In contrast with negative freedom as freedom from coercion, Berlin defines positive freedom rather prejudicially as *freedom to* lead a "prescribed form of life" (EL, 131). In the context of second-generation rights, positive freedom has also been defined in terms of the freedom to survive or even flourish, terms that may seem innocent enough and, as we know, are partly adopted by those who followed him. However, it is important to understand why it is that for Berlin this second tradition of freedom poses a dangerous threat to liberalism and how his unfortunately fairly narrow concerns continue to frame the Anglo-American understanding of freedom today.

For Berlin, the danger of the positive doctrine of freedom follows upon two considerations. First, in contrast with negative rights, securing positive claims translates historically, if not logically, into granting governments the power to determine which of our desires count as rational and worthy of acting upon. Second, these claims are conceived as positive entitlements that do not merely enable but also shape individual choices in accordance with enlightened rational self-interest, social needs, or public duty.[5] Berlin himself happens to support certain minimal entitlements to social or economic equality as part of a liberal welfare state, and hence as necessary props to freedom, but he vehemently opposes including any such claims in the core definition of freedom. This is because he believes that the positive doctrine of freedom, in any of its forms, threatens liberalism with authoritarianism.

Of course, if positive rights signify claims to food, health care, and shelter to survive, one would hardly think the protection of such rights would lead to authoritarianism. On the contrary, one might argue that such rights are essential to democracy and that it is the lack of food, health care, and such that could lead to authoritarianism. Berlin nonetheless argues that if made a part of the very meaning of freedom, even minimal claims for social and economic equality would threaten to destroy freedom. Inasmuch as governments attempt to enforce positive rights, they interfere with individual freedom by channeling private desires for the sake of the public good. Berlin remarks that we may make the pragmatic decision to limit our freedom to some degree for the sake of justice, security, or happiness, but, as he continues to insist, we should not confuse these alternative values with freedom. (We will return not to a pragmatist per se, but to a visionary pragmatist, approach soon—a view that does not just balance freedom with justice, security, or happiness, but incorporates justice, security, and happiness into the very meaning of freedom.)[6] Freedom is the exercise of choice, and, again, freedom, not justice or any other value, is for liberalism the supreme and overriding political value. If we do not secure this core meaning of freedom, we risk surrendering to the state the power to coerce individuals in the name of higher and potentially repressive goals.

And yet, Berlin continues, there are those who do confuse the basic meaning of freedom, and, ironically, among the most confused are the so-called rationalists. These rationalists (not only left-leaning socialists and Marxists but also Kantians and Hegelians) elevate the authority of reason, morality, social duty, or various forms of social responsibility over individual choice, and, by a sleight of hand, call this operation of authority freedom.

The philosophical difference between the two traditions of freedom turns on alternative conceptions of agency. As Berlin explains, positive freedom originates in the determination to be the master over one's own life, through modes of rational self-control or active willing, rather than to be the passive plaything of irrational desires or external forces (the kind of forces set loose in screwball comedy). While the ideal of self-mastery may not at first appear to differ widely from a simple liberal desire to make choices without the interference of others, the determination to be the master of oneself rests on a suspicious metaphysical view. That view is that in each of us there are not one but two selves—a true, rational self and a slavish, false self—and that only the decisions that originate from the true self are freely made. This metaphysical claim becomes yet more dangerous when it is joined with two further claims: that the true, authentic self is found in a solidarity with a larger group identity, or organic "social whole," such as a race, a class, a nation, or a state (here, one can't help thinking about Berlin's association with the English), and that this larger group may coerce members to act against their immediate wishes in accordance with an allegedly higher freedom.

Of course, negative freedom, in contrast, grants the individual a free rein over his or her private life, opening the space for individuals to act according to short-term interests, ill-considered impulses, or even "antisocial" values. For the continental rationalists, individuals who act on destructive impulses or selfish and socially irresponsible desires are the dupes of myths, illusions, or other forms of false consciousness, and thus are unfree. Only individuals who constrain their desires according to norms of public duty or coherent and transparent self-knowledge are said to possess the rational autonomy prized by Kant and other defenders of positive freedom. Positive freedom constrains individual choice in accordance with what is taken by an authority to be rational—an authority that, although perhaps beginning philosophically with the rational self, ultimately, through a "fatal transition," Berlin writes (EL, 150), ends politically with the state. While continental thinkers may posit that rational individuals would never desire to dominate others, and that therefore a rational society would be an egalitarian one without domination or exploitation, Berlin aligns continental rationalism with authoritarianism. "This," he writes, "is the positive doctrine of liberation by reason. Socialized forms of it . . . are at the heart of many of the nationalist, communist, authoritarian, and totalitarian creeds of our day. It may, in the course of its evolution, have wandered far from its rationalist moorings. Nevertheless, it is this freedom that, in democracies and in dictatorships, is argued about, and fought for, in many parts of the earth today" (*EL*, 144).

The English liberal philosophers that Berlin prefers over the continental rationalists are not against reason altogether; they acknowledge the importance of choices that are based on some degree of reflection rather than mere desire or impulse. But for Berlin, reason belongs ultimately to the individual and not to the state or any other mediating party. The continental picture of individuals succumbing to self-deception or antisocial desires if left on their own is not only speculative but highly dangerous because it legitimates the nullification of individual preferences by some external authority in the name of a higher self; for Berlin, the notion of positive freedom carries the potential for the kind of brainwashing or mind-control perpetuated by the totalitarian regimes of Stalin and Hitler. Any externally enforced perfectionist doctrine that demands that individuals master their passions through the moral education of the citizen by the state ushers in totalitarianism under the cloak of freedom. Now one of the weaknesses of Berlin's essay is that it fails to explicitly address how one obvious and unavoidable source of external mediation on freedom, namely, the social education of the liberal individual, would differ from the "indoctrination" of rationalist freedom. As we shall see later, Appiah does explicitly raise this question, but his discussion gives rise to its own set of questions.

We do not need to adopt the metaphysics of the continental rationalists to see that Berlin overstates the case against positive freedom while understating the dangers of Anglo-Saxon liberalism. English liberalism emphasizes individual rights to privacy and property at the expense of civic responsibilities, and as a consequence allows for oppression in the name of freedom. While liberalism may grant entitlements for sufficient food and medicine, education, fair working conditions, and the like as minimal conditions for the exercise of capacities for choice, liberalism inevitability valorizes negative freedom over and above social demands for equality. Minimal needs to survive take second place to individual rights both in theory and in practice. If freedom is to name our most weighty political goal, and thus our most fundamental claim on the state, not to mention a general experience of emancipation, then it is not clear why it should not include positive social and economic rights as part of its core meaning. For how can one be free if one lacks sufficient food or education to live a life without substantial degradation or exploitation? Freedom should signify some degree of respect not only for individual choices but for social equality as well. Contemporary liberal moral theorists agree to varying degrees on the importance of securing adequate resources (what Nussbaum develops in terms of capabilities) in order to exercise negative liberties, but they continue to conceptualize the core concept of freedom as choice (Nussbaum included).[7]

Moreover, the single-minded liberal focus on individual rights, along with the reduction of citizenship to possessing a package of individual rights, obscures yet another basic need that is essential for democracy, and that is the need for solidarity. This claim for securing social bonds, or, as we might say, this *freedom of* belonging to cooperative communities of all kinds points toward the third freedom.[8] Liberal rights to individual privacy apart from claims to both equality and solidarity do not in the long run guarantee freedom or encompass the full range of its meaning. Negative freedom without social equality is domination, and either or both without solidarity fails to generate the networks of care that sustain social harmony.

Our insistence upon the central relevance of the third freedom does not merely add yet one more dimension to the analysis of freedom; it deconstructs liberalism's dualistic framework altogether. Contemporary liberal efforts to salvage some degree of "positive freedom" continue to orient aims back and forth between the poles of the autonomy versus dependency dualism and its many correlates, but this dualistic style of thinking weakens many of the demands that can be made on behalf of not only the third freedom, but the second and first as well. The usual correlates of liberal dualist thinking include not only independence, self-sufficiency, or inner-directed styles of decision making versus vulnerability, neediness, and outer-directed styles, but so-called manliness versus femininity as well. And, given the undeconstructed dualistic framework, the masculine pole dominates the account of ultimate aims no matter how hard one strives to upend it (Nussbaum's tremendous respect for Rawlsian liberty is a case in point). In place of this dualistic framework, I propose a three-dimensional framework centered around the libidinal force of interdependence. The idea is that we cannot understand freedom if we begin our analysis by examining individuals and their needs; instead, we need to understand relationships of interdependence and the ways in which individuals are already connected with others. Individuals do not connect themselves to others through acts of empathy or analogical reasoning; individuals find themselves already connected through their sense of who they are. One important consequence of this interdependence is that we cannot understand—let alone achieve—one dimension of freedom (including liberalism's preferred freedom, negative freedom) without interpreting that freedom through an understanding of the demands of the other two. Moreover, the third freedom, the freedom of belonging, is especially poorly understood by liberal models, and for this reason is crucial for expanding beyond these models.

Still, Berlin is rightly suspicious of those rationalists who appeal to reason to transcend conflicts. It is impossible to eliminate many of the irrational sources of conflict from our lives without risking authoritarian forms of politics. In a perfectly rational society, one has to wonder, what would become of all of us ordinary, hopelessly flawed people? In order not to lose sight of ourselves, that is, ordinary people with the usual vices, I shall take my cues for a vision of freedom not from philosophical doctrines of continental rationalism nor from liberal individualism, but from the libidinal politics of comedy instead. Comedy gives us glimpses into richly subversive forms of negative freedom as well very attractive modes of both positive and social freedom. These modes of freedom serve to combat oppression and instill cooperation, and yet suit the ridiculous, irrational, and stubborn creatures that we all too often are.

However, before turning to a threefold comic perspective, let's examine briefly how a tragic sensibility frames Berlin's cold war–era defense of liberalism's framework for thinking about freedom.

Freedom's Tragic Choices and Liberalism

For Berlin, it is the tragic element of the human condition that gives us a glimpse into freedom's deepest meaning. While philosophers disagree on the nature of the tragic, Berlin argues that only one of our conceptions of the tragic can fully clarify freedom's stakes. And happily for him, that conception corresponds to the sole legitimate type of freedom, namely, liberalism's negative freedom. The continental rationalists, Berlin claims, mistakenly locate the core meaning of tragedy in the conflict between irrational passions and rational duties and then insist that this conflict should yield to reason. Their assumption is that passions and prejudices stem from ignorance and that once we eliminate or control the passions, the grounds for tragedy largely disappear. For such rationalists, freedom is knowledge. That is, once the spell of illusions and ignorance lifts, tragic conflict and violence should give way to a harmonious society directed by rational goals that we would all recognize as our own. This sentimental picture presumes, Berlin observes, not only that we are rational creatures, but also that the ends of all rational beings fit into a single harmonious pattern, and that "all conflict, and consequently, all tragedy, is due solely to the clash of reason with the irrational" (*EL*, 154). Or at least this is the view that one might, and Berlin does, take from continental thinkers.

Those critics of liberalism who argue that freedom must allow for positive interference of the state in individual lives are not only confused, they are dangerous, Berlin insists. While the lack of material means (jobs, skills, or social services) suffered by the lower classes may be a legitimate political and social concern, these kinds of claims are not part of the concept of freedom and should not be redressed by threatening core individual freedoms. Freedom is a matter of making choices, and is threatened directly by other people and not by social or economic forces as the defenders of positive freedom seem to think. Certainly other people or external forces cannot for the liberal be the source of our freedom. While liberals might allow for such social goods as state assistance for the poor and equal opportunity for employment, it would be a mistake to confuse these values with true freedom or, for that matter, to treat true freedom as anything less than our highest social and political value. Negative freedom may rest on support for social services, but the demand of workers and oppressed people for social equality should not be either confused with freedom or allowed to override it.

Claims regarding the true nature of freedom continue to be important both because the notion plays the key rhetorical role in debates about U.S. social and political goals and because it is used to legitimate idealistic interventions beyond our national borders. Certainly the framework for conceptualizing freedom determines what kinds of positions bear the burden of proof in political debate, if they are ever heard at all. And again, Berlin does not mean his view to imply that redressing poverty or ignorance is not a condition for freedom, and in fact, argues that negative freedom is not possible without sufficient food, education, and other resources; indeed, however Nussbaum reconfigures positive freedom in terms of capabilities for well-being, the continued emphasis on negative freedom as the core freedom derails, I argue, attempts to restrict private accumulation in favor of larger concerns for social justice. A visionary pragmatist approach, based on awareness of the actual conditions of human flourishing, incorporates justice as well as security and happiness into dimensions of freedom rather than leaving these values out of the core concept. By contrast, as far as liberals such as Berlin are concerned, freedom should remain sharply and narrowly focused on the individual's right to make choices at all costs—even if these costs include sacrifices that are tragic. Any naive yearning for a society where individuals are not first of all responsible for their own life choices fails to acknowledge the harsh realities of the human condition.

While contemporary liberal discourse may stay clear of the rhetoric of sacrifice and tragedy, and prefer neoliberalism's discourse of winners and losers or the neoconservative moral rhetoric of good versus evil, a tragic view of the human condition still underlies it. This view holds that making decisions is at the center of human existence and that these decisions entail substantial conflicts of value and unavoidable costs, even to the point of ruining lives and undermining the basis for social cooperation. As we have said, Berlin insists on properly distinguishing between the true meaning of liberty and various other values, including happiness, security, solidarity, recognition, and justice. These are all genuine social values, but they cannot be reconciled with each other, let alone collapsed into some nebulous concept of positive freedom, without denying the capacity for choice. Returning to the theme of the tragic, he concludes the argument of his classic essay with the following thought: "If, as I believe, the ends of men are many, and not all of them are in principle compatible with each other, then the possibility of conflict—of tragedy—can never wholly be eliminated from human life, either personal or social. The necessity of choosing between absolute claims is then an inescapable characteristic of the human condition" (*EL*, 169). Freedom is choice.

Now rather than yield to this tragic cold war logic and its aftermath, where games of risk and the rhetoric of choice have become fetishes, we are turning to a comic vision of an irrational, conflict-ridden, yet redemptive social life. From the U.S. Declaration of Independence to film comedy, freedom is not bare choice. Freedom appears more fully developed as the pursuit of happiness.

But before we can proceed to this vision of freedom, we will need to unfold the third and, as we have said, for liberalism the most dubious concept of freedom, along with a view of the tragic that I think may be said to underlie it. As I have remarked in earlier chapters, Berlin mentions this third sense of freedom only to denigrate it as a "hybrid" and terribly confused kind. And yet, as he observes, this third notion accounts for most wars and ongoing struggles against oppression. As Berlin explains, oppressed people seek not only better economic and other material conditions of their lives but status and recognition as well—a kind of mutual recognition that assumes that "my individual self is not something which I can detach from my relationships with others, or from those attributes of myself which consist in their attitude towards me" (*EL*, 156). Thus, the oppressed aim not only for material well-being or even those individual rights that might be provided by a colonizing power but to be recognized as "men" (we might say full citizens) as well. Berlin does not weave into his remarks on this third freedom any consideration of its relation to tragedy. However, we might add to his own remarks the observation that in order to achieve status or recognition, or, to expand the analysis here, a modern concern that evolves out of pre-modern or early modern forms of honor,[9] individuals are often willing to undertake great sacrifices or acts of revenge against either those insults to their sense of self or violations of their friendships and other social relationships that tragic drama calls hubris. Indeed, as Berlin indicates, people subordinated by ethnicity or race might prefer an authoritarian government of their own people over authentic freedom (i.e., the English kind) if that so-called authentic freedom means that they are to be ruled by some other group (e.g., the English, or, as he writes, "some cautious, just, gentle, well-meaning administrator from outside" [*EL*, 158]).

Berlin cuts the discussion of this hybrid concept short because, after all, his topic is freedom, and conveniently for the English, the demand for recognition in anti-colonial movements rests, it seems, on an especially bad case of conceptual confusion. Berlin raises the question of whether freedom might mean something different than English liberalism for an "Egyptian peasant," but he quickly dismisses this question, deciding that whatever a confused people might think freedom means, it should finally be the same for the peasant as for the "Oxford don" (*EL*, 124). Freedom means the absence of state interference. The pity, apparently, is that the non-English are not yet ready for it.

Some years after the cold war, and with the decolonization of Africa and Asia, it might be more apparent to us than to Berlin that if the continental philosopher can be accused of excessive rationalism, and consequently a degree of blind arrogance, so too can the Oxford don. Certainly, in the international legal sphere, the claims of third-world nations for broad international cooperation for assistance in development, aid for refugees, elimination of disease, and environmental safety join alongside positive rights to equality and negative rights to individual liberty. In 1979 Karel Vasak, then director of UNESCO's Division of Human Rights and Peace, named these "third-generation" claims "solidarity rights" and proclaimed that negative, positive, and solidarity rights do not contradict, but in fact they fulfill, the motto of the French Revolution: *liberté, égalité, fraternité.*[10]

Regardless of whether we use the French motto for securing our three freedoms, it's good not to dismiss the demands from third-world peoples out of hand. On the contrary, while Berlin does not mention the tragic in this context, it is easy enough to see that this third freedom, interpreted as the avoidance of hubris and the fostering of social bonds, ties in fairly well with the tragic choral voice that cautions, "Pride goeth before a fall." Of course, as any reflection upon the range of tragic literature immediately attests, the concept of hubris or any other notion of damaging social bonds is not going to lend itself to any simple or single normative analysis. For even if tragic conceptions of social harm appear across cultures and time periods, views on what counts as social harm or hubris vary significantly and are not even necessarily egalitarian. Still we might say that this third locus of the tragic does not turn on a conflict of values (per Berlin's liberalism), nor on the conflict between reason and the passions (per continental rationalism), but on an act of arrogance that damages social bonds. Moreover, I take the liberty to add that given our egalitarian social concerns, we should understand hubris as an act instigated by a dominant party against a weaker one. To clarify further: hubris may include but it does not rest on a flaw in character, as say a Christian ethic might have it; hubris is an act that inflicts harm (often without the agent's awareness) on social bonds.[11] (Here I recall Senator Chuck Hagel of Nebraska arguing on a Sunday morning talk show in the early spring of 2001 that President Bush should send U.S. forces in to liberate Iraq, and that it would not be hubris as long as he invaded with humility.)

It is commonly said that the oppressed laugh to keep from crying. This laughter is a way not just of distancing oneself from present reality but also of calling that reality into question. Laughter may combat assaults by setting up a defensive shield, but it may also shift social perceptions and consequently the social facts.[12] In other words, it can level hierarchies and alter the balance of power. Marx has said that history repeats twice, first time as tragedy, second time as farce. Perhaps this is because farce does not merely repeat history; it also changes its course.

In what follows, I shall reexamine the above three meanings of freedom through the lens of three more or less distinct groupings of comedy.[13] *First,* the genres of farce, camp, and the carnivalesque redirect liberalism's negative freedom away from the valorization of individual choice and toward the destabilization of norms and disciplinary practices that block choice to begin with. *Second,* satire of character and the comedy of manners alter how we might otherwise view the purpose of social intervention in our private lives, and crucially in the soul-shaping need for education. The positive right to education includes the bare-bone skills necessary for economic empowerment, but also the kind of social enlightenment that sustains a free life. In contrast with the traditional (and often elitist) aim of subordinating the passions to reason, comedy cultivates irony together with egalitarian sentiments that we might call an "understanding heart" (I am taking this phrase from George Cukor's 1940 film *The Philadelphia Story*). While this approach to positive freedom through comedy takes the education of character as primary, irony is not to be translated via an ethics of sentiment in terms of humility, nor are the egalitarian sentiments downward-looking pity. *Third,* romantic comedy and comedies of friendship shift the main focus of social freedom away from codes of honor toward the more convivial bonds of affiliation instead. While the former interests are played out in struggles for honor, the comic turn cultivates erotic desires of belonging, citizenship, and even a sense of being "useful" (as *The Philadelphia Story*'s upper-class heiress, Katharine Hepburn, must learn).

Berlin argues that positive and negative freedoms reflect competing views of the tragic and that only the negative concept of freedom is legitimate. Partly as a result of his rather linear approach, his concept of the third freedom rests on an idea of recognition and status that does not contain the notion of equality. I shall argue by way of a dialectic of comedy that the three dimensions of freedom are interconnected and that one dimension of freedom cannot appear fully apart from the other two. In fact, much good comedy (think of Shakespeare's *Midsummer Night's Dream*) draws upon elements of all three at once: negative freedom as the anarchy of farce, carnival, and camp; positive freedom through satire of character and the education of sentiment; and romantic comedy's festive restoration of wounded social bonds.

Negative Freedom, This Time as Farce

Let's look again at negative freedom defined as the absence of external obstacles to a range of possible choices. This definition rests on what *seems* to be a relatively secure distinction between internal and external sources of force, but in fact is not. According to the standard liberal view, the individual makes choices freely when he or she can distance him- or herself from external sources of interference and choose from a range of options.[14] The realm of privacy is that space that an individual has to exercise choice from a range of options independently from what the public might think.

Now it is clear that we require some concept of negative freedom to preserve our individuality, including our rights to personal relationships and self-expression that others may not ever approve or even comprehend. However, the underlying liberal picture of the individual as a discrete substance (known as ontological separatism) does not capture the ways in which prejudicial images, norms, and social perceptions do more than sway identities or distort judgments; they define the horizons of meaning for them.[15] In Foucauldian terms we might say that the bulk of power is productive, disciplinary, and normative—and not just juridical.[16] Theories about the constitutive impact of social forces on our identities and judgments may count as speculative for old-school empiricists such as Berlin. But with image-and-prestige-driven, information-based economies, these forces can strike us as hyper-visible and very real. For example, the absence of available queer identities or the prevalence of anti-gay jokes in the media impacts the ability to individuate and provokes the demand for alternative public and intimate spaces. These forces can be dismissed by a stoic individual as insubstantial threats. In general, what one person or social group perceives as insubstantial or even speculative, another often enough perceives as hard fact. Of course, social norms and perceptions, and their enabling or oppressive force over our individual identities, may not be easy to articulate, and this might lend them an airy appearance. This is especially likely to be the case if one's sense of empirical reality requires total conceptual clarity. The very real impact of these social forces is nonetheless quite evident for our moods, passions, and personal and political identities, and therefore for our freedom. Moreover, these forces often enough take center stage in comedy.

Still, the contemporary post-cold-war-era defense of liberal individualism is more sophisticated than returning to Berlin's classic essay allows. Berlin focuses on cold-war-fueled debates over liberalism versus socialism and communism. The culture wars of the 1990s reframed the major political questions in terms of domestic debates between liberals (John Rawls) and communitarians (Michael Walzer). Then after 9/11 and the increased threat of global terrorism, the culture wars re-emerged on an international scale and altered again the political terrain. Cosmopolitan thinkers, some more deeply than others anchored in Anglo-American liberalism (including Appiah and Nussbaum, but perhaps also Habermas, among others), divided off from those whom I would like to identify as offering diverse elements for anti-imperialist multicultural democracies (a group that could include Judith Butler and Walzer).[17] While the latter approach seeks core meanings of basic terms by examining the concrete person-in-the-world, the cosmopolitan liberal focuses on the abstract individual, in effect consigning relationships, whether they be personal, social, or temporal, to background phenomena: "[W]e can respect persons only inasmuch as we consider them abstract rights-holders. Much of our moral advancement has depended on such a tendency toward abstraction," Appiah writes.[18]

However, from a comic perspective, the detached man or woman depicted as oblivious to (or otherwise able to abstract too readily from) social circumstances is a prime target of laughter (Bergson's theory of the comic is built around it; see chapter 3). Social detachment never has been able to provide a sure means of escape either from the normalizing, subjugating impact of social forces or from the gradients of power that determine our social status, and the invasive nature of these forces should become painfully evident to anyone who is the target of ridicule.

Moreover, as this experience of finding oneself on the wrong end of laughter reminds us, while social forces define us, these same forces also disturb and provoke us. Our subjugation (through the threat of ridicule, for example) is never complete. The question is how to conceptualize freedom from these normalizing, socializing forces when these same forces also enable and constrain us. Escape from the disciplining forces of the social field cannot turn on individual choice because these forces partly constitute the individual and his or her desires and reasoning powers to begin with. The forces that oppress us are not always external to us; they may in fact largely determine who we are as subjects. There is no unambiguous nature lying underneath our constituted selves, and debates over our "true" nature are doomed to be, as Berlin suggests, endless. For this reason, it is too simple to rest *freedom from* oppression on liberalism's negative freedom or to locate the threat to negative freedom in the state's juridical power. We simply have to recall how the ridicule of a dominant group imposes or reinforces disciplinary norms and oppressive social perceptions through its laughter. Against the various nets of social surveillance, negative freedom is the capacity to *destabilize identities and interrupt norms.* And sometimes this liberating force expresses itself as turning the tables on power through laughing back. We find this laughter of the oppressed in the outrageous humor of farce, camp, and the carnival.[19]

How does this comic concept of negative freedom as laughter differ from the liberal concept of freedom as choice? Let's begin with a more straightforward, multicultural critique of liberalism's negative freedom before we offer an alternative notion through comedy.

Walzer argues, rightly I think, that social, environmental, economic, cultural, religious, and other forces affect not only the kinds of choices that are available but much of our identity and even what we take to be rational.[20] We cannot distance ourselves sufficiently from these forces to make the kind of considered choice that is important for a liberal cosmopolitan such as Appiah. For the most part our choices do not precede but come out of these pre-set identities. It's not that choice is not important, but only that choice, even if guided by reason, is not our sole or even our most subtle means of measuring freedom's liberating force. If I understand Walzer's position, and here again I would so far agree, for our socially inflected selves, freedom is less a matter of autonomous choice than a pragmatic endeavor of negotiation and dissent.

Walzer takes marriage as an example. We might believe that we freely choose whether and whom to marry, and that these kinds of private choices are an important part of our liberal freedom. But as Walzer points out, from the sociological perspective, in fact our actual choices largely reflect the conditions in which we were raised. Married couples, for example, predictably share similar socioeconomic and cultural origins. Moreover, marriage is a conventional social practice. Its meanings, obligations, rituals, and typical problems are all prearranged, and these prearranged meanings circumscribe our innermost romantic intentions before we ever say "I do." The liberal snapshot of the autonomous individual obscures the ways in which social practices set our choices. We cannot reflect on the bulk of our background commitments, and choice per se is not our ordinary mode of experiencing agency or freedom. Indeed, what counts as reflection is itself informed by cultural variables, and our responses to our situations are more complex than the bare rhetoric of choice allows. "We move toward freedom when we make opposition and escape possible, when we allow internal dissent and resistance, divorce, conversion, withdrawal, and resignation," as Walzer writes (PP, 18).

Sometimes social norms allow for negotiation and dissent. Other times social norms (think about compulsory heterosexuality) can be all-consuming of our identities and preempt any normal attempt at dissent or resistance. Hence the need for queer camp among other forms of comic subversion. These ironic modalities of subversion push negative freedom beyond the sorts of dissent that Walzer seems to have in mind. Queer send-ups of our sexual identities challenge, disrupt, and disorient not just the coercive policies of the state or discriminatory rules and practices of civil society, but also socio-psychological norms such as heterosexuality. Parodies of gender and sexual identities go beyond the politics of dissent. These parodies mock the prevailing aesthetics of pleasure and pain as well as the boundaries of social emotions like shame and of personal feelings like disgust. They disrupt visceral reactions to images and habits of response that precede and inform any discursive sense of identity. Carnivalesque humor along with elements of irony in camp, farce, and parody are often viewed as abusive and in bad taste, as they must be if they are to disturb our sense of the normal and explore, as the Foucauldians like to say, new bodies and pleasures.[21] In fact, unruly and unconciliatory erotic impulses may compel us to love those whom we please and not those whom by the social norms we ought. To be sure, eros typically ends in conventional forms of social expression such as marriage, and marriage often functions as a conservative institution. But eros can also turn into a strikingly subversive force. On occasion erotic attractions cross social barriers and refuse subjugation at all costs.

Somewhat romantically, the socialist literary theorist Bakhtin envisions the erotic spirit of the carnival as leveling altogether barriers of rank, race, class, age, property, and proper manners.[22] The grotesque exaggeration of images and impulses of the body in carnival-style humor breaks down those defensive mechanisms that rigidly demarcate a separate ego and divide us into hostile social groups. Laughter lets down the guard and opens us to previously unthinkable styles of thought, imagination, and feeling. In Bakhtin's socialist dream, the people (*demos*) would bond together through laughter as did the chorus of fools in ancient comedy.[23] This carnival would socialize (in more sense than one) liberalism's negative freedom. It would translate liberalism's negative freedom into a socialist politics where individual liberty would converge with the social goals of equality and solidarity.

Bakhtin's socialist dream, however, does not cohere with the multivalent understanding of power (through class, race, sexual identity, etc.) that has emerged through multicultural critiques of social power. Persistent conflict among diverse social groups preempts any easy old-leftist ideal of a single whole people. Moreover, the carnival can erect as many social barriers as it knocks down. Think of the use of blackface buffoonery or other derogatory forms of humor for strengthening racist communities.[24]

Yet while the leveling impulse of the carnival can hardly be expected to achieve universal oneness, it does not always reinforce social stratifications either. On the contrary, sometimes it functions progressively. Judith Butler's somewhat ambivalent reflections on postmodern parody, and in particular, the drag performances of gender and sexual identities in *Paris Is Burning* (dir. Jennie Livingston, 1990), illuminate the potential as well as the limits of this kind of political art.[25] Livingston's documentary exposes both progressive and conventional forces in drag. It is the contrast between these elements that is relevant for defining freedom. Queer politics aims to solicit the destabilizing of repressive norms and disciplinary practices, often through irony. Or, as Butler remarks, liberty "emerges at the limits of what one can know, at the very moment in which the de-subjugation of the subject . . . takes place."[26] It is laughter that often enough lays these limits bare.

Liberal theory grounds negative freedom in a sense of personal ownership that begins with the boundaries of one's own body. Queer theory reorients this same basic freedom to the pleasure-seeking desires of a somewhat amorphous body and its comic imperfections. From the comic perspective, our bodies are the sources of desires, impulses, involuntary reactions, noises, fluids, and irregularities beyond any chance of conscious control, let alone any social mechanism for their seamless normalization. Some of these irregularities are deeply connected with unconscious sources of identity, and their repression makes us unhappy. Their expression can liberate us from the soul-crushing weight of conventions.

Moreover, this comic irregularity at our libidinal core is ontologically unavoidable. It's not just that I cannot alter who I am or whom I love, as Walzer might say. The disruptive effect of a ironic element in human existence, the irresistible anarchy of our libidinal lives, accompanies any sober attempt to define rules or establish norms. This is what Butler means when in her essay on *Paris Is Burning* she writes: "Where the uniformity of the subject is expected, where the behavioral conformity of the subject is commanded, there might be produced the refusal of the law in the form of the parodic inhabiting of conformity that subtly calls into question the legitimacy of the command"; or, that all "gender is (like) drag" (*BM*, 122). However, contrary to what Butler may seem at times to imply, the basis for the irregularities is not that all identity is qua performance sheer social construction. The basis for the irregularities lies in our ambiguous yet irrepressible libidinal core.

If we push queer in all of its carnivalesque glory to unravel the concept of normalcy itself, then we might as well add that all social rituals (including Christian marriage) are (like) camp. My point is that the element of the parodic can be used to locate our primary experience of negative freedom, at least from the comic point of view. If liberal freedom is freedom from the state, the carnival can free us from ourselves.

Moreover, our postmodern multicultural affinity for queer politics need not work against a *kind* of transnational appeal—even to cultures that are on their surface quite repressive and unaccustomed to subversion. After all, the freedom of the carnival is older than the concept of negative freedom found in Anglo-Saxon liberalism. It's older as well than Christianity or any of the other major religions.

One clear obstacle to using the comic, especially as irony or ridicule, for a democratic ethics is that laughter can accompany, and may even signify, a sense of superiority. It certainly does in gay-bashing and other oppressive forms of ridicule. The comic can and often does foster the kind of group-based arrogance that an egalitarian political ethics would aim to undercut. Indeed, one scholar, following Hobbes and perhaps Aristotle as well, argues that the sense of superiority accompanies not just some but all laughter.[27] If so, then the comic inevitably reinforces some strong sense of social hierarchy along with oppressive norms, rules of exclusion, sources of embarrassment, or rituals of humiliation. Such a comprehensive view of laughter would undermine our use of the comic to define freedom, or at least, the egalitarian kind of freedom that anti-imperialist, multicultural democracies require.

In fact, not all forms, aspects, or uses of comedy, including irony and ridicule, are politically regressive. The use of ridicule to construct a sense of superiority or an exclusionary community differs from the progressive use of ridicule to deconstruct rigid social barriers. Still, progressive carnival humor occurs at the border of the grotesque—and its ultimate social value may be ambiguous or unknown. Certainly, there is no clear formula for determining the true cathartic value of comedy's transgressive politics. At best we can say that only when styles of transgression converge with our other two social goals—equality and solidarity—might negative freedom open up rather than close down realms of intimacy and allow for a liberating politics. The transgression of rape, for example, may or may not deconstruct norms, but it does not converge with equality or solidarity concerns.

We comic creatures relish scenes of confused identity—think of *Midsummer Night's Dream*. Queer politics accentuates the pleasure together with the ambiguity in spades. In the theater as in politics, the subversion of stultifying norms can be experienced by those who laugh as liberating. Sometimes (contrast queer camp with blackface), this laughter can also be good.

And there we have the first result for our estrogen bomb experiment on the meaning of freedom.

Equality, Positive Freedom, and the Satire of Manners

Here is the classic story of positive freedom from classical Greek to contemporary German political thought: positive conceptions of freedom grow out of the concern that the individual who makes decisions on the basis of impulse alone is not acting freely. Free action requires that we align our impulses, desires, and habits with our better judgments through reason. The single-minded focus on unguided choice does not develop human potential. Untempered, self-seeking individuals slavishly driven by forces that they fail to understand fragment societies. And, in turn, these poorly structured societies deprive individuals of opportunities for self-realization and self-knowledge. Control over harmful impulses and the social environment requires enlightened practices based on rational principles. Unyielding social conflict and tragic violence stem from the failure to abide by informed social duty or rational judgment. A more harmonious world requires the moral education of individual desire to the rational will (Kant, Hegel, Habermas). Self-knowledge as a rigorous discipline of desire rather than slavish devotion to desire traditionally defines the second freedom. Freedom is knowledge.[28]

National Lampoon's 1978 *Animal House* opens with a shot of college classmates, one of whom having barely managed to zip up his fly, walks past a statue of the college founder. The camera gives us a close-up of the college motto carved at the base of the statue: "Knowledge Is Good." Most of the film is about, well, not managing to keep one's zipper up. This comedy, however, is not simply a spoof on knowledge. For as it turns out, the raunchy carnival of fraternity life (John Belushi's lax Delta House in sharp contrast with the hyper-disciplined, blond quasi-fascists of Omega House) leads to a kind of enlightenment. But this is not going to be the kind of enlightenment that the rationalists generally have in mind.

Before we understand what a multicultural comic view might lend to positive freedom, let's examine an Anglo-Saxon, cosmopolitan rendition of the classic formula of reason over passion. Against Berlin, Appiah argues that liberalism cannot rely on negative freedom alone but must set forth criteria of rationality to guide individual choices and that these criteria should be sanctioned, indeed at times imposed, by the state. While liberals are traditionally wary of the authoritarian implications of imposing standards on individuals, Appiah proposes what he believes to be a humble version of rationality in terms of having a coherent life plan: "a desire that flows from a value that itself derives from a life plan is more important than a desire (such as an appetite) that I just happen to have; for it flows from my reflective choices, my commitments, not just from passing fancy," he writes (*EI*, 13).

However, Appiah's rendition of positive freedom does not appear so humble after all, at least not in comparison with a comic perspective on the very same concept. It works out nicely for our interest in the comic that Appiah turns directly to a literary example for support of his rationalist view of freedom, and that his literary example turns out to contain an element of the comedic. For Appiah's example of the rational man is the somewhat sad character of the butler in Kazuo Ishiguro's novel *Remains of the Day*, a novel that is, by the way, written as a comedy of manners. Appiah points out that this character's major life decision to become a servant, and even to take pride in developing his " 'bantering skills' in order to satisfy his new American master," seems at first glance to exemplify the type of socially bound, unreflective person that critics of liberalism (Walzer, but also perhaps Judith Butler) claim to be the norm (*EI*, 8). Appiah suggests that we could view the butler (this butler is not Judith) as accepting servitude in the same way as others would fall into romantic relationships and friendships. Appiah is concerned to address the charge that relationships are important human goods "that we don't 'plan' exactly for" and that would seem to challenge the liberal preference for a life based on reflective choice (rather, or so I am arguing, than the kind of erotic pursuits preferred in comedy). Appiah counters such charges by arguing that even a character such as the butler, who seems to fall into a life of servitude, can give a coherent narrative of his own life. This novel presents an example of such a coherent narrative inasmuch as it is told from the butler's perspective. The capacity for self-making through narration demonstrates, Appiah concludes, that even someone who lives by conventional bonds of servitude, let alone friendship or love, has the capacity to make that choice and to do so on the basis of a rational life plan. The rational life plan lends one the degree of self-knowledge that makes one (in the positive sense) free.

However, Appiah's rationally coherent character (the novel's butler) is also a pathetically comic one. For, as even Appiah remarks, from the reader's perspective the butler is "starchy, self-deceived," and "mildly ridiculous." The butler's life plan to serve his master may be rational and coherent, but it costs the butler any real chance for authentic companionship or real happiness. The external perspective of the reader not only undermines the value of such a sadly ridiculous life, it leads us to question (as I have argued in the prologue) whether a rational life plan is nearly as central to what it means to be free as one might think. The somewhat satiric portrayal of the butler suggests that, at least on occasion, an external perspective (here, the reader's ironic stance) can take us further than a sober act of rational self-reflection (the character's perspective) toward understanding one's freedom. A character's lack of self-knowledge is a prime target of satiric laughter, and this character, despite his narrative, seems to not know himself. Freedom requires a degree of authentic relationship (in this case, companionship) that the butler seems to lack, and rational self-coherency does not provide the means to find this out. On the contrary, the character requires the mediation of his friends to understand himself, and this is what he has failed to do.

Still, Appiah has joined with other contemporary liberal theorists to take us one step beyond Berlin's narrow definition of liberty as negative: "We might need not only liberty from the state and society, but also help from state and society to achieve our selves. Isaiah Berlin taught us to call this 'positive liberty,' and he is deeply skeptical . . . because, among other things, he thought that in the name of positive liberty, governments had been—and would continue to be—tempted to set out to shape people in the name of the better selves they might become" (*EI*, 27). We have come to accept that among various forms of individual betterment, the "state should sponsor scientific inquiry, regulate child labor, and restrict the working day for factory workers; require that children be educated; provide poor relief, and so forth" (*EI*, 27). But if freedom requires intervention, what are the basic parameters for that intervention?

As we have seen, for Appiah (as for most positive theories of liberty) positive freedom turns on some notion of education. Unlike some of his liberal predecessors, Appiah confronts the nature of a rational education head-on, beginning with the claim that the state should promote our ethical well-being by molding us into better persons. The question for Appiah is how could such a perfectionist function of the state avoid a paternalist encroachment on individual freedom, given his liberal aims. Appiah's response is to insist that state interventions should take individual autonomy as of upmost value. A state-sponsored school system that trains its citizens to become rational individuals does not encroach upon liberty, but, on the contrary, strengthens it. In support of his liberal perfectionism, Appiah cites John Stuart Mill's qualitative distinction between objectively higher and more rational forms of pleasure over lower forms. According to Mill, "it is an unquestionable fact that those who are equally acquainted with . . . both [higher and lower forms of pleasure], do give a most marked preference to a manner of existence which employs their higher faculties. . . . [N]o intelligent human being would consent to be a fool" (cited in *EI*, 173).

Now rather than counter Appiah's defense of governmentality with the carnival's celebration of the fool, we might recall that public education is hardly a bad thing, and that it could hardly avoid inculcating norms and disciplinary practices. Whatever *Animal House* might lead some of its viewers to think, universities are more than just party scenes. Carnival humor may rightly release from bondage anti-heroes such as rebels and queers, but comedy's educated fools are not Mill's blind ones. Even the adventures of the rowdy Delta students in *Animal House* lead to some kind of enlightenment, one that is distinctly missing in their uptight Omega House peers. Negative freedom has its significant subversive moments— no doubt about that; but, as the film insists through its irony, knowledge is good. Some idea of positive freedom centered around the social education of emotions is necessary for individuals, schools, and communities to function. Why not inculcate in these individuals the need for a rational life plan?

Let's examine more carefully Appiah's specific argument on behalf of rational soul-shaping. Appiah locates among those major threats to our rational autonomy what he terms "undermining identities." He defines undermining identities in terms of those identities that render our lives incoherent due to the fact that their norms pull in different directions. The force of his argument turns yet again on a specific example (something that happens more often than philosophers admit). In this case, the example is race. Racial identities, Appiah argues, are undermining identities because any notion that we have of race, whether it is biological or social, is "inconsistent with reality." After arguing why this is the case, Appiah concludes that the government should intervene into private lives through public education to diminish the salience of racial identities.

The immediate problem with the dismissal of race as a salient category of social identity is that many people who are racialized, African Americans for example, are profoundly and positively identified with their race, and for good reasons. As long as there is racial oppression, racial identity secures the solidarity necessary for organizing and expressing social goals.[29] Spike Lee's *Bamboozled* offers a persuasive critique of the attempt to deny race (at least in the current U.S. context) as an element of identity (see chapter 3). Delacroix's efforts to detach himself from the strings of racial identity only serve to tighten their pull.

Of course, some racial identities, like other social identities, can be chauvinistic and unenlightening. *Bamboozled* juxtaposes a pseudo-revolutionary, nationalistic hip hop gang (the Mau Maus) with more authentic claims for community, historical memory, and friendship (represented by Delacroix's comedian father, his assistant Sloan, and his friend Womack, respectively). These claims are lost on Delacroix, the black man whose aim to live without a race backfires and traps him in the very role of servitude (the Uncle Tom role) he intended to escape.[30] Racial identity may not be rational, but it is real, and if our notion of positive freedom does not get more real, then it will not take us very far toward important ethical goals.

The question remains as to whether there is some more salient norm for social education than rational autonomy, given that our social identities are constituted through race among a host of less-than-rational sources of meaning.

Comedies can enlighten us through their humor, but this distinctly comic mode of ethical education hardly ever appears as the conquest of reason over desire. On the contrary, characters like the self-righteous pedant or impassive boor, who are bent on seeking coherency at all costs, and especially at the expense of erotic pursuits, are easy targets of laughter. In the screwball film *Bringing Up Baby* (dir. Howard Hawks, 1938), think of the opposing forces of the two female characters on the male lead. The screwball socialite played by Katharine Hepburn tries to pull the scientist (Cary Grant) away from his self-contained life, while the research assistant attempts to swallow him up in it. The screwball character typically wins in film comedy, and this film is no different. The film uses visual images in its first and final scenes to trace the salutary effect of the screwball feminine influence. As the film opens, we view Cary Grant in a pose that is meant to recall Rodin's sculpture *The Thinker.* His pose with Hepburn at the end of the film recalls Rodin's *The Kiss.*[31] The screwball force of the comic, its erotic drive, sets the stage for part two of our estrogen bomb experiment on freedom.

For not only is the rational view not often valorized in comedy, but some degree of conning or even a general atmosphere of illusions may prevail for the sake of the happy endings. Consider, for example, Barbara Stanwyck's use of trickery to win over the boorish Henry Fonda in Preston Sturges's *The Lady Eve* (1941). Indeed, we might say, Stanwyck doesn't just happen to use deception or illusion to win her man as does Hepburn in *Bringing Up Baby.* As if to reinforce the message of what happy endings may require, the film puts its lead character in the role of a con artist and a card shark. Freedom is not always based on transparency; it may be something of a card trick. That is, some salutary indulgence of illusion, myth-making, and forgetting of what cannot be forgiven allows romance to happen, friendships to take hold, and communities to heal.

Still if what the rationalist calls knowledge is not going to foster the well-being of these characters, some kind of self-knowledge typically does. Self-deceived characters are appropriate objects of ridicule, but not because these characters lack rational control. The problem with the boorish characters is that they are not in tune with either their own desires or those of others. In *Bringing Up Baby* and *The Lady Eve,* this is a lesson primarily for the male characters. In *The Philadelphia Story,* it is Hepburn's character who suffers, and this time from a potentially lethal combination of ignorance and arrogance (see chapter 4). In none of these cases is the comic cure a rationally coherent life. On the contrary, the plots of comedy, like much of life itself, are not all that coherent, and the pleasure comes from embracing an element of surprise. The more typical comic cure for our vices has to do with acknowledging our desires and developing a degree of self-irony together with the egalitarian sentiments of an "understanding heart."[32]

Comedies of manners and satires of character typically expose to ridicule arrogance, among other social vices. From such a perspective, we can reconfigure positive freedom as *cultivating the habits and passions that foster egalitarian forms of social engagement.* Despite our critique of the boor, this kind of engagement is not simply a matter of fostering forms of narcissistic enjoyment. The aristocratic Hepburn must also become, as she says of herself, "useful." We might take this type of education as a shift of emphasis from the Kantian dictum that each individual is to be treated as an end and not just a means: for as in the case of Hepburn, the character of film comedy must learn not only to be an end for him- or herself but also to be usefully connected with others. From a comic perspective, positive freedom is less a form of rational self-control or autonomy per se than an attunement of desires. In progressive comedies, acquiring this sense of attunement constitutes the egalitarian element of a character's ethical education. Comedies of manners zero in on those features of character that render friendship, love, or other intimate sources of social enjoyment possible.

At the same time, as we see in *The Philadelphia Story,* enlightened characters do not necessarily transform into more perfect persons, at least in any strong sense. Hepburn does not lose her stubborn quality (she remains the redhead, as Cary Grant insists she should, at the end of the film), and no one (except the hopelessly boorish George Kittredge) wants her to alter who she is. Comedy allows us to live and even flourish with our ordinary vices rather than eradicate them. It is at its core anti-perfectionist.

Characters who are the object of satire's corrective laughter may or may not correct their typical vices, but they do learn to find themselves in relationships that balance their virtues and vices with those of others. This balancing act is the key to the happy ending. The arrogance of a Hepburn finds its counterpoint in the deflationary irony of Cary Grant. Her other two suitors tend to idolize her, which is not what she needs. While the end of *The Philadelphia Story* leaves it unclear as to whether Hepburn loses her arrogance or Grant's irony holds it in check, other films offer a more blunt comment on the limits of our ability to change while insisting upon the salutary nature of our relationships. For example, consider *The Big Lebowski* (dir. Coen brothers, 2003). Clearly in this film, the morally lax ironist "Dude" (played by Jeff Bridges) and the self-righteously arrogant Vietnam veteran (John Goodman) are not capable of any significant degree of change. Their friendship does not act as a source of mutual transformation, but rather as a pleasurable source for the "checks and balances" that each offers on the character of the other.

In this imperfect world, we are not rational individuals, but those funny creatures who require relationships to keep us balanced. Such a perspective brings some degree of awareness of our imperfections and of how to keep them in check, but rarely the ability to transcend them. On the contrary, this awareness of our limits accompanies a sense of the pleasure we take from our need for others. This need for others is a virtue.

The classic Aristotelian formula for comedy locates pleasure in the downward-looking emotions of ridicule and pity. This formula accentuates that sense of superiority that can reinforce social hierarchies rather than knock them down. For this reason, the pleasures that progressive comedies cultivate cannot fit into the classic formula.[33] Their pleasure stems not from downward-looking forms of ridicule and pity but through the pairing of irony with more egalitarian sentiments instead. However, neither irony nor "an understanding heart" can serve a democratic ethics without developing a sense of the gradients of power and the strategies for subversion. The comedy of manners is progressive to the extent that it draws attention to, and undermines, social inequalities rather than reasserting them. Only then does comedy not only entertain but also enlighten. When comedy reinforces the gradients of power, it is anti-education. With a wink toward *Animal House,* we might well conclude that "knowledge is good." That is our positive freedom.

Solidarity: Romantic Comedy and Comedy of Friendships

In a study of Shakespearean comedy and romance, Northrop Frye offers thoughts that may shed light not only on the comic but on life more generally. The forces of the comic, like those of life, he remarks, are hardly coherent; on the contrary, they pull us in two directions at once: "Participation and detachment, sympathy and ridicule, sociability and isolation, are inseparable in the complex we call comedy, a complex that is begotten by the paradox of life itself, in which merely to exist is both to be a part of something else and yet never to be a part of it, and in which all freedom and joy are inseparably a belonging and an escape."[34] It doesn't seem likely that life any more than comedy could yield a coherent narrative or a rational plan.

The carnival of fools disrupt through their laughter those social norms to which they can maintain no allegiance. This exuberant, ambiguous freedom appears anarchistic, and we see that such philosophers of postmodern parody as Butler have been described in these very same terms.[35] Yet freedom's anarchy provides an escape from normalizing mechanisms that defeat our erotic drives. The liberation from social norms cannot do without the unruly moments of carnival, camp, and farce. But we should not have to choose between the freedom that tears us apart from the social fabric and the opposing pull of a comedy of manners that aims to mend it. Social satires and comedies of manners that ridicule antisocial vices keep in check some of the same anarchistic impulses that carnival or camp unleash. Indeed, the negative freedom that releases us from stultifying social bonds is a condition for cultivating the bonds that we desire.[36] Freedom from repressive norms goes hand in hand with freedom to cultivate libidinally rich lives. There we have our negative and positive freedoms redefined. But what of the third freedom?

Berlin depicts the third freedom as an unyielding claim for recognition or status among those who have been slighted or oppressed. In tragic drama, claims for honor often appear as noble or heroic even as they lead to acts of vengeance that damage both oneself and others. But then what might a comic perspective on these very same needs offer?

If tragedy often leads us to appreciate an element of honor or nobility in its broken protagonists, comedy tends instead to mock characters who strive for honor or status as inauthentic or stiff and inflexible or unreal (think of *The Philadelphia Story*'s George Kittredge or *Bamboozled*'s Delacroix and Big Blak Afrika). The tragic spirit acknowledges that life has costs, as Berlin had observed, but it may drive toward the defeat of an enemy even if the violence and destruction boomerangs. The comic sensibility prefers the pleasures of conviviality instead. When the solidarity of communities turns on the exclusion of enemies or the pursuit of revenge, comedies darken. *Social unions, workers' unions, marriages, couples, communities, kinship, friendship, and inclusive rituals of group belonging* are the subject of romantic comedies and comedies of friendship, and of our third freedom.

Resting social freedom on comedy's claims of belonging over tragic struggles for honor and recognition has significant implications for anti-imperialist, multicultural democracies. Recall that philosophical discussions of social identity are often posed in terms of the need of subordinate social groups for recognition, and no doubt this is typically how social groups understand their own aims. The notion of recognition is elaborated in terms of drives for status, honor, prestige, or visibility, drives that in a psychoanalytic vein we might call phallic.[37] It is not, however, the only story we can tell of the third freedom. Suppose we were to "demasculinize" multicultural debates, reorienting these debates around struggles for social and cultural rituals of affiliation instead?

Perhaps Walzer has something like this in mind in his defense of cultural pluralism. He claims that persons are attached to their cultural identities and that they "want to be ruled by people they can recognize as their own—who are familiar with their customary ways and common beliefs" (*PP*, 137). From such a perspective, states should not attempt to diminish the salience of affiliations and cultural identities in order to increase state or national power, but should empower these multifarious social identities along more egalitarian lines.

Still, we might ask how divergent and hostile groups can come together in a single society. Romantic comedies offer one element of a response. Often enough in real life, marriages tend to occur among those who have similar social and cultural backgrounds. Comedies of marriage, however, may heighten erotic tension by pairing characters from antagonistic social groups. *Romeo and Juliet*, Shakespeare's tragedy of lovers from feuding families, is, as is often remarked, a failed romantic comedy, but there are such romances that end up as comedies.

One such example is the 1997 film *Fools Rush In* (dir. Andy Tennant).[38] The film sets up its romantic conflict around two characters whose family and histories originate from opposite sides of the U.S.-Mexican border. Salma Hayek plays a young Chicana artist who marries, divorces, and remarries an Anglo businessman played by Matthew Perry. Certainly, intermarriage between social groups has been and remains an essential strategy for overcoming serious social divisions. Hardly any other social institution provides as much potential for intimacy across hostile borders as does marriage.[39] Of course, in practice marriage more typically conserves traditions, but it can be a progressive force as well, and arguably it is in *Fools Rush In*. The film culminates in the celebration of the couple's child and, therefore, of a future that would cross Anglo-Latin borders and that would be, like any larger American identity, mulatto.

Of course it would be blindly sentimental to assume that racial or ethnic groups might converge anytime soon toward a common hybrid or mulatto identity. As *Bamboozled*'s inauthentic protagonist learns too late, our racialized situation carries sources of meaning and conflict that we deny only in bad faith.[40] Dave Chappelle's satiric skits make much the same point. In "The Racial Draft," the African American team happily allows the whites to choose Tiger Woods for their team if they agree to take the Bush administration's Condoleezza Rice as well. This skit exposes inauthentic responses to racial identity and solidarity. In another skit, Chappelle mocks the myth that white people as a group can't dance (the remedy is an electric guitar), thereby rendering visible through deflationary irony more problematic ones.[41]

Surely it is true that tragic insight into the human condition deepens our understanding of freedom. But comedy also contains unique insights for political ethics. For where better than in comedy do we find that mix of wisdom and irreverence that sustains democracies? Indeed, each of comedy's major genres offers glimpses into freedom's complex meaning.

Carnival's unruly laughter can humiliate and disenfranchise, but unruly laughter can turn into a liberating force as well. The mockery of rigid norms "desubjugates" those who laugh at powerful forces and breaks through identities that constrain more than they enable. The political theater of queer camp exemplifies this power of comedy to liberate us from ourselves. Through the ironic performance of conventional gender and sex roles we can gain the space to reinvent who we are. Negative liberty as freedom from external intervention does not suffice to locate this freedom—not if external norms compose layers of the self and predispose us to understand our desires and choices in ways that work against us. The liberating force of laughter's ironic stance, whether it occurs as camp, carnival, or farce, shifts the core meaning of negative freedom from individual choice to self-liberation. This freedom emerges in the transgression of norms that define our choices and identities in the first place.

Positive freedom is located in the resources and capabilities required to make choices that are good both for individuals and for societies. This kind of freedom allows us at minimum to survive and ideally to flourish. Traditionally, the focus of positive freedom has been on the rational education of desires or, since Kant, the cultivation of rational autonomy. While the comic practices that we find in satires of character and comedies of manner exert pedagogical force, they rarely promote the virtues of what one would call the rational individual. Unfortunately, these practices all too often inflict their irony on characters who deviate from conventional norms rather than on conventional characters who fail to question these norms when they are repressive. Against characters and social practices that instill such norms, we should surely valorize rational autonomy. However, satire's comic gaze on character and manners does not always have to be conventional in outlook; on the contrary, this gaze can draw together normalizing forces to educate us to live in more inclusive, egalitarian democracies. These salutary practices can expose through comic irony the arrogance, boorishness, or greed that undermines social equality. Of course, we cannot eliminate our vices of character completely, and comedy serves well to remind us of our typical shortcomings. But these comedies of manners do not urge us to leave our flaws unchecked either. On the contrary, such comedies promote egalitarian relationships that balance one person's virtues and vices with those of another.

The third freedom, social freedom, has been understood in terms of our need to achieve recognition from others. Cultural images and social attitudes impact not only our social standing but also our psychic life. As Berlin points out, those people who have endured colonization prefer to belong to an authoritarian nation of their own rather than to be ruled by outsiders who fail to perceive them as rivals for power or respect. While recognition is important for a flourishing social life, romantic comedies and comedies of friendship mock those quests for honor or status that struggles for recognition typically imply. These comedies divert characters from zero-sum games for honor and status and toward the pleasures of conviviality. I understand this third freedom as solidarity but shift this term's traditional association from those "phallic" struggles signaled by the old term *fraternité* to rites and rituals that reinvent family, friendship, and intimacy.

To whatever degree liberal theorists affirm the need for positive freedoms, they restrict the core meaning of freedom to individual choice. They may reclaim positive freedom in terms of entitlements to education and other necessary social goods, but they consign these entitlements and the relationships that they imply to background conditions. The individual stands alone in the foreground of analysis, and freedom centers on freedom from external forces. Progressive comedies expand our focus from the individual and her choices to embodied social creatures and new forms of belonging. Rather than choosing one form of freedom over another, these comedies instruct us to keep all three dimensions of freedom in play. Together these three dimensions offer the ground for a democratic ethics, one that invites citizenship for the disenfranchised and joins divided communities for a free social life.[42]

NOTES

PROLOGUE

1. Stephen Colbert coined the term "truthiness" during the first episode (October 17, 2005) of his satirical television show *The Colbert Report*. Cf. Harry G. Frankfurt, *On Bullshit* (Princeton, N.J.: Princeton University Press, 2005).

2. See, for example, the book by University of California, Berkeley, linguist professor Geoffrey Nunberg, *Talking Right: How Conservatives Turned Liberalism into a Tax-Raising, Latte-Drinking, Sushi-Eating, Volvo-Driving, New York Times-Reading, Body-Piercing, Hollywood-Loving, Left-Wing Freak Show* (New York: Public Affairs, 2006). Thanks for these examples to Chad Kauzter, who remarks that the title is itself a piece of comedy.

3. Cf. Remarks by Richard Rorty in *Take Care of Freedom and Truth Will Take Care of Itself: Interviews with Richard Rorty*, ed. Eduardo Mendieta (Stanford, Calif.: Stanford University Press, 2006), 37.

4. Hegel calls this kind of choice arbitrary, merely *Willkür*, which is a "delusion if it is supposed to be equivalent to freedom." See G. W. F. Hegel, *Elements of the Philosophy of Right*, ed. Allen W. Wood and trans. H. B. Nisbet (Cambridge: Cambridge University Press, 1991), 49 [§15].

5. As historian Eric Foner observes, "Despite their devotion to freedom, Americans have not produced many abstract discussions of the concept. There is no equivalent in our literature to John Stuart Mill's *On Liberty* or the essay 'Two concepts of Liberty' by Isaiah Berlin." See *The Story of American Freedom* (New York: Norton, 1998), xiv. On this observation, see also the remarks of John McCumber, *Time in the Ditch* (Evanston, Ill.: Northwestern, 2001), esp. 102. While John Dewey and Martin Luther King, among others, might count as authors of significant statements on freedom, McCumber gives us an explanation as to how cold war politics has occluded such statements from sustained philosophical attention or development. See also Louis Menand, *The Metaphysical Club: A Story of Ideas in America* (New York: Farrar, Straus and Giroux, 2001). I have anchored my own pragmatic approach in Cornel West rather than, say, Dewey in order to better bring out a contemporary multicultural (and feminist) frame to the thesis on freedom.

6. See Greil Marcus's introduction to Constance Rourke, *American Humor: A Study of National Character* (New York: New York Review, 2004), xiv. Rourke's book hereafter cited as *AH*.

7. Martha C. Nussbaum, *Upheavals of Thought: The Intelligence of the Emotions* (Cambridge, U.K.: Cambridge University Press, 2001), 675; hereafter cited as

UT. Cf. Rourke, who argues that American life exhibits a pattern of people who have "known tragedy enough" and who choose to flee oppressive circumstances into comedy (*AM,* 113–14).

8. Kwame Anthony Appiah, *The Ethics of Identity* (Princeton, N.J.: Princeton University Press, 2005), 8.

9. Even those in our society who may seem most rational and autonomous on a liberal account often uproot themselves—usually, these days, to follow a career. One might wonder if the peripatetic habits of the upper middle class compromise their freedom by breaking their communal connections. Of course, there is a huge difference between choosing to uproot and being forced to do so, but the impact on our freedom, if not our autonomy, may be in some ways similar.

10. Toni Morrison, "Home," in *The House that Race Built,* ed. Wahneema Lubiana (New York: Random House, 1998), 5; hereafter cited as *HB.*

11. Toni Morrison, *Beloved* (New York: New American Library, 1987), 219, 226; hereafter cited as *BE.*

12. Ronald Dworkin, "The Right to Ridicule," *New York Review of Books* 13, no. 5 (March 23, 2006): 44. For a discussion of Dworkin's position, see Stephen Eric Bronner, "Incendiary Images: Blasphemous Cartoons, Cosmopolitan Responsibility, and Critical Engagement," *Logos Journal* 5.1 (Winter 2006), http://www.logosjournal.com/issue_5.1/bronner.htm.

13. Robert B. Pippin, "The Ethical Status of Civility," in *The Persistence of Subjectivity: On the Kantian Aftermath* (Cambridge: Cambridge University Press, 2005), 223–38.

14. Shannon Sullivan, *Revealing Whiteness: The Unconscious Habits of Racial Privilege* (Bloomington: Indiana University Press, 2006).

15. Alex Witchel, "The Improviser," *New York Times Magazine,* June 25, 2006, section 6, 37–38.

16. Christopher Caldwell, "After Londonistan: Counterterrorism in the UK," *New York Times Magazine,* June 25, 2006, section 6, 46.

17. On the morals and manners of the stoics see Nancy Sherman, *Stoic Warriors: The Ancient Philosophy behind the Military Mind* (Oxford: Oxford University Press, 2005).

18. "Axis of Evil Comedy, On Tour," in *National Public Radio, "All Things Considered"* (July 28, 2006), http://www.npr.org/programs/atc/transcripts/2006/jul/060728.jobrani.html.

19. Isaiah Berlin's "Two Concepts of Liberty," in *Four Essays on Liberty* (Oxford: Oxford University Press, 1969), 118–72; hereafter cited as *EL.* In an introduction to the volume, he adds the clarification that while freedom should be restricted to its negative meaning, it should be understood as having certain minimal economic conditions, including equality of opportunity, but that these conditions should not be confused with freedom (xlv).

20. Cf. William Connolly's rich discussion of the significance for cultural pluralism of civic virtues such as relational modesty, critical responsiveness, and agonistic respect in *Pluralism* (Durham: Duke University Press, 2005), esp. 123–

26. The political ethics that I develop strongly supports his arguments for cultural pluralism but grounds that pluralism in comedy and laughter rather than in the experience of temporality. However, I am intrigued by Connolly's occasional and suggestive references to laughter in the course of his argument (see esp. 93 and 124–25).

21. Chad Kautzer suggests John Gardner's *Grendel* (New York: Vintage, 1989) as an excellent illustration of the point here. Grendel is the monster-child in the classic Anglo-Saxon epic poem *Beowulf.* The text is thought by some to be a kind of textbook moral tale on heroism and honor. Gardner writes his book from the perspective of Grendel, who, at one point, rather than fight the heroic warriors who come to destroy him (and assume they'll most likely die in the process, which itself would be honorable), makes fun of them. Rather than killing them he humiliates them by throwing apples at them, not only denying them their honorable death, but shaming them, ridiculing them. He torments them because he feels alienated and yearns for companionship and community.

22. Various philosophers have compared and contrasted Stanley Cavell's notion of acknowledgment with Hegel's notion of recognition, including Patchen Markell, *Bound by Recognition* (Princeton, N.J.: Princeton University Press, 2003); Andrew Norris, "Political Revisions: Stanley Cavell and Political Philosophy," *Political Theory* 30, no. 6 (Dec. 2002): 828–51; Falguni A. Sheth, "Bound by Competing Agendas: A Comment on Patchen Markell's *Bound by Recognition,*" *Polity* 38, no. 1 (Jan. 2006): 20–27. Regarding the virtues of comedy, Rourke identifies four: irreverent wisdom, resilience, leveling, and unity (*AH*, 86).

1. LAUGHTER AGAINST HUBRIS

Special thanks to Chad Kautzer for his excellent comments on a version of this chapter to be published in a volume that he is co-editing with Eduardo Mendieta, *Pragmatism, Nation, and Race* (Bloomington: Indiana University Press, forthcoming). Thanks also to Eduardo Mendieta and Harvey Cormier for organizing the "Racism, Pragmatism, and Nationalism" conference at SUNY–Stony Brook in May 2003, where I originally presented the essay; and to Kelly Oliver, Robert Frodeman, and Tim Craker for comments on an earlier version of the chapter.

1. Niall Ferguson, *Empire: The Rise and Demise of the British World Order and the Lessons for Global Power* (New York: Basic Books, 2004); Michael Ignatieff, *Empire Lite: Nation Building in Bosnia, Kosovo and Afghanistan* (London: Vintage, 2003). For a critical overview, see Eduardo Mendieta, "Imperial Religions, 'Clash of Civilizations,' and the People's Church," forthcoming.

2. Cited in Marilyn B. Young's "The Age of Global Power," in *Rethinking American History in a Global Age,* ed. Thomas Bender (Berkeley: University of California Press, 2002), 279; hereafter cited as *GP*.

3. Cornelia Klinger, "The Subject of Politics—The Politics of the Subject," in *Democracy Unrealized,* ed. Okwui Enwezor et al. (Ostfildern-Ruit, Germany: Hatje Cantz Publishers, 2002), 285–302; references to anthology hereafter cited *DU*.

4. At last, for a definitive study of what counts as manly, see Harvey C. Mansfield's *Manliness* (Cambridge, Mass.: Harvard University Press, 2006).

5. The difference between preemptive war and preventive war should be noted here, since the former is technically a "defensive" response to an imminent attack, which is what the 2002 NSS claims it advocates, while the latter is a war of aggression initiated without such a threat, that is, what happened in the case of the U.S. invasion of Iraq, which was a clear violation of international law. The obfuscating rhetoric of the 2002 NSS intentionally blurs this distinction, writing that "we" will "defend ourselves, even if uncertainty remains as to the time and the place of the enemy's attack" (NSS, 19). Of course, even imminent threats are uncertain as to time and place, but the important move in the NSS document is the dropping of "imminent" while still calling it "defensive" or "preemptive." See http://www.whitehouse.gov/nsc/nss.pdf.

6. For an interesting discussion of the novels of *Fight Club*'s author, see Eduardo Mendieta, "Surviving American Culture: On Chuck Palahniuk," *Philosophy and Literature* 29 (2005): 394–408.

7. As a *New York Times* columnist reporting on the ongoing World War in Africa explains, even in a "magical world where great powers always have good intentions," no outside intervention—whether by American, European, Asian, African, or United Nations force—would be likely to solve the problems of ethnic division and conflict that rage in East Europe, the Middle East, or the Congo: " 'Nation building' by outsiders is inherently arrogant and risky, and there are few success stories." See Adam Hockschild, "Chaos in Congo Suits Many Parties Just Fine," *New York Times*, "The World," April 20, 2003, 3.

8. Michael Ignatieff, "The Burden," *New York Times Magazine*, Jan. 5, 2003, 22ff.; hereafter cited as *B*.

9. Thomas Friedman, "From Supercharged Financial Markets to Osama bin Laden, the Emerging Global Order Demands an Enforcer: That's American's New Burden," *New York Times Magazine*, March 28, 1999, 43; hereafter cited as *NB*.

10. William Greider, "Enron's Rise and Fall," *Nation*, December 24, 2001, 1.

11. For the best among a wave of new books on bullying among girls in the schools, see Rachel Simmons, *Odd Girl Out: The Hidden Culture of Aggression in Girls* (New York: Harcourt, 2002).

12. Aristotle, *Poetics*, trans. Richard Janko (Indianapolis: Hackett, 1985).

13. Friedrich Nietzsche, *The Birth of Tragedy and The Genealogy of Morals*, trans. Francis Golffing (New York: Random House, 1956); for hubris as "active sin" see *Birth of Tragedy*, 64; and on the genealogy of moral terms, see esp. "First Essay" in *Genealogy of Morals*, 162.

14. Friedrich Nietzsche, "Homer's Contest," in *The Portable Nietzsche*, trans. Walter Kaufmann (New York: Viking Press, 1974), 36; hereafter cited as *HC*.

15. N. R. E. Fisher, *Hybris: A Study in the Values of Honour and Shame in Ancient Greece* (Warminster, England: Aris and Philips, 1992), 1–2; hereafter cited as *H*.

16. Wole Soyinka's remarks were made at his seminar on African Philosophy and Literature, Feb. 1999, Emory University.

17. Fareed Zakaria, "The Arrogant Empire," *Newsweek*, March 24, 2003, 24.

18. Thomas L. Friedman, "Peking Duct Tape," *New York Times OP-ED*, Feb. 16, 2003, 11; hereafter cited as *PD*.

19. Jonathan Schell, "The Will of the World," *Nation*, March 10, 2003, 3.

20. Samuel P. Huntington, "The Clash of Civilizations?" *Foreign Affairs* 72, no. 3 (Summer 1993): 22-49.

21. Michael Ignatieff, "Why Are We in Iraq? (And Liberia? And Afghanistan?)" *New York Times Magazine*, September 7, 2003, section 6, 85.

Hussein's execution in early 2007, after a highly politicized trial whose legitimacy was never recognized by the international community, has only further incited sectarian divisions, particularly after leaked videos of the execution recorded the sectarian tauntings of the executioners just moments before Hussein's death.

22. Aristotle, *Politics*, trans. Ernest Barker (Oxford: Oxford University Press, 1995), 12880b29.

23. See Richard Rorty, *Take Care of Freedom and Truth Will Take Care of Itself: Interviews with Richard Rorty*, ed. Eduardo Mendieta (Stanford, Calif.: Stanford University Press, 2006), 152-53. Cf. Charles Mills, *The Racial Contract* (Ithaca, N.Y.: Cornell University Press, 1997).

24. Ralph Ellison, "An Extravagance of Laughter," in *Going to the Territory* (New York: Vintage, 1986), 172.

25. See preface in *DU*, 10.

26. Michael Ignatieff, *Human Rights as Politics and Idolatry*, ed. Amy Gutmann (Princeton, N.J.: Princeton University Press, 2001); hereafter cited as *HR*.

27. Martha Nussbaum, *The Fragility of Goodness* (New York: Cambridge University Press, 2001), xiii-xxxix; hereafter cited as *FG*.

28. Sophocles' *Oedipus* in *The Oedipus Cycle: Oedipus Rex, Oedipus at Colonus, Antigone*, trans. Dudley Fitts and Robert Fitzgerald (New York: Harcourt, Brace and World/Harvest Book, 1977), ln 965.

29. Fernanda Eberstadt, "The Anti-American Lifestyle," *New York Times Magazine*, March 23, 2003, 16.

30. Northrop Frye, *Anatomy of Criticism* (Princeton, N.J.: Princeton University Press, 1957), 169; hereafter cited as *AC*. Romantic comedy is often also associated with a critique of the work ethic.

31. Martha C. Nussbaum, *Sex and Social Justice* (Oxford: Oxford University Press, 1999), 12, 11, 6; hereafter cited as *SS*.

32. Toni Morrison, *Paradise* (New York: Plume, 1999), 318.

33. See Patricia Hill Collins, *Black Feminist Thought* (New York: Routledge, 1991), 166; herafter cited as *BFT*. And *Fighting Words: Black Women and the Search for Justice* (Minneapolis: University of Minnesota Press, 1998), 188; hereafter cited as *FW*.

34. Audre Lorde, *Sister Outsider* (Freedom, Calif.: Crossing Press, 1984), 53-59; hereafter cited as *SO*.

35. Toni Morrison, "Unspeakable Things Unspoken: The Afro-American Pres-

ence in American Literature," in *The Black Feminist Reader*, ed. Joy James and T. Denean Sharpley-Whiting (Malden, Mass.: Blackwell, 1984), 25; hereafter cited as *UU*.

36. Toni Morrison, "Rootedness: The Ancestor as Foundation," in *Black Women Writers*, ed. Mari Evans (New York: Anchor Press, 1984), 341.

37. See glossary entry for "wanton aggression" in Aristotle, *Nichomachean Ethics*, trans. Terence Irwin (Indianapolis: Hackett, 1985), 432.

2. LAUGHING TO KEEP FROM CRYING

This chapter was originally presented for a panel with Cornel West organized by Eduardo Mendieta at the Society for Phenomenology and Existential Philosophy meeting in Boston, November 2003. I am grateful to Cornel West, Robert Gooding-Williams, Tommy Lott, and Lou Outlaw as well as the SPEP audience for comments on the presentation.

1. Cornel West, *The Cornel West Reader* (New York: Basic Books, 1999), 475; hereafter cited as *CWR*. The title of this chapter borrows from Langston Hughes, *Laughing to Keep from Crying* (New York: Henry Holt, 1952). See also Ronald Sundstrom, "Laughing to Keep from Crying: Resisting the American 'Racial' Politic through Irony," *Tympanum* 4 (July 2000): 1–35.

2. Michael Agger, "And the Oscar for Best Scholar . . . ," *New York Times*, May 18, 2003.

3. See "On Prophetic Pragmatism," *CWR*, esp. 150–51, 164–65.

4. Note that Cornel West uses "existential" to refer to the role of "death, suffering, love and friendship," and most fundamentally, the basic need of belonging, not in Sartre's classic notion of radical choice; see, for example, *CWR*, 13, 264.

5. Cornel West's afterword in *Cornel West: A Critical Reader*, ed. George Yancy (Oxford, U.K.: Blackwell, 2001), 354; references to edited collection hereafter cited as *CR*; see also West's "Black Strivings in a Twilight Civilization," *CWR*, 86 and 106.

6. Here I am citing the title to the essay that West would prefer of all others to survive (see *CWR*, 87).

7. Cornel West, *Race Matters* (New York: Random House, 1994), 14; hereafter.cited as *RM*. Cf. Cornel West, *Democracy Matters* (New York: Penguin, 2004), 6.

8. Quoted in Pam Houston, "The Truest Eye: Conversation with the Writer," *O: The Oprah Magazine*, November 2003, 214.

9. Cornel West, *Keeping Faith: Philosophy and Race in America* (New York: Routledge, 1993), 72.

10. On the history of the blackface buffoon, the arrogant backwoodsman, and the ironic Yankee peddler in American culture, see Constance Rourke, *American Humor: A Study of the National Character* (New York: New York Review Books, 2004).

11. Cornel West, *Sketches of My Culture* (CD) (2001).

12. Mikhail Bakhtin, *Rabelais and His World*, trans. Helene Iswolsky (Bloomington: Indiana University Press, 1984), 16.

13. *Richard Pryor—Live in Concert*, dir. Jeff Margolis (Terrace Theatre, Long Beach, California, 1979).

14. "Manifesto of the Communist Party," *The Marx-Engels Reader,* ed. Robert C. Tucker (New York: Norton, 1978), 474.

15. Richard Pryor, *Live and Smokin',* dir. Michael Blum (1971).

16. Margaret Cho, *Notorious C.H.O. in Concert,* dir. Lorene Machado (2002).

17. These observations as well as those that follow are based on Michele Norris's National Public Radio interview with Paul Rodriguez for the series *Comedy and Race in America,* aired on December 10, 2002; www.npr.org/programs/atc/features/2002/dec/comedians/index.html.

18. See Michele Norris's National Public Radio interview with Margaret Cho for the series *Comedy and Race in America,* aired on December 9, 2002; www.npr.org/programs/atc/features/2002/dec/comedians/index.html.

19. Henri Bergson's "Laughter," in *Comedy,* ed. Wylie Sypher (Baltimore: Johns Hopkins University Press, 1994), 66-67, 73; hereafter cited as *L.*

20. Sylvia Ann Hewlett and Cornel West, *The War against Parents* (Boston: Houghton Mifflin Co., 1998), xii; hereafter cited as *WP.*

21. On the "acknowledgment" of desire and "avoidance" of forms of sacrifice, see Stanley Cavell, *Pursuits of Happiness: The Hollywood Comedy of Remarriage* (Cambridge, Mass.: Harvard University Press, 1981), 56, 154.

22. For a critique of the language of sacrifice and the nuclear family, see Cynthia Willett, *The Soul of Justice* (Ithaca, N.Y.: Cornell University Press, 2001), 173; and for a critique of these and related concerns see Iris Young, "Cornel West on Gender and Family: Some Admiring and Critical Comments," in *CR,* 179-91.

23. Niall Ferguson, "Why America Outpaces Europe (Clue: The God Factor)," *New York Times,* June 8, 2003, section 4, 3.

24. For brief remarks on Chekhov, see *CWR,* 556; *CR,* 348.

25. See Bernice Kanner's "From *Father Knows Best* to *The Simpsons*—On TV, Parenting Has Lost Its Halo," in *Taking Parenting Public,* ed. Sylvia Ann Hewlett, Nancy Rankin, and Cornel West (Lanham, Md.: Rowman and Littlefield, 2002), 49.

26. An anonymous reader suggested *The Roseanne Show* as an outstanding example of working-class humor that exemplifies this point.

27. Iris Marion Young's "City Life and Difference," in *Justice and the Politics of Difference* (Princeton, N.J.: Princeton University Press, 1990), 226-56.

3. AUTHENTICITY IN AN AGE OF SATIRE

Special thanks to Yoko Arisaka, Lina Buffington, Beth Butterfield, Tom Flynn, Lewis Gordon, Lawrence Jackson, Denise James, Martin Japtok, Bill Martin, Eduardo Mendieta, Darrell Moore, Ron Sundstrom, and the audiences at the 11th Born of Struggle Conference at Rutgers in October 2004; Vanderbilt Philosophy Department Colloquium, December 2004; De Paul's Africana Studies Program, April 2005; and University of San Francisco Philosophy Department Colloquium, April 2005. A shorter version of the essay is due to be published in a collection of essays on black authenticity edited by Martin Japtok and Rafiki Jenkins.

1. For an account of authenticity that emphasizes in the German context the importance of critical responsive to a situation, see Rudolf A. Makkreel, "From

Authentic Interpretation to Authentic Disclosure: Bridging the Gap between Kant and Heidegger," in *Heidegger, German Idealism, and NeoKantianism*, ed. Tom Rockmore (Amherst, N.Y.: Humanity Books, 2000). For authenticity as a social virtue, see Charles Guignon, *On Being Authentic* (New York: Routledge, 2004), 150. For discussions of authenticity and blackness in hip hop, see essays by Paul Taylor, Kathryn Gines, and Lewis Gordon in *Hip Hop and Philosophy*, ed. Derrick Darby and Tommie Shelby (Peru, Ill.: Open Court, 2005).

2. Note, however, that Alessandro Ferrara interprets authenticity as an alternative to autonomy in his *Reflective Authenticity*. Ferrara observes that while autonomy rests on foundational moral or rational principles, authenticity as self-actualization is based on the exemplary universalism of our normative core identities. While noting that the post-linguistic turn requires the recognition of authenticity by others, Ferrara's sharp contrast between autonomy and authenticity obscures the individualism at their root. Authenticity is a non-foundational, non-rationalistic, existential reconstruction of autonomy. In Sartrean terms, it requires that one choose oneself. More significant for my purposes is how one takes up the intersubjective moment of recognition without reducing authenticity to a formal requirement that we think from the standpoint of everyone else. At the same time, the multicultural context puts us in danger of collapse of self-identity into inauthentic social groups such as some forms of popular nationalism or life-world saturated by neoliberalism's socioeconomic forces. See the discussion of Ferrara's work in *Philosophy and Social Criticism* 30, no. 1 (2004), with Axel Honneth and Charles Larmore, as well as Ferrara's response.

3. For an analysis of the racial, ethnic, cultural, national, and political elements of black authenticity, see Lionel K. McPherson and Tommie Shelby, "Blackness and Blood: Interpreting African American Identity," *Philosophy and Public Affairs* 32, no. 2 (2004): 177–78. Perhaps the most well-known satiric return to this question is "The Racial Draft" in *Chappelle's Show*, season 2, episode 1.

4. Todd Boyd explains the significance of authenticity, or "keeping it real," in post-soul and hip hop culture: "At some overt level, hip hop has always been about the cultural identity. . . . [T]his concern over identity is generally bounded by two other primary issues: a politics of location and an overall search for that which is considered authentic." See his *The New H.N.I.C: The Death of Civil Rights and the Reign of Hip Hop* (New York: New York University Press, 2003), 18. He goes on to note that authenticity has to do with "one's perception in the marketplace. It also has to do with one's relationship to capital" (19).

5. This phrasing echoes the nuanced reflections of John McDermott's essay "Transiency and Amelioration," in *Streams of Experience* (Amherst: University of Massachusetts Press, 1986), 63–75. McDermott writes: "If the world as known is in some way a function of the knower, then introspection, sociology, and cosmology are of a piece. Further if self-deception is an irreducible presence in human judgment, the test for meaning is communal and processive" (70); McDermott does not have in mind Huntington's homogeneous community, but a community that is inherently pluralist, or what in this chapter I term the "social."

6. Samuel P. Huntington, *Who Are We? The Challenges to America's National Identity* (New York: Simon and Schuster, 2004), 59; hereafter cited as *WE*.

7. For a persuasive argument in support of cultural conceptions of the nation-state as the locus of ethical cultivation toward universalist cosmopolitan goals, see Pheng Cheah, *Spectral Nationality* (New York: Columbia University Press, 2003), 8.

8. Kwame Anthony Appiah raises the question of the Anglo-Saxon roots of liberalism in *The Ethics of Identity* (Princeton, N.J.: Princeton University Press, 2005), 203.

9. Ralph Ellison, "An Extravagance of Laughter," in *Going to the Territory* (New York: Vintage, 1986), 185; hereafter cited as *GT*.

10. Stanley Crouch, *The Artificial White Man: Essays on Authenticity* (New York: BasicCivitas Books, 2004).

11. On the blackface minstrel show and the blues as the two original styles of the hip among American homegrown cultural idioms, and the connection between hip and blackness, see John Leland, *Hip: The History* (New York: Harper Collins, 2004).

12. It's interesting, in light of Ellison's remark, to read Michael Eric Dyson's *Pride* (Oxford: Oxford University Press, 2006).

13. Daniel Wickberg, *The Senses of Humor: Self and Laughter in Modern America* (Ithaca, N.Y.: Cornell University Press, 1998), 41; hereafter cited as *SH*.

14. On the significance of authenticity for Adorno, see Martin Jay's forthcoming essay in *New German Critique*.

15. Robert Gooding-Williams, "Aesthetics and Receptivity: Kant, Nietzsche, Cavell, and Astaire" (draft 1, p. 30); hereafter cited as *AR*.

16. Lawrence Blum, *"I'm Not a Racist But . . . The Moral Quandary of Race"* (Ithaca, N.Y.: Cornell University Press, 2002), 10.

17. Eric Lott, *Love and Theft: Blackface Minstrelsey and the American Working Class* (Oxford: Oxford University Press, 1993), 3; hereafter cited as *LT*.

18. *L*, Appendix, 252.

19. Jean-Paul Sartre, *Anti-Semite and Jew*, trans. George Becker (New York: Schocken Books, 1995), 97–98; hereafter cited as *S*.

20. Paul Gilroy terms this reabsorption "the 'Beavis and Butthead' syndrome." See *Postcolonial Melancholia* (New York: Columbia University Press, 2005), 134; hereafter cited as *PM*.

21. To attack or denounce vociferously, especially so as to intimidate: *"In years past, [the civil rights leadership] . . . would mau-mau the government or the corporate sector or the white community"* (Joseph Perkins, *Atlanta Constitution*, January 12, 1994). ETYMOLOGY: After the *Mau Mau*, a secret society of Kikuyu terrorists that led a rebellion against the ruling Europeans in Kenya in the 1950s, from Kikuyu *mau-mau*, sound of the voracious gobbling of a hyena. See "Mau Mau Uprising," *Wikipedia*, http://en.wikipedia.org/wiki/Mau_Mau.

22. There are parallels between the message of the Mau-Maus and their leader in *Bamboozled* and the Garveyian message of Ras the Exhorter in Ralph Ellison's *Invisible Man*, "both of whom ardently preach for anything that is pro-black, from

black nationalism to spelling black, *B-L-A-K*." See Guensley Delva, "Black Skins, Black Masks," *Radical Philosophy Review* 5, no. 2 (2002): 210.

23. Tom Flynn warns me that this is too simple a formulation of subjectivity in Sartre's *Being and Nothingness*. One chooses to "be" oneself as "not-being" it, i.e., as not being identical with it because one is always more than it. He also explains that the point of Sartrean authenticity is to live without getting mired in the inertia of an ego (or self). One both transcends the self as one transcends the factical or given and yet must take responsibility for the self that one necessarily transcends.

That said, I will use the reductive formula of "choosing the self" to capture that distancing from the self and its situation as the focal meaning of the Sartrean quest for authenticity. The Spike Lee film shifts the focus of authenticity from the element of transcendence toward that second element of responsibility for one's situated identity. This gestalt switch is significant. The altered focus shifts our attention from a negative freedom and its romanticization of alienation toward a social freedom and the romance of belonging.

As will become more clear in chapter 5, however, my aim is not to reject negative freedom either, but to reinterpret it through queer theory and camp humor. Queer camp locates freedom in the destabilization and disruption of norms, though, and not in a consciousness that transcends them. One might be able to reduce both of these discussions of freedom to a Sartrean frame, but not without losing the specificity of the philosophical contributions of African American and queer culture, respectively.

24. Jean-Paul Sartre, *Being and Nothingness*, trans. Hazel E. Barnes (New York: Washington Square Press, 1956), 111; hereafter cited as *BN*.

25. Jazz and Negro culture critic Anatole Broyard works directly out of Sartre's study of the inauthentic Jew in his "Portrait of the Inauthentic Negro: How Prejudice Distorts the Victim's Personality," *Commentary* 10, no. 1 (July 1950): 56–64. He defines authenticity to "mean stubborn adherence to one's essential self, I mean his innate qualities and developed characteristics as an individual, as distinguished from his preponderantly defensive reactions as a member of an embattled minority" (57); hereafter cited as *PIN*.

26. Tom Flynn points out that Sartre changes his mind in his later work, and that even in *BN* (part 3) in a section on Being-for-Others (e.g., "shame" consciousness), Sartre addresses an ontological dimension of the self that depends on others. I am using Bergson's discussion of shame, ridicule, etc., in comedy of manners to integrate, expand, and elaborate upon multiple dimensions of the being-for-other for the core meaning of freedom and authenticity in a way that Sartre does not consistently do. This requires that I use the literary concept of character and emphasize the concrete situation in place of more abstract discussions of subjectivity, consciousness, being, and nothingness.

27. Bergson himself does not develop the significance of social mediation through family, friendship, or community for individual identity in his own work. For a discussion of his later mysticism, see Leonard Lawlor, *The Challenge of Bergsonism* (London: Continuum, 2003), 104.

28. While Sartre comes to agree with the general tenor of this claim, he never fully develops a theory of freedom that can handle our thick social identities. He does not ever see in cultural and social groups a source of pride and positive meaning apart from strategic goals of social change that would eventually render them defunct. I shall discuss this concern further in chapter 5 as I look at contemporary identity politics and multiculturalism. Cf. Broyard, who, despite writing as *Commentary's* jazz and Negro culture critic, acknowledges to some small degree the positive value of the culture of the Jew but not of the African American (*PIN*, 63).

29. Tom Flynn points out Sartre's critique of the "liberal democratic 'friend.' " My point here, and this is important, is that Sartre insists the Jewish identity and other thick social identities have only a strategic relevance for combating racism. After racism is defeated, there would be no need to preserve such an identity. In other words, Sartre sees no positive cultural meaning in being a Jew, etc. This is a point to which I shall return in chapter 5. Still I agree here with Tom Flynn that Sartre's dialectical method could be used to recognize cultural particularities in the context of multiple social relations (viz., what Hegel calls the concrete universal, and Sartre terms the "singular" universal).

30. I leave as an open question the argument for postcolonial nationalism in the neocolonial South; for a subtle argument in favor of the latter, see Pheng Cheah's *Spectral Nationality* (New York: Columbia University Press, 2003).

31. Charles Taylor also indicates the importance of a social component of authenticity, but he does so in such a way as to separate manner and content. See his *The Ethics of Authenticity* (Cambridge, Mass.: Harvard University Press, 1991): "Self-fulfilment, so far from excluding unconditional relationships and moral demands beyond the self, actually requires them in some form" (72–73). He then distinguishes between the content and manner of action, and understands authenticity to refer to manner and not content: "Authenticity is clearly self-referential: this has to be *my* orientation. But this doesn't mean that on another level the *content* must be self-referential" (82). As we shall see, the Spike Lee film suggests that authenticity comes through a strong sense of belonging to a larger, if conflict-ridden, history, and acknowledging debts and responsibilities accordingly. This orientation is not just mine, but necessarily one I come to through others, and so is *ours*. Hence, the question of black authenticity emerges as an important question that cannot be disentangled from individual authenticity in Spike Lee's film. This kind of question is elided entirely by the discussion of recognition and authenticity in his *Politics of Recognition,* which presupposes the possibility of a common horizon that privileges the dominant group without dealing with underlying conflict.

32. This recuperation of the self through friendship traces back to what Charles Taylor identifies as the dialogic basis of authenticity in "The Politics of Recognition," in *Multiculturalism and "The Politics of Recognition,"* ed. Amy Gutmann (Princeton, N.J.: Princeton University Press, 1993), 36. While he examines the issue from the point of view of the dominant group, Spike Lee's film replays the question of recognition from the point of view of a historically subordinate

group. See also Robert Gooding-Williams, "Race, Multiculturalism, and Democracy," *Constellations* 5, no. 1 (March, 1998): 18–41.

33. In this climactic scene, Spike Lee presents us with a vision borrowed from the romantic comedies of the Hollywood that he is known to dislike. Stanley Cavell has argued that these Hollywood comedies reinvoke for American culture the aristocratic dreamworlds of Shakespearean romance. These dreamworlds of romance had been forgotten for centuries when comic writers were inspired instead by Jonsonian mannered comedies of bullies, bitches, and brutes—characters too vicious for the noble passions of love and true friendship (*PH,* 170). Suppose Shakespearean romantic comedy does indeed provide the basis for much of the Hollywood comedy that Spike Lee dislikes. Spike Lee's Jonsonian comedy of manners reclaims the romance of friendship for characters who are more than the bullies, bitches, and brutes they are made out to be.

34. Sartre sketches some elements for a vision of friendship and authentic love in *Notebooks for an Ethics,* trans. David Pellauer (Chicago: University of Chicago, 1992). Perhaps we have developed one version of such a vision here. In this case, the background is the racial turmoil of contemporary American society.

35. Lawrence Jackson, *Ralph Ellison: Emergence of Genius* (New York: John Wiley, 2002), 339–40.

36. On Ellison's own gesture toward isolation and the political fallout, see Lawrence Jackson's "Ralph Ellison's Politics of Integration," in *Oxford Companion to Ralph Ellison,* ed. Steve Tracy (Oxford: Oxford University Press, 2004), 171–205; and "Ralph Ellison's Invented Life: A Meeting with the Ancestors," in *The Cambridge Companion to Ralph Ellison,* ed. Ross Posnock (Cambridge: Cambridge University Press, 2005), 11–33. As Jackson points out in the latter essay, "Ellison declared that Richard Wright and Langston Hughes, men who had started his career, were his literary relatives, . . . but, like a father, uncle, or brother, he did not choose them. . . . Ellison symbolically allied himself with the icons of Anglo-American literature" (21).

37. Compare Martin Beck Matuštík's call for a new critical theory of multiculturalism that balances existential freedom with remembrance of authentic cultural traditions in a cosmopolitan world in his "Contribution to a New Critical Theory of Multiculturalism," *Philosophy and Social Criticism* 28, no. 4 (2002): 473–82.

4. ENGAGE THE ENEMY

I am grateful to the audience at a Pennsylvania State University philosophy colloquium, November 11, 2005, and especially Claire Katz, Dan Conway, Emily Grosholz, and Shannon Sullivan, for helpful comments on this chapter. A version of this chapter will appear in Shannon Sullivan and Dennis Schmidt's *Difficulties of Ethical Life* (Fordham University Press, forthcoming).

1. See especially Carl Schmitt, *The Concept of the Political,* trans. George Schwab (Chicago: University of Chicago Press, 1996).

2. Ernesto LaClau and Chantal Mouffe, *Hegemony and Socialist Strategy: Towards a Radical Democratic Politics* (London: Verso, 1985).

3. Chantal Mouffe, *The Return of the Political* (London: Verso, 1993), 4. For an important reflection on Mouffe, see Noelle McAfee, "Two Feminisms," *Journal of Speculative Philosophy* 19, no. 2 (2005): 140–49.

4. Michael Ignatieff, "Who Are Americans to Think That Freedom Is Theirs to Spread?" *New York Times Magazine*, June 26, 2005, section 6, 42ff.

5. Jacques Derrida, *Politics of Friendship*, trans. George Collins (London: Verso, 1997), 277; hereafter cited as *PF*.

6. John D. Caputo, "Who Is Derrida's Zarathustra? Of Fraternity, Friendship, and a Democracy to Come," *Research in Phenomenology* 29 (1999): 185; hereafter cited as *DZ*. For a Nietzschean critique of Derrida's politics of friendship, see John Lysaker, "Friendship at the End of Metaphysics," *Soundings* 79, no. 3–4 (Fall/Winter 1996): 511–40.

7. For a defense of Aristotle's city of prayer as a true aristocracy, see Jill Frank, *A Democracy of Distinction* (Chicago: University of Chicago Press, 2005), 138–42.

8. Chantal Mouffe, *Deconstruction and Pragmatism: Simon Critchley, Jacques Derrida, Ernesto LaClau, and Richard Rorty* (London: Routledge, 1996), 77.

9. Stanley Cavell, *Pursuits of Happiness: The Hollywood Comedy of Remarriage* (Cambridge, Mass.: Harvard University Press, 1981); hereafter cited as *PH*. For excellent commentaries on Cavell, see Andrew Norris, ed., *The Claim to Community: Essays on Stanley Cavell and Political Philosophy* (Stanford, Calif.: Stanford University Press, 2006); and Espen Hammer, *Stanley Cavell: Skepticism, Subjectivity, and the Ordinary* (Oxford: Polity Press, 2002).

10. For Stanley Cavell's observation of the difference between Dewey and Hegel, see his interview in *The American Philosopher*, ed. Giovanna Borradori (Chicago: University of Chicago Press, 1994), 125.

11. Paul Taylor and Robert Gooding-Williams are both currently engaged in examining the contemporary relevance of these films for racial politics.

12. On the sexual radicalism unleashed by the 1920s, and redefinition of marriage culminating in the twentieth century, see Stephanie Coontz, *Marriage, A History* (New York: Viking, 2005), esp. chapter 15, 247–62.

13. For a discussion of the contemporary relevance of pragmatism, see Michael Walzer, *Politics and Passion* (New Haven, Conn.: Yale University Press, 204), 159–61. For speculation on the effects of the eclipse of pragmatism, as well as the blacklisting of Hollywood screenwriters during the McCarthy era, see John McCumber, *Time in the Ditch* (Evanston, Ill.: Northwestern University Press, 2001), esp. 90 and 94.

14. Susan Bordo, *The Male Body* (New York: Farrar, Straus and Giroux, 1999), 161; hereafter cited as *MB*.

15. Northrop Frye, *Anatomy of Criticism* (Princeton, N.J.: Princeton University Press, 1957), 182.

16. Cf. Walzer, chapter 2: "Countervalence is, in a way, a response to the structuralist critique of liberalism. It makes for an informal constitutionalization of social life; as the state is divided and balanced, so is civil society" (25–26).

17. Alexander Walker, *Sex in the Movies* (Baltimore: Penguin Books, 1969), 244–49; hereafter cited as *SM*.

5. THREE CONCEPTS OF FREEDOM

Special thanks to audiences at University of Georgia's colloquium on the *Legacies of the Enlightenment,* organized by Tzuchien Tho, including my commentator Charles Rozier; at the University of North Texas Philosophy Department colloquium organized by Robert Frodeman in April 2006; at Trinity University in Hartford, Connecticut, in April 2007; at Southwestern University in Texas in April 2007; and at Stony Brook's Undergraduate Philosophy Society in April 2007; and to Gabe Rockhill for organizing a session at New York University in Paris, June 2007.

1. For an earlier version of the poster, called "Biological Warfare," see Guerrilla Girls, *Confessions of the Guerrilla Girls: How a Bunch of Masked Avengers Fight Sexism and Racism in the Art World with Facts, Humor and Fake Fur* (New York: HarperCollins, 1995), 19.

2. Mark D. Jordan, *Blessing Same-Sex Unions* (Chicago: University of Chicago, 2005), 207.

3. Cf. Etienne Balibar's call for a feminization of power in *We, The People of Europe? Reflections on Transnational Citizenship,* trans. James Swenson (Princeton, N.J.: Princeton University Press, 2004), 202.

4. Berlin carefully rephrases and corrects parts of his original 1958 essay on two freedoms in the introduction to *TL* in *Four Essays on Liberty,* where the essay was reprinted in 1969. On the importance of having doors (opportunities) that are open, more than just the lack of external obstacles, see esp. xlviii.

5. For a defense of the priority of positive rights over negative rights, see Joy Gordon, "The Concept of Human Rights: The History and Meaning of Its Politicization," *Brooklyn Journal of International Law* 23 (1998): 689.

6. On visionary pragmatism, see Patricia Hill Collins, *Fighting Words: Black Feminist Thought and Search for Justice* (Minneapolis: University of Minnesota, 1998), 189–90; and Stanlie James and Abena Busia, eds., *Theorizing Black Feminisms: The Visionary Pragmatism of Black Women* (New York: Routledge, 1993).

7. Martha Nussbaum, *Frontiers of Justice: Disability, Nationality, Species Membership* (Boston: Belnap Press, 2006).

8. Quentin Skinner, "A Third Concept of Liberty," *London Review of Books,* April 4, 2002, 16–18; hereafter cited as *TC.* Albrecht Wellmer, "Models of Freedom in the Modern World," in *Endgames: The Irreconcilable Nature of Modernity,* trans. David Midgley (Cambridge, Mass.: MIT Press, 1998), 3–37; hereafter cited as *E.*

9. Charles Taylor, "The Politics of Recognition," in *Multiculturalism,* ed. Amy Gutmann (Princeton, N.J.: Princeton University Press, 1994).

10. Stephen P. Marks, "Emerging Human Rights: A New Generation for the 1980s?" *Rutgers Law Review* 33, no. 2 (Winter 1981): 435–52; Karl Vasak, "A 30 Year Struggle," *The UNESCO Courier* 31–32 (Nov. 1977): 74–93; and also Karl Vasak, "Pour une troisième génération des droit de l'homme," in *Études et essais sur le droit international humanitaire et sur les principes de la Croix-Rouge en l'honneur de Jean Pictet,* Studies and Essays in International Humanitarian Law

and Red Cross Principles in Honor of Jean Pictet, ed. Christophe Swinarksi, 837–45 (Geneva: Martinus Nijhoff Publishers, 1984).

11. For more on hubris, see Cynthia Willett, *The Soul of Justice: Social Bonds and Racial Hubris* (Ithaca, N.Y.: Cornell University Press, 2001), esp. 7–16.

12. Debra Berghoffen distinguishes fact from facticity in the existential philosophy of Jean-Paul Sartre, with just such a possibility in mind (conference presentation, "Sartre at 100," Emory University, December 2005).

13. Interestingly, Robert Crease approaches the same topic of liberation through dance, and comes up with some parallel insights. See his "The Pleasure of Popular Dance," *Journal of the Philosophy of Sport* 24 (2002): 106–20.

14. See Howard McGary, "Alienation and African-American Experience," in *Theorizing Multiculturalism,* ed. Cynthia Willett (Oxford: Blackwell, 1998); and Ann Cudd, *Analyzing Oppression* (Oxford: Oxford University Press, 2006), for rich explanations of the importance and limitations of the distinction between internal and external constraints for liberal concepts of freedom.

15. For an excellent defense of ontological separatism along with chosen identities and autonomy, see the introduction to Catriona Mackenzie and Natalie Stoljar, eds., *Relational Autonomy* (New York: Oxford University Press, 2000), 3–34. For a lucid statement of the ways in which external norms inform our identities from the inside out, see Noelle McAfee, "Two Feminisms," *Journal of Speculative Philosophy* 19, no. 2 (2005): 140–49.

16. Michel Foucault, *Power/Knowledge* (New York: Random House, 1980).

17. The cosmopolitan liberals de-emphasize social and cultural differences and corresponding group rights, and rest normative claims on principles or arguments that are accessible to all rational individuals and that aim to view individuals as basically all the same. These liberals claim that our common humanity transcends cultures and customs, and is based in the individual capacity for rational autonomy. They differ among themselves as to the degree to which they believe that social mediation (such as public debate) is required to establish normative claims, but they all exclude social differences from overly burdening their fundamental normative claims. For example, both Habermas and Appiah claim a rational basis for normative judgments, but Habermas anchors moral judgments in consensus-oriented debate and Appiah emphasizes individual autonomy and textured moral judgment.

For the multiculturalists, normative claims require that we factor in, rather than abstract from, thick social identities, embodied passions, and historical memories at the most basic level of any kind of philosophical analysis; the assumption is that individuals are oriented by their various cultural, social, and/or economic positions. Multiculturalists differ among themselves as to the degree to which they focus on various socioeconomic and cultural conflicts as sources of difference. Judith Butler valorizes singular individuals and invented forms of kinship, while Michael Walzer gives pride of place to traditional and established ethnic communities. Both write of the central role of passionate attachments, and not reason per se, as the basis of individual meaning and social bonds.

18. Kwame Anthony Appiah, *The Ethics of Identity* (Princeton, N.J.: Princeton University Press, 2005), xv; hereafter cited as *EI*. Interestingly though, Appiah's interest in abstracting the individual from practical circumstances and habits is almost entirely gone from his most recent book, *Cosmopolitanism: Ethics in a World of Strangers* (London: W. W. Norton, 2006). Given this latest book's attention to unconscious and affective patterns of thought, there are very rich tensions with its proposed cosmopolitanism, which traces back to Kant and the stoics.

19. For examples of queer camp, see Ann Cvetkovich, *An Archive of Feelings: Trauma, Sexuality, and Lesbian Public Cultures* (Durham, N.C.: Duke University Press, 2003), 39, 252–54, 266.

20. Michael Walzer, *Politics and Passion* (New Haven, Conn.: Yale University Press, 2004); hereafter cited as *PP*.

21. See Ladelle McWhorter, *Bodies and Pleasures: Foucault and the Politics of Sexual Normalization* (Bloomington: Indiana University Press, 1999).

22. Mikhail Bakhtin, *Rabelais and His World*, trans. Helene Iswolsky (Bloomington: Indiana University Press, 1984).

23. These significant elements of Bakhtin's discussion of the carnival are emphasized in Michael Holoquist's prologue to *Rabelais and His World*, xiii–xxiii.

24. Ted Cohen points out that humor often enough constructs a community through appealing to a common background among an ingroup and the eviction of an outgroup. See his *Jokes: Philosophical Thoughts on Joking Matters* (Chicago: University of Chicago Press, 1999).

25. See Judith Butler's "Gender Is Burning" in her *Bodies That Matter* (New York: Routledge, 1993), 121–42, hereafter cited as *BM*, and her "Conclusion: From Parody to Politics" in *Gender Trouble* (New York: Routledge, 1990), 142–49.

26. Judith Butler, "What Is Critique? An Essay on Foucault's Virtue," in *The Political: Readings in Continental Philosophy*, ed. David Ingram (London: Blackwell, 2002), 13. For related discussions of desubjugation as freedom, see Saul Tobias, "Foucault on Freedom and Capabilities," *Theory, Culture and Society* 22, no. 4 (2005): 65–85; Wendy Brown, *States of Injury* (Princeton, N.J.: Princeton University Press, 1995).

27. F. H. Buckley, *The Morality of Laughter* (Ann Arbor: University of Michigan, 2003).

28. For background on pragmatist approaches to this theme of education and democracy, see John Dewey, *The Public and Its Problems* (New York: Gateway Books, 1946); and John Stuhr, "Neither Mission Impossible nor Mission Accomplished: Democracy as Public Experiment," *Kettering Review* 24, no. 3 (Fall 2006): 18.

29. Lionel McPherson and Tommie Shelby, "Blackness and Blood: Interpreting African American Identity," *Philosophy and Public Affairs* 32, no. 2 (2004): 171–93; hereafter cited as *BB*. See responses to this essay in *Symposium on Gender, Race, and Philosophy* 1, no. 1 (May 2005), http://stellar.mit.edu/S/project/sgrp/.

30. Orlando Patterson points out (in a review of Shelby's work) that thick claims of culture and community can be obscured by the "moral and intellectual needs of the black elite and upper-middle classes." See his "Being and Blackness:

Review of *We Who Are Dark* and *Creating Black Americans*," *New York Times Book Review,* Jan. 8, 2006, 10–11.

31. Stanley Cavell notices this juxtaposition of images. See his *Pursuit of Happiness: The Hollywood Comedy of Remarriage* (Cambridge, Mass.: Harvard University Press, 1981), 117, 121.

32. Cf. Eduardo Mendieta's claims regarding the importance of moral psychology for citizenship and national character in "Racial Justice and the Supreme Court: The Role of Law and Affect in Social Change," in preparation for a volume to be edited by Jorge Gracia. Mendieta contrasts a moral psychology based on respect, gratitude, sacrifice, loyalty, and deference with one based on contempt, disregard, arrogance, and derogation. He discusses how these affects are conditioned by laws.

33. Chad Kautzer suggests contrasting this chapter's view of equality as the equality of imperfections, vulnerabilities, and idiosyncrasies that we mutually recognize and become conscious of through humor with the view of Thomas Hobbes from *Leviathan* (New York: Penguin, 1982), chapter 13: "That which may perhaps make such equality incredible, is but a vain conceipt upon ones own wisdom, which almost all men think they have in greater degree, than the Vulgar; that is, than all men but themselves and a few others, whom by Fame, or for concurring with themselves, they approve. For such is the nature of men, that howsoever they may acknowledge to be more witty, or more eloquent, or more learned; Yet they will hardly believe there be many so wise as themselves: For they see their own wit at hand, and other mens at a distance. But this proveth rather that men are in that point equall, than unequall. For there is not ordinarily a greater signe of the equall distribution of any thing, than that every man is contented with his share."

34. Northrop Frye, *A Natural Perspective: The Development of Shakespearean Comedy and Romance* (New York: Columbia University Press, 1965), 104. Cf. Ronald Sundstrom, "Laughing to Keep from Crying: Resisting 'Race' through Irony," *Tympanum* 4 (July 2000): 1–35, which joins Appiah to advocate, with regard to race, finding solidarity but practicing irony.

35. Linda Martin Alcoff, *Visible Identities* (New York: Oxford University Press, 2006). On Judith Butler, she writes: "[H]er radicalism is much more sympathetic to anarchism while mine is a variant of communism" (294n8). For further exploration of negative freedom in queer theory, see Shannon Winnubst's *Queering Freedom* (Bloomington: Indiana University Press, 2006). For a discussion of the contrast between concepts of self, freedom, and narrative resources in queer theory and feminist theory, see Lynne Huffer, " 'There is no Gomorrah': Narrative Ethics in Feminist and Queer Theory," *Differences* 12, no. 3 (2001): 1–32. What we might call the carnivalesque left should be viewed as having roots in the "lyrical left" of Greenwich Village before World War 1; see Eric Foner, *The Story of American Freedom* (New York: W. W. Norton, 1998), 166–67.

36. Cf. Albrecht Wellmer's *Endgames: The Irreconcilable Nature of Modernity* (Cambridge, Mass.: MIT Press, 1998). Wellmer's focus on freeing the rational self-

determined individual occludes to some extent the libidinal core of our nature and requires that eccentric behavior be perceived as reasonable from the point of view of community rationality (*E*, 22–24).

37. Charles Taylor, "The Politics of Recognition" (see above). See also Alex Honneth, *The Struggle for Recognition: The Moral Grammar of Social Conflicts* (Cambridge, Mass.: MIT Press, 1995). The concept of recognition can be traced back at least as far as Aristotle. For a discussion of adding insult to injury, and the role of love and friendship, and locus of freedom in the spirit, see *Politics* VII.7.1327b36. See *Politics* V.11 for strategies to break the spirit that are useful for tyrannies.

38. Paul C. Taylor, "The White People Are Melting: Marrying Mexico in 'Fools Rush In'" (unpublished).

39. Here I would take the film, or at least Taylor's reading of it, as a remarriage comedy, to pose a subtle critique of Richard Rorty's reliance upon intermarriage to overcome social tensions, and his refusal to find any value in multiculturalism. See Rorty's remarks in *Take Care of Freedom and Truth Will Take Care of Itself: Interviews with Richard Rorty*, ed. Eduardo Mendieta (Stanford, Calif.: Stanford University Press, 2006), esp. 156–59.

40. We might extend his claims to include race, but, if so, only as Ronald Sundstrom suggests, with that appropriate degree of irony that prevents race or any other social identity from hardening into a regressive Omega-style (*Animal House*) one. See Ronald Sundstrom, "Laughing to Keep from Crying: Resisting the American 'Racial' Politic through Irony," *Tympanum* 4 (July 2000): 1–35. Eduardo Mendieta argues for the political necessity of a racial identity in "Communicative Freedom, Citizenship and Political Justice in the Age of Globalization," *Philosophy and Social Criticism* 31, no. 7 (2005): 739–52. The simple carnivalesque celebration of the "browning" of the United States occludes serious claims for reparation and racial justice. The remarriage metaphor is part of a larger redefinition of the third freedom in terms of the repair and reinvention of social bonds based on intimacy and conviviality rather than recognition and status. As Eduardo Mendieta has suggested, in some respects my project joins with what Albrecht Wellmer proposes as "communal freedom" (see Wellmer's *Endgames*). Mendieta explains that Wellmer's proposed third freedom serves as an alternative to Habermas's overly rationalist conception of "communicative freedom." And as Mendieta points out in the above-mentioned article, the history of these third concepts of freedom is discussed in Quentin Skinner's "A Third Concept of Liberty," *London Review of Books*, April 4, 2002, 16–18; see his note 7, 752.

41. *Chappelle's Show*, season 2, episodes 1 and 3 (Comedy Central, 2004).

42. While Salma Hayek, the actress behind the Chicana artist in the romantic comedy *Fools Rush In*, performs Frida Kahlo in the film *Frida*, which she co-produced (2002), she is not the "Frida Kahlo" who "signs" an early version of the Guerrilla Girls' poster "Estrogen Bomb," called "Biological Warfare." This connection between the two performances of Frida is just a happy accident.

INDEX

Cynthia Willett is Professor of Philosophy at Emory University. Her previous books include *The Soul of Justice* (2001) and *Maternal Ethics and Other Slave Moralities* (1995). She is the editor of *Theorizing Multiculturalism* (1998).

Lightning Source UK Ltd.
Milton Keynes UK
UKHW010141300921
391396UK00007B/316